THE NEAR WOODS

THE NEAR WOODS

Millard C. Davis

Illustrations by Matthew Kalmenoff

1974
ALFRED A. KNOPF
New York

THIS IS A BORZOI BOOK
PUBLISHED BY ALFRED A. KNOPF, INC.

Library of Congress Cataloging in Publication Data:
Davis, Millard C., date.
The near woods.
1. Forest ecology—United States. 2. Forests and
forestry—United States. I. Title.
QH104.D35   574.5'264   73-20757
ISBN 0-394-48592-2

Since this page cannot legibly accommodate all permissions
acknowledgments, they will be found on the facing page.

Manufactured in the United States of America
First Edition

Grateful acknowledgment is made to the following for permission to reprint previously published material:

Thomas Y. Crowell Co., Inc.: for an excerpt from *The Desert World* by David F. Costello. Copyright © 1972 by David F. Costello.

Dodd, Mead & Company: for excerpts from *North with the Spring*, *Wandering Through Winter*, and *Near Horizons* by Edwin Way Teale.

Harcourt Brace Jovanovich, Inc., and the Estate of Robert Frost: for excerpts from *The Journal of Henry David Thoreau* and *Travels in North America*, Volume I, page 20, by Peter Kalm, edited by Adolph B. Benson.

Harcourt Brace Jovanovich, Inc.: for an excerpt from *Remembrance Rock* by Carl Sandburg.

Holt, Rinehart & Winston, Inc.: for portions of "In Hardwood Groves," "Reluctance," "Mending Wall," "Stopping by Woods on a Snowy Evening," and "Come In," from *The Poetry of Robert Frost*, edited by Edward Connery Lathem. Copyright 1923, 1930, 1934, 1939, © 1969 by Holt, Rinehart & Winston, Inc. Copyright 1942, 1951, © 1958, 1962 by Robert Frost. Copyright © 1967, 1970 by Lesley Frost Ballantine. Reprinted by permission of Holt, Rinehart & Winston, Inc.

Houghton Mifflin Company: for excerpts from *A Natural History of American Birds* by Edward H. Forbush and John B. May, *The Appalachians* by Maurice G. Brooks, and *The Works of Thoreau*.

McGraw-Hill Book Company: for excerpts from *Fieldbook of Natural History* by E. L. Palmer. Copyright 1949 by McGraw-Hill, Inc.

Oxford University Press: for material from *A Sand County Almanac* by Aldo Leopold.

Random House, Inc.: for "The Flow of the River" from *The Immense Journey* by Loren Eiseley. Copyright 1953 by Loren Eiseley.

Betty Flanders Thomson: for an excerpt from *The Changing Face of New England* by Betty Flanders Thomson. Copyright © 1958 by Betty Flanders Thomson.

John Wiley & Sons, Inc.: for an excerpt from *Introduction to Parasitology* by Asa C. Chandler and Clark P. Read.

To Mother and Dad,
who kept intact our Near Woods

Contents

Foreword

Woodlands, great or small, have always been a major part of the American scene. We find them forming a backbone to the seacoast, closing over a marsh or brook, resisting the spread of cities as remnants in parks and small neighborhood groves, stretching in overwhelming vastness over seeming wildernesses, and finally thrusting toward redoubts on mountaintops. Most of us can find one sort or another of such woods. These chapters, then, take up the wooded scene that is not so far away; in fact the near woods, where one might like a guide—here offered.

A few of the chapters, in part or whole, have appeared in *The Living Wilderness, The Conservationist*, and *The Science Teacher*. I thank the editors and publishers for permission to reprint this material.

Friends who have helped along the way as field guides themselves, or in other ways, are many, but I wish to thank especially Dr. James H. Zimmerman of the University of Wisconsin; Dr. Richard B. Fischer and Dr. F. H. Butt of Cornell University; Ben Osborn, formerly of the USDA Soil Conservation Service; Mrs. Mary E. Hawkins, Editor of *The Science Teacher;* Mrs. Rachel L. Horne, Director of the Nature Education Center, Washington Crossing State Park in Titusville, New Jersey; and Mrs. Virginia Welch.

Especially I thank my wife, Ginny, who had to wait the longest. The book begins and ends with woods we have known together for years.

June 21, 1973   MILLARD C. DAVIS

THE NEAR WOODS

1 | *Forests of Land's End*

America's forests begin down by the sea. Though great lengths of seacoast are famous for their rocky, conifer-strewn backbones, for most of the coastline the forests are anchored in sand, at once protective and uncertain. Here beaches, gradually rising, sap most of the force of the waves. Only sea winds and sea mists roll over the greater expanse of beach into the dune forests, where true stability is achieved only by conquering the sand itself. And this is the real burden of the forests of land's end.

The dune land is a restless zone. The brow of a sand hill has a most temporary existence, being born and destroyed in the wind. If the hill is to remain, to grow, to wall the tides back, it must break the disorder of the wind's free flow. The first steps begin with beach grass. It is the warp and the woof of many dunes, and especially those of the typical Atlantic coast strand I have come down to again and again.

In spikelets on crests, in gust-cut swales of the flat drift beach where the path is now to the north, now west, or stranded and broken on a wave-lashed slope, this sand reed measures land's end. From each clump tough stems creep out over the sand and eventually, at the tips, sink long wiry roots. Sand catches in the growing leaves, and the dune begins to be shaped. In this partnership roots, leaves, and rhizomes bring order to wind drift. An ordinance in Massachusetts once required colonists in some coastal areas to tie up dunes by spreading this natural inhabitant. Beach grass will itself be replaced by other plants when new sand comes no longer.

At the same time the advance of beach grass to the sea is restricted by tide and spray. Noon breezes come in off the sea, and in their turbulence salt spray toboggans up the beach. Experiments indicate that a four-mile-per-hour stream can carry ten-millimeter droplets nearly thirty feet, one-hundredth-of-a-millimeter ones almost three thousand feet, providing they burst from the breaker at least five feet above ground level. So even the town beyond the beach shows chloride damage. Yet dune grass resists. At least part of this tolerance depends upon the low wetting qualities of the blade cuticle. And while the strain of whipping in the wind may in time crack the blade's surface, thick-walled protective cells surround the food-making and other cells inside.

The close association of wind and grass bends many blades permanently toward the lee of the prevailing winds. In this protecting crook, weedy sea rocket is apt to grow as solitary individuals next to isolated tufts of grass. These broad-leaved plants are usually the first pioneers into the drift beach zone, just above the last seaweed windrows and in the trough where autumn and winter surfs pound. The sand is smooth, hard packed from being too low, and too well protected to be regularly churned by wind. By noon this part of the beach is hot underfoot. Here the shadows and deep green of the radishlike sea rocket leaves contrast sharply with the sere flat stretches of sand. So succulent are the blades of sea rocket that when I opened the magazine I was using for a plant press one summer, they were plastered to the pages. Sea rocket grows in fairly sparse plantings. Such wide spacing of small individuals suggests it is a means of evading drought and starvation as is found among desert plants —and the drift beach and headlands are effectively a desert. A neighbor, dusty miller, follows the same rules with a slightly different approach. These individual plants, too, are usually small, seldom as much as a foot long from base to bowed flowering tip, but they tend to cluster in thick scattered colonies. This spatial arrangement is true, as well, of a relative of dusty miller, the famous sagebrush of the cooler southwest American deserts, the Great Basin desert, and upper elevations of the Mojave.

Dusty miller, luminescent and soft, symbolizes the dune land. A wiry mat of fine white threads that may act as both heat reflector and windbreak masks the chlorophyll-green leaves. The low-key glow of it lasts past death as an iridescent paleness. The plant expresses all that is gentle and everlasting about this kind of beach. I once cut into the stem of one of these plants. Under the ribbed jacket hundreds of sand grains were packed like jewels.

Yet to some the crusty, small-leaved pinweed better represents the hardy life here. Its orange blossoms cap a low existence. It exists, but often seems dead-alive.

Above these pioneers the headlands rise angularly. Their upward climb is a race against descent. Every day wind pulls away a layer of sand curtain to reveal the old roots that still stabilize buried dunes—dunes known once to children whose grandsons now sit quietly in the shade downbeach.

As one goes up the dune, stepping from depression to depression and noting how they swirl away behind, it becomes evident that the crown is cut up by grassless furrows, that the grasslands are increasingly a tangle of repressed larger plants. Seaside goldenrod pitches sluggishly in cross winds. Its fleshy leaves, thickened in defense against wind-carried chlorides, cluster around a stem hardly two feet tall. The leaves are bulkier on the seaward side, where a mechanism has been built by the plant to slow the movement of chlorides through its tissues. Often, nearby, beach pea vine labors uphill, spills downhill, sometimes attains a height of a foot or better in a wrenching grip on beach grass or golden-rod. Its presumptive blossoms of June suggest short stacks of artistically fluted organ pipes. A week later the inflated pink blooms, unmistakably legumes, belly out from the shadows. On one of my initial swings across the dune ridges I stopped to examine a few flowers that had scarlet

beach plum   wild rose   bayberry   white-footed mouse   poison ivy   beach grass

seaside goldenrod   sea rocket   dusty miller   herring gulls

pustules from wind damage, and incidentally tried a bite into one of the leaves. It tasted pleasurably like garden peas.

Grasshoppers inhabiting the beaches are apt to match the sand in a startling fashion. After they alight, only their shadows will give them away. But a lively beach locust flying over tumbling dunes and slipping in and out of stringy beach pea can bring a full-grown man to his knees long before the insect has tired from being pursued.

Here and there Virginia creeper drapes across an open slope. It usually appears at its fullest on the back side of the greater dunes, where it is buffered from direct ocean breezes. Farther downhill the innocent leaves mingle with the slightly broader ones of poison ivy, a weed that is too often a barrier to walking in the hollows.

My wife and children and I have often spread our blankets here on the inshore sands when the wind is up but the sun is warm. Pools of open sand are staggered across the slope, forming an irregular clearing that separates herbaceous from flowering shrub communities. The trough also forms a calm corridor for insects flying to and from the nectar flow. Occasionally a crane fly, worn from laboring in gusty winds that hold to no bed, lands on one of the dark roots projecting from a nearby sand cliff. It swings around until the local breeze breaks over its belly. Black-and-green solitary bees zigzag up the hill toward embedded beach plums in blossom. A few white locusts prefer our particular sand bay and the trails nearby. Their staccato flights are accompanied by a brief crackling of wings, end in a dive and a lurching landing in the sand. Down the grassy way toward the open beach and the lines of tide I can see pits and scufflings we and others have made. This dune is edging toward that farthest point, though our climbing the offshore side may briefly have disrupted a portion of its advance. By midafternoon the fine coating of sand blown over our blankets reminds us that the world moves whether or not we stand still.

Above us the spring nectar flow is creating an insect garden, as it does every June. Most of the back hillside soon lies beneath the white petals of beach plum, and the odor of nectar in flow and of ripening pollen draws multitudes of insects all afternoon. This stand of a single species looks as if it were two kinds: trees down in the gully appear to be considerably larger than those near the crest. In point of fact, it is only that the upper tiers of beach plum are partially buried and their ebony sticks project like a tiny, crooked forest. Cottontail rabbits and mice browse in the thick cover. I once even found a small nodule of black smut encrusted on a plum stem barely eight inches tall.

Songbirds rarely come to the open beach. It is the land of the restless sanderling, the mirror of the plodding gull. Yet a few hundred yards from here a shrubless hollow attracts robins and sparrows in the cooler hours. One morning before five-thirty my young son and I stole up to the rim of this bowl. Across the amphitheater a dark arc was losing its grip as the shadows of the night sank. Two or three black birds were flitting back and forth across the far sandy wall. No other life was in sight. We broke the morning scene and slid in shade down into the broad shallow marsh lining the bowl. Filled by the sea of the tidal water table, it was apparently without life, at least above microscopic size. Enough drift rot had accumulated to give the surface an oily tint. Successive changes in level were marked by concentric russet and black margins; the barren surrounding apron suggested a poisoned environment. As we left the salt-marsh flat and began to climb back up the slanting sand, we cut across lines of tracks that wrote brief natural histories. They showed where gulls had plodded a few steps beside the pond with the outgoing tide but had done little investigating. The gulls might take beetles here, but these probably fall mostly to songbirds along the upper trails. Inch-long weevils, which frequent all the dunes, had left dragging tracks suggesting the continuous tread of tanks. We saw that a few rabbits had made very short dips into the hollow.

The back of this "cellar of the dunes" is tied together by a heavy thicket growth, a harsh fencing that populates the lower inshore side of other dunes up and down the beach. A hedge of wild roses often dominates these shrub zones immediately behind the beach plums. It merges unattractively with a ragged belt of plant "rough stuff." False Solomon's-seal, bayberry, greenbrier with its cutting stems, poison ivy, black rasp-berry in hutlike sheaves—these plants and many more grow one on top of the other in a wholly inhospitable screen.

Quite suddenly, however, the waste lot falls away. Rugged oak and pine cast their shadows on a weak ground cover. Hurricane force and the killing chlorides of salt spray produce typical shoreline anomalies, which are perhaps most noticeable here in the pines. The espalier canopy of pitch pine stretches away from the sea, whose windblown salts have killed growth tissue on that side, and points vigorously landward. Older trees often show hurricane damage in an erratic clustered growth of sur-viving twigs; the trees have a ball-like rather than a uniformly balanced foliage.

While the surface layer of dune sands may also have a heavy coating of chlorides, the salts either stay on top or are leached quickly through by rains. As a result, roots of coastal plants are little affected by the chlorides; most injury is to aerial parts, such as growing tips and places exposed after abscission or leaf fall. Pitch pine does well on poor soil and can even resist fire, so it often occurs in such weather-worn habitats of the dunes. Its scraggly appearance gives it an unkempt, un-wanted look—a tree that was never young.

Scrub oak also tends toward brutal habitats. A dwarf species that is often a six-foot shrub at maturity, it branches profusely and becomes knotted with anything growing nearby. When that is pitch pine the result is a small mesh fence. In a clearing of an oak-pine complex I once dis-covered a number of sand wasp diggings. The doughnut of dirt around each hole was considerably darker than the surrounding sand. I was far enough upland that this could hardly be due to a damp subsurface, nor was the dirt likely to be the kind that forms the base of inland dunes. I rubbed some between my fingers. This was sand and finely broken fire-wood. Suddenly I could see the history of those ancient pines staked out among the young oaks and pines here. Fifteen or twenty years ago a running blaze had wiped out the plant community. The dunes lay charred and peeled except for a few guarding pitch pines. Then winds drew carpets of sand across the land. Beach grass and shrubs moved in. Finally, like the offal of ungrateful guests, the shadows and acids of oak and pine destroyed the pioneer ground cover. The old forest was repeating its conquest.

In time, pines and oaks will cross the dunes now tied in place by beach plum. The honey flow will cease, the bees' hum will be lost in the night of a changed land. Only by walking again toward the sea will I find the old grounds, one step farther ahead in distant summers.

2 | *A Land of Fields and Forests*

The first Europeans who landed on the sandy coast of America soon found large grasslands, suitable for grazing, and these gave settlers a welcome purchase on the continent. The coves where both ships and early farms found shelter were fringed with tidal marshes, and these offered the best immediate grazing grounds. Then, as the pioneers ventured inland, surprisingly magnificent fields appeared along the watercourses.

The edge of the sea along the southern New England and Middle Atlantic coasts still has some areas of grasslands suitable for grazing that go on for acre after acre. With a little experience their signs can be read in the nature of the soil and water. Shoreline elevation is, of course, one of the best indicators. In the lower marshlands man and beast sink too quickly for comfort into the ooze, which is always wet and in many places inundated with each high tide. Stunted smooth or salt-marsh cordgrass, along with its companions, salt meadow hay and spike grass, indicates areas that are especially salty. Some of the younger sandbars may be identified by sparser acreages of cordgrass. Yet it may be worth grazing even here, for cordgrass ranks high in protein—about 3 percent or so. Salt marshes are, therefore, among the best wildlife zones on the continent.

An upland salt marsh may be best identified by wavy mats of the choice yellow meadow hay. Spike grass usually runs with it, interpersed with stringy sprays of sea lavender, chufa, and black rush. Red-winged blackbirds, bitterns, and other marsh-loving birds do more nesting here than anywhere else along the coast. Often their curious companions will be hermit crabs, whose burrows go down to the waterline and have top-side entrances that are apt to be funnels of different-colored sand and mud. I remember once standing in one of these drier wetlands when an autumn storm began to shake the grasses and rattle the branches of sea lavender and marsh elder. The muted tones of scattered pink blossoms faded as darkness fell, but a lone albino blossom, reluctant to go, stood out like a last shout from the grass.

The seashore grazing that is farthest from the tides often occurs among thick stands of black rush, a relative of the lily. The land is more solid here, and in the past houses came down to meet the sea. Wise builders constructed them at a respectful distance, though, and today they still stand among the yellow autumn plumes of rubbery-leaved sea-side goldenrod. Hunters filter through on their way to bag clapper rails. Their dogs can sometimes be heard chasing one of the birds down a twisting path through the grasses; later, if the bird was lucky, it may appear swimming in the marsh, only its bill cutting the water surface.

Such places were eventually sold with pride at being marshland plantations. Even now you may find the imprints of horses' hooves in old meadow sod that has been uncovered by stormy waves, or a corduroy road leading to the sea. Salt marshes were once considered such good grazing that not only was their sedge hay brought up to the farms on scows, but cattle were brought down to the meadow. Some escaped and became wild.

But, fine as the coastline grasslands were, nothing really compared to the open swaths upriver. And in spite of the fame that prairies farther west were to gain, many of the eastern meadows were actually far superior for grazing. Drought is practically nonexistent in the east; in the mid-west drought and terrific hot and cold spells periodically bring life to a standstill. In the east grass grows for the better part of three seasons, or at least for two and a half in the old colonial states. The problem was that not only could grass live a good life but forests could also. The natural competition somewhat restricted the river meadows, though settlers did report amazingly large meadows inland. Thoreau speaks highly of grasslands along the Concord River. "To an extinct race it was grass-ground," he says, in *A Week on the Concord and Merrimack Rivers,* "where they once hunted and fished; and it is still perennial grass-ground to Concord farmers, who own the Great Meadows, and get the hay from year to year."

As a matter of fact almost all of New England eventually became famous as a land of meadows. Seaside thatch, still used on roofs in some historical restorations, was matched with equal grandeur by tall grass from uplands only slightly farther west. And there the trees helped. Where good trees grew along a waterway, beavers made better dams. The resultant ponds swelled out and eventually filled in with fine silt topsoil. Then the grasses spread and turned the old beaver ponds into rich high-country pastures. So the trees came to indicate excellent soils, which drew farmers. And the prospect of beaver pelts attracted everyone who could hunt or trap.

Beaver meadows and others in clearings were naturally small, and so farms in New England and neighboring westerly areas were somewhat two-by-four as compared to those in the south and midwest. The New England farm of stone fences meeting at angles is a familiar scene even today, when farms there are all too few. And yet, circumscribed as they were, these little plots yielded elegantly—as much as forty-one bushels of corn from an acre in Connecticut. The people just learned how to interpret the hints pointing to the best land—buttonbush and sedges for the wetter lowlands, white birches for the good soil on the uplands. And white pines often told them where the glacier had deposited a load of sand or sand and gravel.

Today's representative fields are not always the best examples of what was, of course, for all too many have become compressed, nearly barren, hummocky pastures. Cows bunch together where the grass is thickest or spread out very loosely, each seeking her own clumps. On poorer farms that still retain unused or sparsely used acres, however, the autumn picking of puffballs may be unsurpassed. Such land has many fertile niches, and the fat puffballs along a hillside look like scattered gray loaves of bread. Sliced and fried, they are a kind of essence of fall. By comparison, the thatchy thickness of these former farmlands may perhaps be inferred from a note by Thoreau in his *Journal* for August 31, 1850:

> I notice that cows never walk abreast, but in single file commonly, making a narrow cow-path, or the herd walks in an irregular and loose wedge. They retain still the habit of all the deer tribe, acquired when the earth was all covered with forest, of traveling from necessity in narrow paths in the woods.

West of New England, huge grasslands startled the first comers. A Jesuit priest, Father Raffeix, wrote, in a letter of 1671, that between New York's Owasco and Cayuga lakes one could find a wide plain bordered by great forests. The Indians evidently controlled the nature of such plains by burning over the fields every year. This kept the territory in a state of grasslands, shrubs, small trees, and mixed hardwoods, a favorite habitat for deer and a varied land that attracted an exceptionally wide collection of wildlife. It also kept the view clear for the Indian hunter. To Europeans the hilltops seemed to make up a vast plain broken only by wooded valleys below. I have no doubt that fires were more frequent on the summits, since flames tend to travel upward. (Thus any spark that escaped from the valley floor was almost certain to provide a reaping blaze above.)

Indians had been living on the land that is now New York since at least 10,500 B.C., so one can hardly tell its history without including their long-term effects. Without a doubt they kept parts of the East open as prairieland. The early Europeans saw it and used it, but they allowed the woods to come back, spread by flying seeds and the nuts carried by squirrels. These plains have largely disappeared into farms, cities, and forests, and we tend to consider their little bluestem grasses and other fire-tolerant species as western prairie types. Actually, prairie now begins in Pennsylvania. New Yorkers are losing what few prairie stands they still have, for invading species are apt to win when competition takes place in soils kept moist by the moderate annual rainfall of the typical northeastern growing season.

Today's northeastern "plains" are mostly abandoned small farms where timothy, goldenrod, and brambles are being overrun by pines, oaks, ashes, and maples. The oldest barns, with their "snug Dutch" roofs, may in some cases go back to the late 1700's. Their builders helped bring on the transition from expansive meadow to old fields and encircling woods. When I was a boy I used to swing through the edge of one of these small forests, which was made up primarily of young white pine. A friend and I played a sort of pioneer game of tag six or seven feet above ground as we quite literally ran across the encircling layers of boughs, speeding from one tree to the next like squirrels. Most conifers put on a whorl of branches each year, and these woods near our house were made up of successive soft green tiers laid side by side.

South of the old Indian Plains the settlers found different land: heavily forested tracts, often on limestone, which were similar to many parts of their European homeland. Forests here had long ruled the land, with only occasional fires opening it to fields of any great extent. In going from Philadelphia to Wilmington, Delaware, on October 3, 1745, the Swedish traveler and scholar Peter (Pehr) Kalm noted:

The greater part of the country is covered with several kinds of deciduous trees; for I scarcely saw a single tree of the evergreen variety except a few red cedars. The trees of the forest were tall but branchless below, so that it left a free view to the eye, and no underwood obstructed the passage between them. It would have been easy in some places to have gone under the branches with a carriage for a quarter of a mile, the trees standing at great distances from each other and the ground being very level.

These great deciduous trees gave the early Swedes and Finns a chance to ply an art that persists today mostly in reproductions, the fashioning of bowls whose curling grain could come only from knobby swellings on the trunks of oaks, ashes, and red maples. All but those of oak were eminently successful. Oak burls, as the virally induced knobs are called, suffered from worms and rot.

The settlers were less pleased with one inhabitant of the near woods, pileated woodpeckers, which flew out from their rectangular holes in trees to attack corn. The *tillkraka*, as the Swedes called it, landed on ripe ears and ripped them apart with its axlike beak. The big bird, which normally feeds largely on insects, may have learned to look the corn over for crawling meals. Or it may have found the new agricultural product tasty in itself. Whatever noise the pack made in the fields, the sound of its nickname surely repeats on our tongues the whacking sounds the Nordics heard from the woods surrounding their plots.

Because certain game laws have been stringently applied for some time now, we are able to hear today another noise that engaged the early Pennsylvanians and others. That is the gobbling and calling of wild turkeys, some of which apparently weighed more than forty pounds. A few of the fatter ones are said to have exploded on the impact of a bullet.

Speaking of noises, a third one might have been the racket of a few people acquainting themselves with some of our snakes. All in all, the serpents seem to have caused little real trouble. De Soto had marched through Florida and surrounding territory without incident from either rattlers or coral snakes. William Bartram, a trained American naturalist, whose famous botanist father lived near Philadelphia, investigated much of the southeast from 1773 to 1778 and wrote in his *Travels* that rattlesnakes were harmless unless attacked. John James Audubon acknowledged that their rattle was fair warning. Nevertheless, an inquisitive and cool snake might join a warm sleeper in his bed, and so Indians sometimes raised their cots on sticks. Two canoers are reported to have slept on board rather than go ashore. One rattler wriggled through the pews of a church in session and was dispatched. A companion followed and was likewise sent to its maker. The sermon never stopped.

Not all of Pennsylvania was densely wooded, however. Then as now some of the midwestern prairie country began in the western part. Across the Susquehanna floodplain grass grew so tall that a man on horseback could get lost in it. From here to the far-distant western side of this vast sea of grain, settlers showed a fear of prairie depths, and many were reluctant to move west simply for that reason. Cattle that strayed might never be found again, even by men searching on horseback. Also, grass fires were prevalent and smoke clouds could roll for miles, from horizon to horizon, as they tumbled forward. Eventually, of course, the farmers did break through and succeeded beyond any measure hitherto known. On short-grass prairies cattle drives eventually became famous for the monstrous numbers of animals involved. In one celebrated case a thunderstorm descended on more than thirty thousand of the beasts from eleven herds —and it was ten days before the 120 cowpokes involved had them re-shuffled and finally moved on again.

Scots and Irish were among the first early settlers to choose grass-lands over great forests and, as the southern colonists did later, they went westward on grass. It actually made empires for some. Bluegrass moved with them and conquered other species, even colonizing the tops of the low eastern mountains, where it produced low fields, or balds, in place of more rugged growth. Hardy in winter, it fed cattle the year round, and so a bluegrass economy developed at elevations of five hundred feet or more above sea level. It was, of course, an economy always under pressure from encroaching forests.

Part of the early south's reputation for being rich farmland came from tobacco. But along the coastal plain this single-crop agriculture soon resulted in worn-out fields, which eventually turned into old fields of grass and weeds and finally into second-growth woods. Curiously, by rapidly depleting the land tobacco robbed the colonists not only of good food crops but also of houses, or at least the ability to build lasting new ones. The first comers brought ax and saw into forests that had probably never before resounded with the noise of chopping, aside from the whanging of woodpeckers on dead or dying trees. If they chose, these builders could build to stay, for the wood of the original magnificent oaks, maples, chestnuts, and hickories became even more solid as it dried. Today the outer veneer of flaking gray chestnut boards that are over two centuries old can be peeled away and there will be solid wood beneath. The inferior second-growth wood simply does not have the same durability. The difference is reflected in the amount of personally inscribed woodwork we still find in the oldest homes. Many were planned to last for generations and remain in excellent condition today.

When the southern plantations faded and the more adventurous farmers moved westward, they followed not only bluegrass but oaks. Where oak flourished, gravel beds were often the underpinning, and grain would grow there. Buckeye, maple, and walnut indicated land well suited for grass. An oak woods lets in more sunlight, and the substory is often wiry and tangled. Maples give more shade, and consequently the floors of older maple woods are quite bare. That is why we find in them the best shows of early-spring wild flowers. They thrive here where competition is slight, held down by the dawn-to-dusk gloom that rules except in spring. Then, when the woods are sunny and warming but the leaves are still in bud, they burst into bloom. The flowering is swift, both to come and go, and so we call these small plants spring ephemerals. Either kind of woods, oak or maple, is apt to leave fine pastures and cropland after it is cut down.

The advance west necessitated new ways of living off the land, and so the housewives who gathered food learned to watch what their cows ate to see what might be safe for their families. Some settlers doubtless had already practiced another trick of survival back east and tried it again now. Young deer, when tamed, would remain around the homestead but sometimes trotted off to the forests during the day for food. There they would make "friends" and, returning home at dusk, would entice their companions with them—wild deer. The decoys were especially successful during mating season.

Interpreting the changing land became a most demanding art, as Archer Hulbert has shown in his book *Soil: Its Influence on the History of the United States*. Some farmers were lured away from bluegrass fields by the apparent richness of canebrakes, which had served the loosely rooted Indians well. Unfortunately, cane soil is pauperous compared to that of bluegrass. But the wiser homesteaders did learn to follow the good fortunes of blue ash up in coves of the Great Smoky Mountains and down in the Mississippi Valley. New England aster always meant promising soil. Clover indicated they could raise wheat. Along the Red River, poor soils that were "crayfishy," as viscous as jam, and phosphate-thin showed their true colors in the low willow oaks and elms and other sickly trees growing there. The calcium-rich soils in Illinois were better. Down by a river these were often identified by tall sycamore trees; farther from water, the sycamores were replaced by butternuts, walnuts, and ashes, while wild cherry, linden, and ash took over on the uplands. Calcareous soil of the Illinois prairie could be foretold by sunflowers, whose place was taken by ragweed after the land had been farmed.

Land speculators played tricks with this art of interpretation, however, earning fortunes for themselves but burdening credulous easterners with what must often have been horrible trips into poverty. Much of the value of the land east of the Rockies, Hulbert points out, was reckoned in terms of its oaks. On good, well-drained soils they often became giants that stood thickly shoulder to shoulder. Thus oak soil was commonly accepted throughout the east as worth buying and perhaps moving onto. But farther west, where oaks were squat or dwarf, though hardy, fairly large tracts of oaks stood for the worst land—as the speculators well knew. The history of the midwestern prairie and its "oak openings" is worth looking at more closely, and we shall return to it.

Still farther west, in trapping country, few people wrote east to tell of their good fortunes as they successfully wrested fields out of forest land. Many could not write; others simply kept the secret to themselves. Unluckily for later missionaries, too often it was the first dedicated prelates who leaked the story out. As in New England, the best beaver country also had the best soils and so was ripe for agriculture. Indians began settling down to a life of farming and so, in time, did bushels of homesteaders from farther east. Soon the dispossessed trappers came to resent missionaries for having spread the word. The situation sometimes backfired on the missionaries in another way, too. Their efforts among the Indians now had to contend with prosperity—communities which had already been "saved" by successful farming.

Agriculture in California proved a boon to easterners, however, Hulbert says. So varied were the soils and climate there that a wide range of land practices was tried. California served as a testing ground and school. Eventually the word went back to the westward-moving farmers and helped them design a way of surviving in the dessicated land that lies between the Sierras and the one-hundredth meridian.

Let us return to the great midwestern prairie, which has its own peculiar wooded tracts and which has become known as the breadbasket of our country. In the section I know best, Wisconsin, most of the prairie is now remnant. It has fallen to farms, cities, towns, and now the return of woods. But enough remains to show aspects of the giant that once lay naturally through the center of this continent.

On one of our walls at home is a photograph of a purple cone-flower. This is essentially a sunflower with a large central disc and long ribbony rays drooping from the edges. The blossom in my photo is pale, not because of poor film exposure but because the soil had been dry most of that spring and all summer. The scene is typical prairie, where ability to endure drought is a regular characteristic of plants and animals that have been around for any length of time. Pale as it is, the blossom further stands out against a dark background of near woods. This, too, is typical of Wisconsin prairie, where forests have always threatened to take over.

Once, when standing in an upland meadow, I could see enough of the prairie–forest conflict and the meeting of eastern and western plants to suggest that this was a representative view of the way one part of America had grown together since the European invasion some three hundred years before.

Seen from the edge of the highland hill, the valley below often has long dark shadows. On clear days sunlight sweeps only briefly up the north–south cut. To watch this interval of penetrating yellow down there in the black and green, I stood that noon on a distant brow, where running gusts were parting the grass now this way and now that. I had come to this lookout point by following the lay of the land and some directives. A thin path led north along a barbed-wire fence. I stopped off where it turned to the right and barely divided scalloped patches of Canada thistle. At the corner the shade of an old sentinel bur oak met and also parted company with the fence.

From this vantage point I could see how the valley divides and subdivides the landscape. Deeply etched lines lead to finely dissected watersheds west of the Wisconsin River. Narrow defiles weave down through oak forests until the streams find a farmed opening. Then they leap out onto plains as flat as an ironing board. Sometimes you cannot see the streams when you drive by on a road cut low along the far bank; their sinuous beds have been sliced straight down into windblown, or loessial, soil. I have learned to follow their distant lines by watching the course of yellow-tinted new twigs of black willow—the only native willow to achieve tree stature here.

Once, when helping to survey a farm where designs were being put forth toward diverting such a lowland creek, I was witness at the proposed death of one of these old trees. The willow, as it stood astride a crook in the one little drainage outlet the land had, and half strangling the stream, had a bad habit of snarling all the water rights of way in spring by tying up the leaf-and-twig rafts that like to be off at flood time. The farmer would have sacked the willow some time before, but every machine he owned seemed likely to sink its roots in the mud also if he tried to haul the tree out. Yet, while he probably admired the reputed soil-draining properties of the tree, he still couldn't see having several acres of good bottom land soak out every spring when overwhelmed by meltwater and rain.

Just how that conflict between man and nature was ended, if at all, I never heard. I do know that the parties I was representing stood for the good and the evil of advising that the creek be straightened or the willow taken out. I came as close as one can, perhaps, to living the conflict—by ruining my shoes in the muck where young corn was dying in rows as I listened to the bees in the catkins. By luck, I happened to be reading Aldo Leopold's *Sand County Almanac* during those days, and I chanced on a paragraph that could have been written out in this field. No doubt Leopold's heart also was on two sides when, seeming to press a single point home, he wrote:

> The government tells us we need flood control and comes to straighten the creek in our pasture. The engineer on the job tells us the creek is now able to carry off more flood water, but in the process we have lost our old willows where the owl hooted on a winter night and under which the cows switched flies in the noon shade. We lost the little marshy spot where our fringed gentians bloomed.

If I now go back to the old bur oak at the brow of the hill, I fall under the spell of another view. The choice between prairie and pasture here was made over a century ago, but the lone oak got to stay. So it stands, a tree that evidently no one wanted or wants out. Its long arms arch over the juncture of mountain and valley, and in the grinding sound of the bark being tested by wind is the voice of a tree that long stood fast in prairie storm and stillness. While now its accompanying music is the line song of pasture wire, for several centuries the background tune was one played through prairie grass.

And that is how the limbs came to parallel the horizon. Once they hovered over the heads of turkeyfoot and switch grasses. That was back in the days when grass was *really* grass. A man got his view of the long shadows below from saddleback or by climbing bur oak of one of these scattered "oak openings." I have never been surrounded by acres of the eight-foot variety of grass, but having been in some of Wisconsin's highly regarded preserved prairie, I imagine the experience was kin to that which we used to have as children running through a neighbor's corn. After the fun, we nursed fine sawtooth slits in our skin drawn by corn leaves. Corn, incidentally, which later took over much of the prairie, is a "grass" that probably came from Central America. It grows rapidly rather than carefully and doesn't sink thick roots deep into the soil, as most of our other prairie plants do.

What happened to all the upland prairie? Well, the Indians had kept it free of trees by burning it every so often. They had learned how much richer a field comes back after burning. The sun warms the ground earlier, and new shoots get more sunlight. The warmth also affects soil bacteria, which then release more nitrogen to the new plants. The coolness of night reaches the plants more easily, too, since there is no cover; the plant chemicals' reactions slow down, and energy is conserved. Less carbohydrate is burned up and lost at night. The end result of the burning was prairie more palatable to the buffalo, which were now easier to see. Grasshoppers also enjoy prairie grasses. David Costello, in his book *The Prairie World*, says: "Although there is no proof in history, I could imagine that the thousands of dead buffalo described by explorers as resembling gigantic pumpkin patches on the endless plains could have been there because unbelievable multitudes of grasshoppers had left no living plants for them to eat."

Of the trees, only a few bur oaks, with their protective coats of cork that reach even the green twigs, held out through fire. Their rounded tops filled with ragged nests of branches were a familiar sight in Indian land. So was the prairie—now up, now down, as hunters found *their* vistas improving when they burned the grass to see the buffalo. And though it may have been a pleasant thought that shaggy old bulls occasionally sidled up to the bur oaks to rub their itching fur, the Indian soon found that a good prairie smoking coralled their prey and even cooked some of it for them. This left standing that lone bur oak at the edge of a mountain-hill. Only when Europeans came along did the vista into the valley permanently improve. Well, things down there became easier to see, anyway.

The white settler, too, left the old oak, possibly for romantic reasons or at least as a place to sit in the shade and have lunch and a nap—until he had to give way to his cows, who had similar inclinations. Probably there were one or two burs elsewhere on his hillside. If old letters tell the story right, these oaks, too brittle for timber, were valuable for fencing and as logs in the fireplace. Wisconsin winters there frequently paused in the below-zero twenties and more than occasionally sank into the minus thirties. So the extra bur oaks went. A wry note should be added to point out that here, as was to be the case all over this land, European fire power was in the end greater than that of the native Indian.

The upland prairie gradually changed, so that in most ways the first farmer saw what I saw. The grass shortened. The prairie giants fell before his scythe and then, under heavy grazing, blinked out like cooling sparks. Within perhaps a decade the prairie grasses had given way to exotics like bluegrass, quack grass, orchard grass, clover, and dandelions. The first deed to ownership of the slope I stood on and the valley below was recorded in 1854. Shall we say, then, that the end of the Civil War saw the end of this part of the old Wisconsin prairie? And the beginning of a happier life for the thirteen-lined ground squirrels so common here now. Curious to many people for having rows of spots between their stripes, curious in their own nature as they sit up very erect and peer around, these squirrels prefer the short to the long grasses.

Today, as I walk this meadow where my shoes grow dusty from brushing through the tops and curled blades of Kentucky bluegrass, I write to a friend that we should save the green land of these rugged little mountains. This territory, possibly untouched by the glacier, is perhaps a relic of an even more distant past. So again a conflict is embedded in my wish. To save the Old World plants on this preglacial front yard? We have to start, or stop, somewhere. I would turn this small place over to prairie now. We can re-establish the broader prairie frontier later.

We could begin with color. In a wet summer, green is the cheerful response of bluegrass, which was born in a moist climate. But pale brown is its shade in this dry place. Prairie grasses evolved under drier conditions and remain green during some of the worst droughts. So we can help the *constant* summer green of prairie grasses to take over. And in fall more reward will come in the field, for these grasses take on tones we have long associated with trees, especially in New England—pinks, mahoganies, and yellows.

Prairie grasses and their companions sink their roots deep and put a lot of faith in them. More than 90 percent of their bulk may be underground. As a matter of fact, during the first year of growth so much energy goes into rooting that twelve inches of root may develop for each inch of top. Like trees, the prairie grasses store carbohydrate in the roots over the winter. Its slow transfer out of the leaves, and the response to cold, bring out the autumn colors, just as in trees. In September you can identify prairie patches on these midwest hillsides by the flush rising above the drying tans of European bluegrass.

Where I was standing, by the lone bur oak, beneath which bobolinks often swirl about, I could see another change coming over the land. The grasses along the southeastern flank of the slope were being overtopped by red oak. Sixty-year-old trees had edged in, indicating that back around the turn of the century someone had let a few of the rockier acres go. Hardy vervain, which was once accustomed to lifting its blue spires six feet high or more—the insects could find it on the prairie—had survived the farmer's cows by having a bitter taste, but now it was likely to lose out to the new invaders. The red oak had followed the receding glacier north from more southern forests.

Even before the oaks would take over, however, a brief competition might occur in the field at the shrub level. Two red cedars—the sort often seen from the roadside, where they colonize steep, stony landscapes that have escaped from pasturage—were poised on a south-facing ridge.

A hundred feet below, a clumped prickly ash had found a home among sandstone boulders. Eventually the offspring of both were likely to mingle out there in the grasses, and their shade would kill the grass before the oaks got a chance. The shade would also eliminate the goldfinches that sang on their looping flights across the open meadows and waited for thistledown to appear among the grasses and provide lining for their nests. Thistledown acts as an absorbent—a diaper, as it were—for the waste products of the young. (Sometimes, however, the down is so packed that it *holds* water, and goldfinch chicks have been known to drown in their beds.) The delay in nesting has also a side value, says Dr. James H. Zimmerman, of the University of Wisconsin Arboretum; it saves goldfinches from being parasitized by cowbirds, which lay their eggs earlier.

The two tough cedars took me back a long way, to the Atlantic coast, of all places. Stories from travelers centuries ago tell of the pungent odor of red cedar that greeted their ships. The Indians burned these and other trees to drive game to slaughter—a familiar act in a different scene.

In this same meadow I found Rugel's plantain, which is native to our country. Another broad-leaved plantain, which was brought by Europeans, spread so fast, however, that today it is the common one of our lawns and fields. The Indians called that one *mokamon*, meaning "white man's foot," because it followed his footsteps.

Not all of Wisconsin's driftless mountain slopes and hillsides have such a fluctuating history. On steep, fast-draining south- and southwest-facing slopes the native plants have found a bit of thin-soiled garden as yet unsuited to man's use. The late Norman Fassett, pioneer Wisconsin plant taxonomist, once named them "goat prairies," because only a goat would go up that sort of place.

Many of them appear today along road cuts. Their rocky, angular balds bake in the summer sun, catch little drifting snow in winter. Exposed rubble promises to chatter away underfoot. Even from a mile or more away the mass-wasting, or slowly downward-sliding, soil appears as a ringed series of concentric terraces or paths that go nowhere. A friend in a government office in Madison calls them "cat steps." We once climbed one of these goat prairies to get a closer look.

Dark splotches of weeds helped us grind our way upward. The roots had gripped a number of the more fertile footholds. This kind of growth is found especially where the rock base is limestone, for it holds moisture better. Many of these greener areas include prostrate juniper, *Juniperus horizontalis.* One old spread-eagled tree can look from a distance like a colony of something else. A close relative, *J. virginiana,* or red cedar, is apt to stand nearby, tall and often perfectly Christmas-tree shaped. But where we were walking the growing conditions are so difficult that one specimen we estimated to be about a hundred years old was barely twenty-five feet tall. A few of the horizontal trees probably were as venerable.

On the same small knoll were several dozen intermediate junipers, genetic hybrids of amorphous shape. Over one was draped the nearly complete cast skin of a blacksnake. Its apparent freshness suggested that somewhere nearby was the temporarily blinded snake. It failed to remind me we were in rattlesnake domain, however, until later, when a shiver passed over me as I recalled how I had been scrambling among stones. A photograph of a little skullcap flower bearing blue bell-like blossoms under capping sepals is my record of lying full-length where most people *walk* with care.

The peculiar pyramidal shape of a buckthorn bush, a European guest on that limestone prairie, indicated that cattle had been grazing here. Evidence of their topiary work often appears in shrubs and trees that look like cones, hourglasses, and so on. It all depends on where the cows are chewing nowadays. Deer have the same effect, as may be noticed in fields or along the edges of woods.

Another European visitor, Kentucky bluegrass, had taken over some of the moister spots on the hillside. A ring of exceptionally tall bluegrass had sprung up around a "cow pie"—if the cows keep away for the season the grass gets to grow. No one had yet browsed the stalks and woolly leaves of the mullein next to the higher ledges, either. Like much of the other growth, this is a European plant that can usually be counted on to do well in its adopted land. Without regard to actual growing conditions, I made a species list here and found seven natives, five Europeans, and one world citizen. If this goat prairie had been on sandstone, the drier conditions would have precluded the European plants' gaining a foothold.

The insinuations of native goldenrod appeared about us like ghosts of the prairie. A weathered locust tree carried the elliptical injury holes of departed locust borers, but I never found the goldenrods that the adult beetles gather on in late summer. Several yellow-collared scape moths fluttered away before me like bits of burned paper. They must have gone elsewhere to find the goldenrods which they, too, frequent in August and September.

One day in June, with that same friend I journeyed from one goat prairie to another. Under the high noon sun I became a collector of quotations. He figured that the best maxim of prairie management was "Take half and leave half." On a wind-swept ridge we stood nearly as tall as some stunted aspens that, in proportion to their thickness, should have been forty feet tall. Still, the top of the ridge had been grazed. It was typical of the sort of situation where "two-story agriculture" is found, where there is ridge, ridge top, and valley. The eight-year-old government car that had brought us there was a monument to the economic depression the nation was then feeling, and my friend felt that "if the financial crisis holds out much longer the service is going to have to get antique licenses." We had been photographing for a few hours, and as he snapped his last shot he observed that it was "the one the shoemaker threw at his wife—the last and the all."

As we swung over a rusted barbed-wire fence, the variation in strands caught his eye. Three of the four were genuine rustics. One, a single string with occasional looped barbs, suggested the thorny twigs of Osage-orange trees, which long ago formed some of our earliest fences.

Times and places gone before seem omnipresent sometimes. That day held a number of reminiscent occasions. The tall threads of mossy sandwort I pulled from one hillside prairie were relatives of an old acquaintance, the pine-barren sandwort that forms doughnut-shaped rings on sandy beaches down the Atlantic coast. Fuzzy, sunlight-reflecting western sand plantain, flourishing immediately beneath the lowest strand of that fence we crossed, had come east. Its Old World relative, common plantain, had journeyed west. Finally, furry hound's-tongue had ridden west with the pioneers and found a home. When I saw it the red blossoms were bobbing on both south- and north-facing slopes in Wisconsin. The fuzz and the fur on these plants probably help allay the dessicating effect of wind, for they slow the prairie gusts to a cooling breeze around leaves and stems.

I suppose these three—sandwort, plantain, and hound's-tongue—symbolize the movement and adaptability that have typified the United States ever since its beginnings. Their hardiness has given them a place throughout this land where the tension between field and forest became so much controlled by the European incursion.

3 | *Across the Fields and into the Woods*

More than any other places, fields have a mood. For Thoreau it might have been the feeling of wildness engendered by a fox snuffling in snow on a winter night; for John Burroughs it could have been a restful warmth aroused by the hum of bees leading across a meadow into the near woods; to Edwin Way Teale it might well be the promise of change that comes with misty burning colors of autumn, soon turned under by snow. "I tread down vegetation these days with no tinge of regret," Teale says at the browning of fall. "A greater, more destructive foot than mine has been before me." To me the mood is of mellowing age as a field becomes a woods. It is a mosaic that is always in motion. I have a favorite photograph of one old field showing a melding land of chocolate goldenrods with gray-shocked heads, auburn broomsedge grasses, green pyramids of red cedars, luminous red flowering dogwoods, and a looming background of tall trees gone up in the many-hued yellows and scarlets of autumn. An hour, even a minute, later the scene was different.

Over all else there is a shift from field to forest that takes place slowly, step by step, over many years. It is called maturity, or succession.

It can begin as primary succession with barren rock, and end with rooted trees digging in for security. I know a mountain forest in Vermont where no such permanence has yet been achieved and every large storm uproots a few of the taller trees. One year, after a hurricane that had rerouted itself and crossed through central Vermont, the top of this mountain was strewn with giant sticks. In some places the forest had been so flattened that it appeared plastered down like wet hair.

Most succession today is secondary. That is, the land has already had good growth, but the growth has been destroyed and the cycle is more or less starting again. Man is often the culprit. Typically, a fairly mature situation will have been set back a half century or so, usually when a forest was cut down or a brushy field burned. After a total fire, an area may go back to something close to primary succession, namely, lichens spreading over rock like flat gray-green pansies, followed by mosses in the small soil the lichens have created. Mosses growing on a woodland floor are a sign of disturbance, for their microscopic spores can germinate only in soil that is free of litter. On old lichens the spores find a natural environment. This is often fairly rich in minerals that the lichen has derived from rock or log, and it is damp due to the lichen's water-retaining properties. For the minute spores, it is much more rewarding than lying high and dry on last year's pile of fallen leaves.

Swiftly rooting and fruiting plants eventually come in, such as ragweed, horseweed, and evening primrose. They can hardly take over soon enough, though, for in plant-poor fields the soil structure breaks down fairly easily; more nutrients are lost from barren fields than are stolen when we harvest crops. A badly mauled field may initially come back as something suggesting a ragweed plantation, especially if the soil is moist. This is actually a lucky event for the owner, since ragweed has that curious ability to join with soil bacteria and add nitrogen to the ground. So it is that, shortly after cutting, a wheat field will come back as an elegant stand of ragweed—fortunately! We have already noted that prairie farms often attracted ragweed after the crops had been harvested. Good tobacco crops, which are infamous for the amounts of nutrients they strip from the soil, require a previous crop of ragweed or similar land conditioner. Legumes such as clover or trefoil are widely used for preconditioning a field in this way, but few people add ragweed deliberately. This suggests something about lawn mowing, especially in that little bare spot where the ferny fronds of young ragweed are just beginning to appear: let ragweed grow, at least until just before its flowers open. The conflict of interest can sometimes be resolved elsewhere, however. I know a person who once introduced small ragweeds (name unknown— *nomen obscurum*) to the border of his garden for their ferny appearance and light-yellow flowers. He even staked them up properly and was dismayed when they drooped at first from the shock of being transplanted. They made nice border flowers, but his children were soon suffering as never before from hay fever. This ended the conflict before it really arose.

Ragweed and companions are truly "pioneers," as they are known to ecologists, and most of them thrive on the combination of a few local factors. They need plenty of light and heat, but they are frost-hardy and can take a fair amount of drought. Their seeds travel easily, although plant families are more apt to arise around last year's parents from a concentration of seeds that have scattered near each base. Eventually, like burgeoning cities, the social lines merge and a broad stand of "weeds" may develop.

While the first-stage plants in a succession are annuals and biennials, the next stage sees an influx of a group whose individual plants have come to stay as long as possible—the perennials. These include many of our most attractive goldenrods, as well as Queen Anne's lace, lobelia, and that imitator of strawberries, cinquefoil—but bearing five leaflets to the cluster, as its name says. One of the common grasses to fill in all the spaces between other plants is broomsedge. So tall and vigorous is this bunch grass that its shade and demand for water can eliminate neighbors altogether. Even asters and ragweed have been known to fade before its aggressive tufts. As a group the perennials love light and have rather shallow, matted roots, which tend to eliminate annual and biennial competitors. The final setting of this stage may often be seen best in the picturesque dead stalks of evening primrose that, on its way to extinction, gives winter fields a less barren look.

As the years go by, the few woody plants become many. Poison ivy winds through the grasses and climbs the more frequent red cedars and dogwoods. Dr. Hal R. De Selm, of the University of Tennessee, once wrote me that in various fields of Tennessee and North Carolina grass stands are commonly ornamented by catbrier, Japanese honeysuckle, and trumpet creeper vines, and by such shrubs as blackberry and raspberry. Herbaceous legumes such as tick trefoil and red clover add nitrates, as ragweed did in an earlier stage, and their success leads swiftly to a heavy growth of woody thickets. Gray dogwood, later one of the first forest-edge shrubs to give way as tall trees advance, may be a dominant or large thicket plant. Sugar maple, now appearing here and there, is a climax, or final forest tree in its own right where cold weather prevails. Yet it probably won't survive the thicket, but must wait until smaller trees have paved the way. Another interesting visitor is sensitive fern, so called because it is very sensitive to cold and dies quickly when autumn frosts hit.

Dr. De Selm also observes that some fields in Tennessee and North Carolina may also have a halfway stage in which broomsedge grass is blanketed by honeysuckle, poison ivy, and trumpet creeper before cedars, pines, or hardwoods—such as sassafras—rule the scene. Bittersweet along with the honeysuckle makes thickets that in winter resemble igloos joined wall to wall, a common passageway running through all. Eventually, the substructure may collapse as the climbing vines kill off their own supporting bushes. The little feet that run under there, protected from weather and hunters alike, will soon have to pad elsewhere.

Our suburban life has so restructured the land that we now are a nation of thickets. Truly wild beasts have fled or been wiped out: black bears, wolves, and bobcats. Ruffed grouse and screech owls have not fared much better. Cardinals and blue jays *have* adapted very well to our residential thickets, though the less well known veery and wood thrush haven't.

The transition from thicket to forest may support less animal life than any other stage on the road to maturity. The trees are often not large enough for woodland birds but are outsize for thicket ones. I remember the late Leonard Bradley, president of the Connecticut Botanical Society, saying ten years ago, "In Connecticut it takes twenty-five to thirty years to reach this stage from fields; people entered Connecticut thirty years ago and bought farms and then left them alone. This is why birds in Connecticut are thin now." I wonder how the birds are doing there today. It is possible to actually watch a thicket develop and gradually become unacceptable to white-eyed vireos for nesting.

Birds obviously have their own successional patterns, as do other animals. And man. As a species we seem to prefer the transition zones. Not wholly open fields burning under the sun, nor deep woods where gloom pervades. Our esthetic senses and perhaps our instinct for survival lean toward open places with scattered groves of trees. In parts of Africa these are found naturally today very much as they were in man's early evolutionary history there. We seem to reiterate the preference in our city planning by designing parks with a similar mixture of open and closed spaces.

Birds use the land according to their inner dictates, and one can learn something about a place by the way certain birds treat it.

While most songbirds sing from branches or hidden places near the ground, those that nest in broad meadows or prairies sing while flying. So it is possible to discover open places by waiting in a roadside that is banked by shrubbery and simply noting the bird songs. That of the goldfinch seems to repeat its bounding flight. Bobolinks fly way up, almost out of sight, and their falling notes may be our first notice that they are about. Horned larks (true relatives of the Old World skylark) also frequently sing from very high in the sky, though once on a cold morning I heard one courting from a row of grasses between pastures. To these songs one can add the slurring whistle of meadowlarks and the asterisk-like reedy voice of red-winged blackbirds (possibly the most populous bird in the United States). The last two are not as good indicators as the others, however, for they are notorious perch singers as well.

Again, while walking through a field that is within the ranges of vesper sparrows and horned larks but where none have appeared, one might guess that dense, tall grasses are dominating the scene and keeping these two species out. The eastern meadowlark, which many ornithologists have dubbed an indicator bird for its territory, may be present to give a positive picture of the lay of the land; where such birds are frequent, their distinctive nesting grounds should also turn up. These are primarily wetter and smaller pastures, where a hutchlike dome of grasses often surmounts the bird's nest.

While it may be a surprise to find frogs in such fields, too, they are well known for following belts of soggy lowlands that take them far from open water. But toads are really the most typical amphibians of old fields—they are better able to live through dry times. Being amphibians, toads still have to undergo the aquatic phases of their life cycle—the egg and tadpole stages—in wet places, so in fields they depend heavily on spring and summer rains. The presence of either beast is likely to indicate not only nearby standing water but also watery paths through the field.

Mammals can also be such indicators. Examinations of abandoned fields in the Southern Atlantic and Gulf states have shown that pine mice and meadow voles become especially noticeable as perennial broomsedge grass begins to take over. In Michigan, prairie deer mice and cottontail rabbits enter recently abandoned fields; meadow voles join them as perennial grasses start to dominate, and the deer mice finally leave when mixed herbaceous perennials come in. If you were shown an exhibit of small mammals from that area, you could guess the nature of the plants by correctly identifying the animal species. Similarly, sandy or peaty areas may be indicated by numerous tunnels of moles, which prefer loose soil.

Life is not always pleasant for these little fellows. Two of their worst enemies are owls and hawks, which patrol the same acres by night and day respectively, a twenty-four-hour vigil. For white-footed mice the situation is even worse during winter, since they have the habit of running on top of the snow rather than in tunnels beneath it. Where they come in contact with each other, white-foots will battle for property rights with meadow mice or voles. Which is usually the victor can be seen by the networks of tunnels and the number of short-tailed voles racing from one grass clump to another. Bend some grass aside and note how many of the clumps have entrances. Even during winter as many as 140 or more voles may share one acre of field. Where field plants are more spread out, the less aggressive white-footed mice do better. It is possible to catch them by their long tails, fully half the total body length. Their aerial nests in trees show considerable care, and may even be a redesigning of an old bird's nest. Such travels also make it inevitable that theirs are sometimes the feet that scratch annoyingly as they cross an attic floor or race around inside walls during winter. A walnut or acorn left behind with two openings bitten in its shell is a sure indicator of this visitor.

As shrubs and small trees become more obvious in a field, the bird population makes perhaps its most distinct changes. In the east, thicket birds often include chestnut-sided warblers and towhees. The evolution of our land becomes more dramatic when one realizes that at the time John James Audubon was working his way through America chestnut-sided warblers were seen but rarely—Audubon himself saw just one alive. Only a hundred or so years ago few really large open areas existed in North America east of the Mississippi. Audubon expressed it simply by noting that a squirrel could cross the eastern United States to the Mississippi River without ever touching ground—namely, by racing from tree-top to treetop. We have traded the huge pileated woodpecker, whose rectangular openings we still find in trees—some present, some ghosts of the past—for catbirds. Cowbirds—which were once known as buffalo birds since they followed the herds, and which possibly evolved the habit of laying their eggs in other birds' nests because of their constant movement—now take to nesting in thickets.

We should be glad for those bird species that have done well in our openings, however. As the grasses continue beyond their normal growing period and so yield more grasshoppers, we may need the birds to counter incipient swarming and the resulting plagues.

You think we don't have them, that locust invasions are limited to faraway places? Well, as a matter of fact, in some parts of the United States such events have taken place in *very* impressive fashion. The possibility has already been raised with regard to the starving of plains buffalo. One roaring insect storm that was actually seen was estimated to contain a total of 125 billion locusts during raids along the Mississippi Valley and into Texas from 1874 to 1877. Swarms from this country have struck north into Canada, and Canadian hordes have winged south. On Mount Cook in Montana, at an altitude of about eleven thousand feet, a glacier records what was surely the wrong route for one mass flight. Layers of Rocky Mountain locusts were laid down, and today the black streams migrate slowly back down the mountain. According to carbon-14 tests made in 1952, the deposits were then forty-five years old "plus or minus" a few hundred years, as such calculations are stated. C. B. Williams, in his book *Insect Migration,* wryly observes that this suggests the locusts might have landed there 350 years ago or might be due in another 250 years.

Insecticides used against these and lesser plagues have sometimes backfired in their results. True, the grasshoppers eat them and die, but before dying or while still undecomposed many of the insects may be devoured by mice and other predators. Inside these animals the insecticides are concentrated, death or illness in compact packaged form for the next feeder in line. So mice eat many of the poisoned grasshoppers, and owls and hawks feed on the mice, ingesting massive quantities of the insecticides—which are, again, likely to kill or maim them or their young. The situation is similar for predators and prey of marine and fresh-water habitats, where insecticides may take even longer to break down into something relatively harmless. Rachel Carson made the actual and potential results abundantly clear in her book *Silent Spring.*

As we move through the grassy, weedy fields to more wooded ones we often notice a change in insect voices. Of the long-horned grasshoppers (those with long antennae), the so-called "false" katydids are probably the most widely recognized form. The long green wings with their flat sides suggest slim, quiescent leaves. The males are apt to be scattered in a field, often perched in elderberry and other small trees, and the low scratch of their voices rises uncertainly. I find it almost impossible to catch a male by tracing the low tics of his call. Rarely can I get within ten feet of his stage before he slips away among the many curtains.

For years two giant elms at the edge of our lot have been the calling towers of one or two of these insects. Perhaps fifty yards out in the woods two or three other males have also taken up residence in trees. Late in the afternoon they speak, trading calls across the creek. One of the katydids in the elms appears to initiate the conversation. He often begins with a sharp click. If this draws no response he will try several more. By dusk the voices of the katydids have been reaching back and forth across the creek for two hours or more.

At nightfall fields and especially woods are transformed into a vibrating room of sound. The topmost positions are taken by "true" katydids, insects with bulging wings that produce the familiar "Katy did, Katy didn't" song. I think of this as a rather guttural sound, perhaps saying something unromantic like *crunch, crunch.* One night my wife and I were taking a short cut home along a back road in New Jersey when we entered a sumac grove full of katydids. I stopped the car and began searching the treetops with a flashlight. The grunts came from all over the canopy, but I couldn't locate even one katydid. Eventually I became convinced I was looking in the wrong place, that what I was hearing was the snorts of pigs in some way transmitted to this sumac copse and reflected downward by the leaves. Anyway, I gave up, much to my wife's rightful delight.

One of the more interesting aspects of a field that is changing to woods is the horizontal view, a view that reveals the whole story of succession. From the side, the horizon is seen to slope gradually upward from grasses to tall trees. This is beautifully illustrated in one field I know well from literally thousands of hours there.

Northeast of a large eastern city a country road climbs through hillsides that roll away from the usually placid Delaware River. Half a mile up this north bank a road of red shale dust and broken stones breaks away from the highway like a wandering thought and pursues more seclusive ways. It enters a part of the state where a few hundred acres of fields and woods have been left behind by advancing and passing waves of civilization.

As recently as sixty years ago most of this land was under farmland. By the close of the Second World War a curving field, now fronting a woods and giving access to it by a well-worn path, had begun to spring up from some back-lawn fescues and a few abandoned farm furrows. Today weeds mingle with grasses; shrubs and small trees dot the landscape. Finally the scene blends gently into a dark oak-hickory forest.

So may pieces of land that I know personally or have seen in fleeting illuminating moments of passing have similar backgrounds. These are the ragged, unkempt fields and woods lying between suburbs and rocky hillsides, along meandering creeks where marshes or swamps still linger, in a corner where lots adjoin, in "waste" places beside the highway—I see these last all the time.

In my imagination I can take a fairly straight path through such fields and into their woods, just as I can in reality within this one I know so well, and the trips are very much alike. Differences exist, of course, just as differences leap out from even the most familiar spots every time I walk to and in our American woods. The similarities so far outweigh the disparities, however, that I am at home in many places I may pass only once in a lifetime.

At the edge of my familiar field, bunches of hairy broomsedge grass linger where the land most recently went wild. In late autumn its spearlike stems stand out among companionable tufts of timothy by being an autumn red. In the past these must have made colorful brooms as they stood, bound to knobby stick handles and leaning against a cabin wall. Farther out in the field the grasses are joined by legumes such as clover and trefoil, which spread their triple leaves with increasing frequency. The nitrates that their associated root bacteria have added to the soil over the years since the land was farmed have helped pave the way for a wide variety of species.

The white, asterlike flowers of daisy fleabane string through the grasses and appear in all sorts of open spots, adding a brightness from spring into fall. The plant comes early to bare spots but is one of the first to depart as grasses enter. Sod and leaf litter are its enemies. Once native to only a few small areas of North America, daisy fleabane found the opening up of our land by Europeans to its liking and soon became a regular companion to civilization, going backward to Europe as well as westward.

Perhaps the most prominent wild flower in taller parts of this field is early goldenrod, first to blossom and then nodding in yellow fountains as summer matures. An accurate species-by-species identification of goldenrod defies all but an expert, especially during winter, so I look for just one or two clues to a few species. My favorite tip-off is the ball gall on the stem of Canada goldenrod and only Canada goldenrod. It is caused by a fly, whose creamy white larva may be found inside throughout the snowy months. By late March the worm has turned into a brown, rice-sized pupa. During May a small fly with dark zigzag bands on its wings punches out—through a window that it had made some months before as a larva!

Not all parts of the field have this concentration of fleabane and goldenrod. Another part has a high population of Indian hemp, the bark of which was peeled off by Indians and used as twine. But what segregated it pretty much to that one place? A possible answer might lie in the effects of sunlight.

Last July I was with a group of naturalists who were comparing two sites that were really two different slopes of the same hillside. One slope curved so that it faced south and southwest, while the other looked west and northwest, completing the arc. Measurements showed that each had a gentle rolling tilt of from zero to six degrees. Thus the south-facing slope was not only being baked by the sun most of the day, but it also

ragweed   horseweed   broom sedge   Queen Anne's lace   goldenrod

                          red-tailed hawk

red cedar   dogwood   poison ivy   shagbark hickory   oak

white-tailed deer

received much the same effective sunlight as would a level field several hundred miles farther south. At first we were going to sample a great many of the plants and animals on both slopes and see what the differences were, but, frankly, it got too hot to try either site for very long.

We liked the thought, though, that these two parts of one hill might tell us what things were like farther to the south and north, and that without moving more than a hundred yards or so we could see quite a lot of the whole picture. The south-facing slope would be perhaps a better place to collect crusty fleabanes and goldenrods, to see butterflies vibrating their wings in the morning *before* breakfast as they tried to break the night chill. On the other side we would have better luck in tracking down plants like Indian hemp, which prefer more moisture, together with dew-loving mosses. The nearby woods was too small, but had it had a greater expanse we might have found *there* on the south side oaks and hickories enjoying the fullest sun, and on the north side sugar maples and beeches cooling it over with hepaticas and mosses through which crawled an occasional red-backed salamander.

The principles we kept as simple as possible, but we agreed that our south- and southwest-facing sections receive more direct sunlight and were more likely to be dried by the prevailing winds. As temperature and evaporation rate rise, air and soil moisture dip. Tough-skinned plants take over. In more northerly aspects, though, temperatures are lower and moisture lasts longer. Evening dews arrive earlier and linger into midmorning, important for, among other events, moss sperm, which swim over to the eggs on another green moss stalk. Humus and duff are deeper. In these respects our north slope was likely the richer.

From April through August of the same year a friend of mine kept a species list of the herbaceous plants (those that make little if any wood) growing on those north- and south-facing slopes and in the woods nearby. We then chased down as well as we could the places of their origin. Out of 230 species, we found 161 native Americans, 64 guests, and 5 that seem to have roots common to both North America and Eurasia.

My friend had not separated out the field plants according to site, but it is possible to guess at the locations of the natives and the guests. One might first ask: Which are those that get the worst and which the best places on our land? Many of our native wild flowers have always lived in very harsh environments, such as those goat prairies of the midwest or in deeply shaded woods where they bloom briefly between the passing of heavy frosts and the expanding of leaves overhead. Others live dangerously in the thin strand between a stream or lake and trees or shrubs that like an occasional flooding. So when we gaze out over much of our best open land, full of dancing blossoms, we can see some of the results of a real "open door" policy—most of our best-known flowers are immigrants that docked at American seaports with two-legged Europeans. Betty Flanders Thomson says, in her book *The Changing Face of New England*, that visiting English herbalist John Josselyn was impressed enough to write in his *New England's Rarities Discovered*, of 1672, that forty or so new weeds had arrived since the English settled in New England. Thomson lists "the native New Englanders that are both common and conspicuous among the field flowers: milkweed, cranesbill, robin's plantain, steeple bush, asters, goldenrod." Not many.

Roger Tory Peterson has had the pleasure of tracing the more ancient routes that some of our smaller guests possibly have traveled. He has seen the same plants flourishing in Greece and neighboring countries. Why might they not have ridden to Rome with voyagers from the eastern Mediterranean thousands of years ago? Then have accompanied Caesar's legions to Britain? Our knowledge of plant migration is terribly incomplete, even though books dealing with the identification and uses of plants turned up fairly early in medieval Europe and England. Unfortunately, the artists who drew the pictures for them followed ancient descriptions of species that had flourished in the Near East, perhaps along with some knowledge of local flora. Too often the result was a composite that had lines of two or more kinds of plants. And pure botany was not alone in suffering. The people themselves fell prey to sickness in spite of remedies that might have been useful when ascribed to the right plant but were worthless or worse when using a native one that looked like one in a book.

A great many plants were brought over out of need. A short list of some valuable ones would surely include oats, wheat, sugar beets, cabbage, red clover, alfalfa, peanuts, potatoes (from the Andes Mountains), and tomatoes. Think how far back many of these go in their association with man! I cite just two: clover and the grapevine.

Red clover, especially rich on our north-facing slope, has long been esteemed as nutritious fare for cavalry horses. It was one of the first English introductions into New Zealand but was a failure until bumblebees (which pollinate it far better than other insects do) were sent for. Superstitions have been gathering around clover for centuries; even in ancient times five-leaved ones were believed to be a bad omen, four-leaved ones good. Grapevines, very heavy weights on dogwoods and ashes along the northwest line of our field, go back to the *most* ancient times. They have been cultivated in Europe for an estimated ten thousand years or more. When the settlers brought theirs here an American grape aphid, or plant louse, quickly attacked and destroyed the roots. Then the insect went abroad to sack European vineyards as well. The plague ran freely and disastrously until finally one man saw how Europeans and Americans might find surcease through unity. Charles V. Riley, an American scientist, endeared himself in the late 1880's to Europeans, and especially to the appreciative French (who subsequently awarded him with a gold medal) by proving that grafting of European vines onto root stocks of resistant American plants would eliminate the parasitic insect. He helped the Americans also, for the European grapes, cultivated and selected carefully for millennia, had the qualities our tastes prefer.

Most of the plants that farmers brought with them were small edible ones, but many others are more familiar today as the things we simply ignore, mow down, or pull out. Since they illustrate one phase of field succession, let us consider them for a moment as plants in nature and see what qualities they have for living there. Then we will ask ourselves: How many could go on without us? How many do we see still living around relict farms, and where might they best survive?

Curiously, the answers are to be had in our own front yards! Most of our crops have ecological characteristics identical to those of the common plants we call weeds—especially the ragweeds, dandelions, plantains, and others that come in on bare spots on the lawn, do very well in spaded gardens, and otherwise make their presence known about as soon as anything the ground may have been *prepared* for. One reason for this sudden take-over of an opening is that they arrive quickly and spring up rapidly. Another is that some weed seeds have the ability to lie in wait in the soil for at least sixty years, then to burst forth as leaves and roots at the right trigger—which may be only a brief turn in the light, such as one might provide by spading the soil! So our crops, ecologically or behaviorally speaking, are "weeds," too.

A few personality quirks of such plants that affect their survival, wanted or unwanted, in the farmer's fields, are worth noting. First, they are pioneers of open ground, with its somewhat drier soils and full, intense sunlight. So the farmer bares a plot of ground, lays in his seed, and expectantly looks forward to the harvest. But if he grows his crop in too crowded a fashion, it will tend to self-destruct. Weeds are born pioneers, with a desire for lots of elbow room. (We are not really certain which part of the scale *man* is on, I might point out, but neuroses and crimes in cities suggest that we, too, have these weedlike characteristics.)

Second, weeds come and go quickly, leaving the next wave of activity to future generations. Left alone, most will disappear beneath the choking blanket of other plants. This is the fate of abandoned crops. I once saw a cornfield that was equally corn and horseweed, both crops being over six feet tall. Very shortly both annuals would be wiped out by species that last longer. In fact, cultivated plants may actually *acquire* shorter lives. Annual winter rye, for example, has been derived from perennial wild rye. Cotton is a tropical plant that is a tree in its natural habitat but in temperate climates becomes an annual. For our needs, it must flower and fruit before autumn frosts kill it.

Finally, for this brief account, the weedy types can take punishment. Rip one out of the ground, and it may still produce seeds with its dying gasps. Dandelions left lying around after a home owner has put in a long, tiring session on the lawn will still get in some licks, even dropping seeds into the nice bare spot that has just been exposed. And the seeds are born by the carload. But remember that the offending, densely seeded spike of crab grass has its counterparts in the heads of wheat, oats, rice, and corn. As a matter of fact, crab grass and barnyard millet were both cultivated annuals that have degenerated to common weeds of the less attractive type.

Where might such plants survive best without us? Doubtless many would simply drop out of existence in their present form, since our emphasis on heavy succulent production is not always consistent with nature's needs for tougher and more elongated stems. The fleshily over-developed roots of carrots and turnips attract pests to feed on them. Their excess of water leads them to freeze easily. And, worse, these weaknesses are generally followed by a failure to produce seeds until the second year, which obviously might find the plants all dead. Roots are not alone in this kind of degeneration under the thrust of civilization. Some plants, such as wax beans, have taken to growing yellow leaves, which are poorer than green ones in producing the plant's own tissue. Other than such weaknesses, which have come with the easy life, many of our vegetables might go back to the rugged little habitats of cliff debris, eroding stream banks, active ant hills, well-exposed ground hog dumps where the initial entrances have piles of soil, and so on—wherever there is a plot of sunlit ground kept free of competitors, usually by one form of disturbance or another.

At the bottoms of hills occur some of the more interesting, if less disturbed, places of that field where we had been examining the successes of weeds and other growth on the two different slopes. In spots these are wetlands where moisture collects, even becoming marshy here and there. The fate of such lowlands appears to have been written in already, however—they will soon be succeeded by grasses. But while they exist I have investigated them often. The most memorable recent occasion found our group, who had hitherto been working on the upper reaches of the north and south slopes, standing up to our ankles in the water of a fast-drying marsh at the foot of the north-facing slope. Here damselfly nymphs wriggled occasionally, as though reviving now and again from a dream. Small black polywogs bumped along the receding edge of the marsh. Where the shoreline was beginning to turn gray under the sun we did some collecting of insect larvae, digging out the partial remains of a dragonfly nymph with a *shovel*! One sight I shall long remember was the starchy white leaves of duckweed. They lay everywhere, on darker ground giving the appearance of gay flowers sewn to coarse, somber cloth. As a matter of record by my calendar, within another two weeks the bottom here had shriveled to crazed cakes of plaster. Where snails had been clustering about our feet before, later they lay in piles like so many cherry pits. In time only some of the hardier sedges and the last low alders and buttonbushes would identify the spot as former marsh.

People often avoid such low sections of fields at first because they are uncertain of the footing. When they do learn to recognize some of the plants and animals that tell them wet parts of the field are at hand—or underfoot—they are usually less reticent about walking in unfamiliar places. For instance, the first time I saw a buttonbush shrub up close I had stepped carefully into a firm-appearing cowlick in the grass— promptly filling my shoe with water. The incident remained with me. Five years later almost to the month, and several hundred miles away, I was standing safely on a small rise in a field viewing the prickly white globes of buttonbush blossoms while I was dry and comfortable, and comfortably wiser.

It is only transient enjoyment if we do not sometimes seek out these low places for their own gifts. Like Thoreau, one must at least occasionally track down the low meadow and "live deliberately." I remember sitting with a small group near the base of a wooded hill in Wisconsin one March evening, intent on a quiet, damp meadow that began only a few yards below. A chill was coming down onto our backs, changing the meadow from a gradually darkening one to a land of low, silvery mist. As twilight became only a thin oystershell gleam rimming the western horizon, a certain intensity of light came over the field below. The moment for woodcock song and dance was swiftly approaching. We were listening for a bird that had once been hunted especially by a small dog that still bears a part of its name, the cocker spaniel. Ours was a hunt for sound. Suddenly we picked out the beeps. Certainly had no one been there to tell me *"now . . . now . . . now,"* I would never have noticed. Very intermittently, and seemingly from widely separated places, they pierced the dusk and thin sheet of fog to keep us alert. Then I heard what resembled a faint purr or the rippling of wind past a scrap of paper held out the window of a moving car. It was the woodcock's wings as the bird rose—some say it flies to one hundred feet in the air. I did not hear the warbling, tumbling descent. But then, in my only spring season in Wisconsin I *had* heard that pirouetter of the evening sky. How elegant that its nearest relatives should include sandpipers and snipes, that the woodcock is an upland shorebird.

The surest evidence that my favorite field above the Delaware has been let go to seed is red cedar. These tall, slim pyramids stand as front-line sentinels of the invading woody plants that one comes upon while walking closer to the tall trees beyond. Here and there a straight row of these junipers (they are not really cedars) shows where the former fence line ran; birds used to sit on the fence and excrete the seeds from the berrylike cones. Cardinals weave strips of the outer bark into their nests. Evidently these strands, like the old-blood wood we have for a long time used in chests and closet panels, also repel insects.

White-tailed deer, which tend to enter fields in the wake of shrubs and small trees, often leave as one of their winter marks damage which begins near the ground and goes up to waist height. It is especially noticeable on red cedars, in the form of browsed twigs which often end in tongues of bark that the toothless upper front part of the deer's mouth could not rip away. Rabbits almost invariably snip the twigs off cleanly and at an angle, as though new hedge clippers had been used. Often all the lower branches of a red cedar are eaten away by deer browsing, and the trunk is bared to view; the upper foliage swells out above the browse line like an elderberry. I can often tell how bad a winter the deer have had in this field by the height of the browsing. Sometimes the take is limited to one side of a cedar, and then the tree has a bent figure, as though it had been kicked in the "breadbasket."

Deer feeding can actually change the nature of a clearing or beginning woods. Deer's favorite copses include crab apple, flowering dogwood, hornbeam, and red maple. This leaves succession open to other species. Thus in an area heavily populated with deer the woods that follows upon an old field may be considerably different from the usual type only ten or so miles away.

Far less conspicuous than red cedars, of course, but more promising of the eventual rise of a woods in my field is the sprinkling of short seedlings of white ashes, black cherries, dogwoods, black haws, maples, and hickories among these signs of long-term abandonment. Another indicator is the clattering *"drink-your-tea"* call of towhees, birds which nest on the ground or near it in brush or open woods. You may see only a flash of white from the tail feathers as one flees with your coming, but that is enough of a field mark.

White ashes are typical of those trees which promise that a true woods is imminent. They grow swiftly and tall and can sweep a field. They rarely travel alone but, rather, are accompanied by a mixed variety of other kinds of trees, giving the future plenty to choose from. Their rusty, nut-brown buds lend a warm color to winter landscapes. In midsummer the fallen needle-nosed samaras may be found standing on end in the leaves of weeds, where their shafts have thrust through after a long dive. One large fellow stands prominently just inside a main entrance to these woods. The way its branches sway in the wind suggests that the wood has plenty of spring, and, in fact, white ash is used for baseball bats because it adds an extra zing to the hit.

Within this first quietness of the woods we often hear the *a-olee* melody of the wood thrush, the bird John James Audubon loved the most, opening and closing the night. It is usually mid-July before its song is stilled, unless the woods goes dry, and then the bird wings southward. In any case, it is rarely seen at all, and one must settle for the wood pewees calling from directly above the entrance and flitting through the canopy. Typical flycatchers, they sit straight up when perching, which makes them easier to identify. Their song will continue toward dusk after those of most birds of the field have quieted down. Woodland birds seem to be active longer and call later than those of more open areas. Possibly this is because it is cooler inside under the trees.

4 | *Homestead Remnants*

One autumn, on weekend journeys home from college, I began to notice the small farms strung along the cross-states road I traveled both ways in the slowly fading light of late afternoon. Farming was a dying custom here, and, like the golden glow of the passing season, like the very houses set back down the road, the twinkling lights were going out one by one. I suppose it was my being a passer-by that made it seem so, but the closing out *felt* unnoticed.

And so I saw some things that promised to go without being seen from the farm side of the walls, either, and for a good many years to come. I doubted that any of the paintless doors, locked behind their owners or not, would ever be opened again from the inside to view a level scene. It was nighttime for their day, and I wrote lines that went:

> The leaves are falling by a door
> That guards dim starlight on the floor.

A farm along this road would almost invariably begin with a stone wall. Once the wall may have stood straight and stockily tall. Now it sloped, like the well-worn Green and Taconic mountains. Birches and wild black cherries that had long ago been left as mere quirts in the wall now rose as kingpins against which the sag could lean every so often. As rocks had drifted down the pile away from their sockets, the gaps they left had eventually become open skylights for grass to take aim at. And where the frost heaving had not been too jarring, a shrub or so had also climbed through.

Beyond one particular wall a hill showed signs of heavy wear that seemed likely to have helped decide the abandoning of the farm. I took a chance one day on trespassing, and stumbled over rocks and ducked under barbed wire to get in. The cows had left little upright greenery there other than widely spaced tall thistles. The ground itself was very treacherous with pits and hummocks from their plodding—I began to appreciate the natural rubbery tension in the human ankle that kept mine from snapping to one side or another without warning. In one hand I carried a geology pick, for the bedrock was slate and I wanted to look for fossils along the flat, curving terraces on the hillside that had stood out from even a half mile away. Once on the terraces, I appreciated their graceful swing. Always they moved slightly upward or downward, as they had been carefully laid out by cows over Lord knows how many years. These were the "cat steps" I had noticed from a mile or so distant in Wisconsin. The geology pick proved a tiresome tool on the platy, trodden soil—I finally settled for breaking slates apart, farther on in a roadside cut, and looking for signs of the beasts known as graptolites. These primitive animals, now reduced to H-shaped carbon film, had lived and presumably died in quiet stagnant waters around 350 million years ago, after perhaps 50 million successful years. In their own way the graptolites (which I never turned up) had been "one H of a" long-term tenant on this land.

The final scene I recall of the broken farms is one of scattered boards. They are, even before red cedars, the first woody sign of human abandonment. They reflect disintegration. The integrity, or soul, of the farming operation is breaking down or apart. Is this when shed roofs begin to sag? They say that that comes from snow lying on top, but I think the first weakening of timber may occur inside.

Only a month earlier I had witnessed such physical disintegration carried out to an extent far greater than I could ever have imagined. A hurricane had deviated wildly from the path such storms had taken regularly for decades. Like a top spinning crazily through a room of toys and ricocheting off in a new direction every time it encountered something solidly grounded, the hurricane had rambled along valleys and scaled hills crabwise, flattening here and distributing bits and pieces with largesse there. A crew of us, traveling main highways and back roads, found shack after shack that once had been, now identifiable only as slabs and fragments blown over the hills. Of one home, a wall leaned against a black Cadillac, while the worst rags you ever saw, presumably laundry and including a small print dress, extended to the grass on a rope that stretched from a pole. The clothes had been pulled to their utmost by the last departing current and now pointed off in a tangent to the direction of the gale.

Thus we learned to what an extent tenant farming had gobbled up operations in this state. All those shanties stood for a sort of slavery that had crept in. Now an X-ray, in terms of nature, had registered the patches of sickness. I don't know what the ultimate result was, whether or not the governor stepped in with his crew to change the economic pattern. *Our* crew helped to repair some of the places. We had to be careful—most of the walls still standing could be punctured by resting a hand on them too heavily. I heard that one farm lost to mercy killing, or outright braining or stabbing, 98 out of 104 cows. The major difference in loss seemed to be, though, that the little fellows were not insured, whereas the landlords were—though maybe not against wind.

Farms on mountainsides would seem to be another matter. Their life often appears to be lonely, isolated as many of them are. In the Great Smoky Mountains I have seen curving loaves of hillsides where a farm could be seen just peeping over the ridge, like a low flat crab scrabbling up to see who or what was there. The demise of a farm in such uplands may begin with a "tear" in the sod well below the best pastures—this is a gully caused by soil erosion. The rent moves upward year by year. Eventually it slithers under a fence down in a rarely visited part of the property where herds almost never graze. Unchecked, it continues climbing upward, its open jaws of broken sod yawning wider by the yard. Pioneering weeds, shrubs, and trees follow. And so in the end it swallows a generation or so of dreams, filling in the gap with plant tenants that had been temporarily pushed aside.

A series of gold rushes that seriously depleted labor on farms all across the country began in California about 1849 and continued here and there through the latter decades of the nineteenth century. Connecticut, which was about 63 percent farmland in 1820, lost many settlers to the gold rushes. By 1910, 45 percent of the cleared land had reverted to forest.

In one episode of his career that is rarely mentioned, during August 1875 General George Custer reported the discovery of gold in the Black Hills area of South Dakota. By autumn, his report had brought more than fifteen thousand prospectors pouring in. The town of Deadwood attained its notoriety from Wild Bill Hickok's presence there. Prospectors charged onto the Sioux Indian reservation, followed by the Northern Pacific Railroad, and soon the Indians went on the warpath. Less than a year later, on June 26, 1876, Custer and his troops paid part of the bill for the unwanted tenancy when Custer's command was destroyed at Little Big Horn. This was a sort of *Indian* declaration of independence. But four months and five days later, chiefs Sitting Bull and Crazy Horse and their warriors also went down to defeat. Farmers were the eventual winners, re-creating in the west what they had left behind in the east.

What happens to a farm that has been left untended for a century or more? No one plows, no one mows, and the meadow and wood lot return. For without man's continual support most of his creations cannot go it alone. It's a nice lesson in man as a part of nature, not a partner.

I once walked up the road to one of these abandoned farms and became aware that I was in the vicinity of the house when I noticed a white pine in the midst of the maple-birch forest that now dominated the land. In the clearing formerly kept open by house and lawn this tree had at one time found enough light to continue growing for a good many decades. Perhaps the site of the house had been chosen for its nearness to the pine, needles of which fell and were joined by mosses on the house as an insulating "pine-moss" roof. It was in its prime then, after an ancient fire had opened the original forest. Now, like the farmer's last candle of many years ago, it was being snuffed out in all-pervading darkness.

A more recent sojourner had laid down the road I came in on. Small tree trunks had been dropped across low places, giving it a corduroy backbone where flat. Still, there were occasional dips, which probably had been scooped out by floods and then left as resting steps for teams of horses and oxen plodding up the slope. These "thank-you-ma'ams" also broke the force of all but the worst downpours, and so were a defense against washouts. In the best days of the farm there had been a public road here, too, but fate had preserved it only as a ditch I could see off to the side. In that form, though, it might outlast the neglected road I was walking on. With real luck it might preserve itself as an ever deepening gully that steadily pulled the old homestead and the corduroy logs down with it.

I left the road to enter a grove of uniformly small trees. Red maple, black birch, oak—all had about the same girth. They indicated that this part of the forest had once been a field and had been let go all at the same time. Probably I would have found, had I compared trunks carefully, that those of the maples and birches were fairly uniform, maple to maple and birch to birch. Their seeds spread easily, and those of a single generation might sail out to cover a whole field, thus producing new trees all the same age. I would wager two bits that the oak trunks, however, graded from larger to smaller as they approached the center of the field. This is because acorns are heavy and travel more slowly, making their swiftest advances when squirrels carry them, which isn't very far. So these would be trees of successive generations.

Evidence of human activity marked quite clearly the line between an old forest and the young one that had taken over the field. A stone fence carrying a thick cloak of leaves trundled along the border humbly and wormlike. At the lower end of the former field, it appeared to be about half as tall on the upland side as on the other. As a matter of fact, the offside was even steep and clifflike. Evidently each year when the farmer had tilled here he shifted his topsoil six inches or so farther downhill. Finally, between his shoving, the forest heaving and redepositing, and mud flows, the upland had gradually been worked downward. It made for a flatter place to seed where it had filled in next to the wall. Such a sudden flat meadow in the midst of a decline is similar to those made by beaver ponds that have silted up. Each has had a dam that for a while checked the natural eroding of topsoil.

Stone fences can be counted on to resist the wasting away of the land for many decades if they have been well constructed. A northern farmer looking to a long, fruitful future probably needs a three- to four-foot trench for his base, lest frost heave the wall over—as will happen when even well-set rocks are rested above the frost line. A sound wall is usually shaped like a pyramid, with its base its widest part. Such long-lasting walls or fences are particularly associated with New Englanders, who had innumerable boulders to choose from among those left by the glaciers. It was a very mixed assortment, called glacial erratics, which in general does not match the make-up of the bedrock.

Such lasting fences as this farm had are often dependent upon geography. Along parts of the coastal plain and in the south and west, where exposed stones are less common, rail fences take over. A zigzag "Virginia fence" might wrap a mere two-hundred-acre farm snugly in enough wood to have wiped out a twenty-acre forest. Hulbert says that in places where wood had to be bought it could cost more than had been paid for the farm acreage itself! He also points out that many southern farmers went westward not because of worn-out soil, as tradition has it, but because of the eventual elimination of wood suitable for fencing.

Unromantically, the stone fence I had found may have been built not in response to personal initiative but, rather, to the force of local law. Farmers in various parts of the country were enjoined to fence in their cattle, with the owner of any despoilers paying for damage done to a neighbor's crops. Where wood was required, all kinds were used, prime forest timbers going first. On September 22, 1748, Peter Kalm said of the Philadelphia area:

> Chestnut trees were commonly used for this purpose, because this wood kept longest against rotting and a fence made of it could stand for thirty years. But where no chestnut wood was to be gotten, the white and black oaks were taken. Of all kinds of wood that of the red cedar lasts the longest. . . . Hickory . . . is not good for fences since it cannot well withstand rotting after it is cut.

And the folk there paid dearly for their wood, too. Much of the original forested land was owned by well-to-do people who sold it at the highest possible prices. What's more, they were willing to hang on for some time waiting for prices to rise. As a result, old-field red cedar came to hold the better farms together.

Times change, and so do preferences in fencing materials. The farm I was investigating was uniform as to stone, and the wooden gates had gone. But I have seen the evidence in other places. So it was that 102 years after Kalm's note—on May 12, 1851—Thoreau commented that black locust

> was one of the earliest trees introduced into Europe from America (by one Hobin, about 1601); now extensively propagated in England, France, and Germany. Used for trunnels to the exclusion of all others in the Middle and Southern States. Instead of decaying acquires hardness with time.

Trunnels were nails made from wood, or "tree nails." Today black locust is grown here in managed forests, and every now and then you will pass property where a roadside sign offers locust fence posts for sale.

During Thoreau's time Osage-orange trees were becoming popular in the midwest as living fences. With their thorny twigs they could form a very formidable boundary as a hedge. But barbed wire was invented in 1874, and most of the hedge fences we find now in the country are wire ones. They often become refuges for weeds, grass, shrubs, and trees, which here avoid being chewed by cattle or mowed. Only last summer I had an old-field plot that was 120 by 110 feet plowed up and left alone to see what would take over. To satisfy another bit of ecological curiosity I got a friend to help me stand three gigantic posts in holes we dug along a diagonal line across the field. We then strung a strand of barbed wire along the tops of the posts. Our hope is that birds will perch there and drop seeds, the result in time being a line of bird-toted species. It should make for both interesting research and nice showcasing.

In cities as well as on farms, hedges have long been a major part of the scenery. Privet was used early as well as today. Peter Kalm observed that privet fences surrounded a number of fields and gardens. Unfortunately privet lacks spines, and cattle, hogs, and other four-footed guests push through all too easily. Kalm recommended switching to hawthorn.

In woods where the trees form an almost completely closed canopy, such as on that abandoned farm, only a stone wall would be likely to have remained in good form. Log and other wooden fences would have moldered away. Living fences would have gone wild and then been shaded out. I know of one woods where a string of black haws might have been one of the latter. Each year they become more spindly and produce fewer leaves and fruit.

That even the stone wall here had been no defense in the end against encroaching maples and birches reminds me of Robert Frost's poem "Mending Wall." In it the poet is close to error when he says:

> He is all pine and I am apple orchard.
> My apple trees will never get across
> And eat the cones under his pines, I tell him.

The fact is that one or the other grove is likely to drop seeds on neighboring property and eventually shade out the crop there. At any rate, it seems that the forest of *this* farm did take over a last remaining apple tree, for its twisted and open bole lay raggedly near the farmhouse foundation. The tree had had a half dozen feet or so of trunk, indicating it had been cared for. Apple trees gone wild branch close to the ground and continue to do so steadily as they grow.

Apples and pears have been present around human dwellings for thousands of years, at least as far back as the neolithic lake dwellings. Both European and American orchards have had a history of producing so much fruit that even total strangers passing by were allowed to help themselves to at least the fallen ones. The principle is similar to the Biblical one granted Ruth, when she was allowed to glean near Bethlehem.

I suspect that this solitary apple tree had been just as solitary in its day, however. There seemed to be no evidence of a full-scale orchard, not even the spotty four or five trees such as can sometimes be found today in suburban developments, one tree every three or four lawns or every hundred yards. This tree had probably been tended for its family-size load of fruit each autumn and also for the spring blossoms. On a large tree they light up the sky; even a modest flowering brightens the front lawn and carries the sounds of honeybees for days.

Colonists often kept hives of these insects, which the Indians soon referred to as "the white man's fly." But the life of the bee was not always as pleasant as simply visiting blossoms. In *Letters from an American Farmer*, J. Hector St. John Crèvecoeur tells how he opened the gut of a kingbird that was hunting near his own hives and took out about 171 honeybees! He spread them on a blanket in the sunlight and watched in amazement as 54 revived, licked themselves, and went back to their labors.

The fact that the old homestead here, though little more than a rough basement, had remained in any shape at all for today's inspection is testimony to the way people used to think. The frame had probably burned down, but the stones had evidently been carefully laid. Houses and barns were *supposed* to last for generations, even centuries. And so fine woodworking around old entrances and elsewhere tells about more than just the art of the individual owner or his ancestors. It speaks deliberately to the future like hieroglyphics in stone. The designs are our Rosetta stone, a glimpse and a key into the worthwhile past.

I missed finding a springhouse on the farm. Perhaps I might have turned one up at the far bottom of the long slope. But I see them often now in other woods here and there. They have a deep chill. The "dislocated" stones of their inner walls are rarely that, but were really shelves planned to hold goods. Here is how Thoreau immortalized one in his *Journal:*

> It *was* a delectable place to keep butter and milk cool and sweet in dog-days—but there was a leopard frog swimming in the milk, and another sitting on the edge of the pan.

5 | *The Woodland Marsh: Richest of the Rich*

"If he cries," said Supreme Court Justice Bowlong in Carl Sandburg's *Remembrance Rock*, "I shall tell them it is the Future they hear crying." Judge Bowlong was speaking of a healthy baby, but he might have been speaking of one of the multitude of voices that call out lustily from a vigorous marsh. And when the marsh is threatened by woods which are closing in more tightly every year, that cry is one of the long successional Future.

In the economy of nature marshes rank as one of the banks. They steadily become richer with topsoil, fertilizer, leaves, and living and dead organisms. The only hint of bankruptcy is in their potential for rising so high in gathering so many of these riches that the ground rises, and they fill in completely. Then the marsh is no longer. Within a forest the trees take over.

I know of one small shallow lake where plants growing out in the water are nearly a forest themselves, and where shoreline woods are year by year moving out as the open space silts in and shrinks. It is a remarkable demonstration of the way a lake becomes a marsh and the marsh is almost immediately a thickly wooded swamp or just a wet forest. My visit there, about three years ago, was by innocent invitation. Little did any of us realize when I accepted what could happen on an expedition which really had begun with rather limited aims.

I had been driven to the lake by a friend and his wife simply to band some marsh birds called least bitterns. She hopped out of the car first, to enter a copse of cattails and explore for the needle-nosed birds close to shore. Alone, she could slip silently and stealthily through the leathery blades. He and I drove on to pick up a canoe and enter from another bank. The day's adventures, though beginning slowly, were under way.

We had soon slung the light metal craft between us and were headed down toward the water. As we passed through a grove of trees my friend commented on their fairly great height and yet youth. "Generally, the faster growing, the weaker a tree is. Good examples are silver maples [now overhead] and box elders." Some grew near our recently built apartment house, and he observed that developers like to use them for their rapid rise in height. "Cottonwood is an exception," he added. I could certainly agree with him, at least in part, for a large box elder outside our kitchen window had already acquired a promising-looking split in the main trunk. A few weeks later a huge limb, eight inches in diameter, crashed to the ground on our sidewalk. I punched my fist into its center and came out with a handful of very punky material. Wet and soft as balsa wood, that stuff belonged in a teddy bear! Could a landscaper be sued if such a limb bounced off someone's head or bashed a baby carriage sitting under the pleasant shade—which had been provided all too soon?

Down at the lake, we could see that there was a lot of blue sky, and he observed that this was a warm day for April and the rising air was carrying off some of the dust overhead. So there would be more sky to see. Then he spoke of the mixing of warm and cold air, high and low air pressures and storm fronts, and darkening clouds. This was a curious portent—but more about that later.

Swish went the smooth metal skin as we slid the silver boat down a last few grassy and sedgy feet of shore into the water. A natural hedge of sandbar willows accompanied us for twenty or so yards into the lake.

My companion pointed out the half pyramid they formed, its peak being the part farthest inshore (except for some tumbledown pieces that were testing higher ground out of the water). Sandbar willow, he said, sends out roots and creeping stems, and new trunks grow up from these; this growth continues year after year, until a single shrubby tree becomes a thicket. As the lake filled in with silt and muck this sandbar willow followed the silt like a finger pointing toward open water. Each year a band of new willow trunks came up as a lower and further step of foliage. We could have counted the steps and told the age of the whole semi-individual, or clone. But too soon, I thought, we lost track of it as we marched without pause into the water and were quickly chest deep.

My guide was soon weaving his way down almost undetectable paths through the tallest wedges of cattails I have ever seen. Huge mats, or floating islands, of them were anchored to the bottom by hemplike roots that slammed them shut behind us—forever, I thought, closing off our escape should we try to retreat. Every now and then we did err, as it seemed we were not always quite on course to the thread-thin corridor that was to lead us to open water and contact with his wife.

Muskrat lodges appeared now and then like inflated ancient landmarks. Really old ones furnished nesting for black terns, while new ones attracted mallards and teals for both nesting and resting. My friend pointed out that muskrats cut down a lot of cattails while feeding and building nests. The stems are left standing leafless underwater. This kills off the emergent weed and results in muskrat runways—down one of which we were shoving, I presumed. These larger channels were also deeper, fine for many fish, but the water was rising ever higher on our rib cages. "Bitterns and herons feed in this deeper water," my friend commented with pleasure—though I noticed it was still too clogged by cattail fencing for us to roll into the canoe and paddle a bit. The shift from a dense cattail plantation, which might really be a single individual with many shoots, to one simply of barrier packs favored the nesting of many birds. I guessed that more and more species were arriving above us even as we plodded along.

A slight shift in the air pressure zones up high had begun to bring a few wispy clouds and a little bite into occasional gusts of wind when we broke out of the forest of green spears and entered a water lily paddy. In no time we had rocked the canoe back and forth between us, one being very experienced and the other just getting his sea legs, and we flopped in over the gunnels, along with a hatful or so of shipped water. We were undeniably cooler there for an instant, but soon the pressure of attaining some sort of momentum through the carpet of lily pads had our temperatures rising. Anyway, our feet were warm. For today, the bottom muck had a certain warmth from having been decaying several hundred years without stop, and in our boots the process did not cease. We would only be making a chilling mistake if we tugged them off and dumped the ooze overboard simply out of esthetics and an unaccustomed feeling of constant pressure.

Well, the upshot was that we were a bit late catching up with the lady, who had had to plunge on after the bitterns alone. She was especially eager to see how the population as a whole was doing and to count and band some of the young. Unfortunately, while the adult bittern is familiar to most of us—at least via photographs—as a long-faced individual who poses rigidly among the reeds, beak up straight as a church steeple, the youngsters are as agile as an army of spiders and run away through cattails with about as much ease. Their feet are remarkably adept at grasping the blades and stems like little fingers. Not only that, but the six-inch fellows dodge. They seem to have the sense of humor one might expect from any individual who thinks (successfully) that hiding is standing with your nose up.

I recorded here some action on the bird chase that eventually developed with everyone down in the water. Crash! Cattails parting and someone wet. "How many do you have?" Pant or gasp. "I don't have any yet." (Fifteen minutes had already passed, and we were chest deep again.) "I'm going to try—" Splash! We, or she, I believe, caught one, banded it, and placed it in the floating Styrofoam picnic box for me to photograph.

I think that it was about then that I stumbled and slapped the Styrofoam lid in two.

We were ready to leave after we had enjoyed watching a least bittern infant peck its way free from its pale greenish egg. My friend averred that this minute specimen was indeed "a least least bittern."

Dark clouds had brought a gloom over the lake, and a slick breeze was snapping the cattail flags as we pitched each other and ourselves into the canoe. My friend and I dipped our paddles furiously but rhythmically into open water once again, and we were soon racing before the occasional raindrops while his wife organized the boxes, cameras, and so on amidships. Within minutes our prow whispered and then hissed as it cut into pond lilies that grew rapidly thicker. Deeper and deeper I thrust my paddle, finally straining even to drive it past a vertical position. I looked down into the massed lily pads and mumbled, "I sure don't remember working this hard coming out!"

With that notice of our predicament, there was a moment of agitated exercise near the center of the boat, a parting shot that went something like, "Well, I'd better get out!" and a *kerchunk* in the water. My friend's wife had lightened our load. Though not her own—with her shoulders awash, she began knifing a brown furrow through the lake without further word. The last we saw of her was a gallant splitting of nearby wind-lashed cattails, until we drove up in the car a good twenty minutes later.

A day such as that comes rarely.

More usual encounters with marshes can be as brief as a pause between appointments elsewhere to climb a roadside fence for a better view of a gem that has been noticed now for the first time. I remember one such occasion well. I had first been drawn up short by the pale green plate the marsh made beside the wall of a forest. The squared shape of its corners spoke of an old farm pond that had been left to the wilds. A thick skin of duckweeds indicated that it had once accumulated a rich content of nutrients, which were now fertilizing this massive bloom of one of our smallest flowering plants. I stepped closer and with a brush of my hand parted several hundred flat seedlike leaves. The water was so dark as to defy my finding anything but nearly microscopic life chugging by. As surely as a board cover laid over the marsh, its green roof had become a ceiling of death to weeds, nymphal insects, and fish that had doubtless once lived below. Sunlight had probably not penetrated the water for two months, it now being late in June.

The marsh was quite young, though aging fast under the duckweed regime. Nothing larger than sedges was encroaching upon it as yet. Soon I would expect to see the brown bats of cattails thumping each other out beyond the sedges. I did notice one fairly certain sign of the future, though. To my right rested a fallen tree with a few arms raised and held akimbo. A number of its upper branches had evidently been sheared off long ago, possibly to allow a telephone line to pass through. I considered it to be an incipient perch, a preconditioning of the marsh for the arrival of red-winged blackbirds when cattails filled in dense enough to support their nests. It would be an arrival of mixed blessings for the local farmers. Red-wings stand in line behind the plow to pluck up larvae that have been thrown open to the sun, but they also can fill the sky with a tornado of birds as thousands of them attack corn and other grains at harvest time. During this season, incidentally, the musculature of their gizzards grows stronger with the diet change to harder food. They and other marsh birds are vectors, or carriers, of equine encephalitis, a disease that is then transmitted to man by mosquitoes.

Thirty or forty yards away a pond somewhat similar in size and shape lay half within the woods. The greater portion of this one was shaded even at noon by a venerable maple which had seen many changes come over its part of the world. Huge branches made jerky right and left turns, showing where new growth during various springs of the year had been forced to take new directions over a long lifetime. No large limbs existed toward the road side. I could not get in close enough to tell, but either they had been lopped off to keep the pasture and later the pond clear or companion trees of the forest had long ago so cut them off from sunlight as to cause the tree to abort them.

Their death had meant life for this pond, though. Slender pipeworts were poking up through the water's sunlit surface, yellowed by that finest powder, pollen from fringing shrubs. Submerged pondweeds gave an interior green mirroring that of the surface. Tall brown heads of last year's sensitive fern were filling one corner of the bank with their fruit, while a loose cluster of skunk cabbage leaves added a rank sense of vegetative luxuriance.

Such scenes of life and death are but small-scale glimpses into what is actually one of the most productive of all our temperate zone communities, the half-submerged reed marsh that is dominated by cattails. The best environment for these plants would be a large shallow marsh with a gently graded shoreline, a dip of six feet per thousand feet having the potential for yielding a large crop. That dying lake I was taken to might have been a good example of such a marsh in the process of being created. The massive roots of cattails have been dried and crushed to make a high-quality flour. Their seed hairs are useful for insulation and have been used in place of kapok; more than three hundred thousand can occupy a single cattail head. Farming was easier because cattail neck rings for the horses helped prevent burns from horse collars. Some people even used the battening of the cattail head as down in their beds! Unfortunately, the soft fibers coalesced into lumps after a while, and the practice faded. High-grade cattail leaves are used to waterproof barrels, and some chair caning has long been made from the leaves. A two-acre marsh that is producing well may yield nearly a thousand dollars' worth of barrel waterproofing and chair caning alone each year.

Most of us have to settle for esthetics rather than cash crops, however. And there is excellent scenery down by the marsh. One may go only part way and treat it simply as the conclusion of a very pleasant walk under red and silver maples and through a wiry grove of willows to the alder fence at water's edge. There, if the season is autumn, one can appreciate that final crackling sound like tissue wrapping paper—the dying leaves of dayflowers. If it is spring, a few moments may be spent following inquisitive manure-toned flies as they poke about and finally settle on an emerging skunk cabbage. I myself always enjoy following a marsh from the first really damp sidelines out to the center, from wetland shrubs such as buttonbush to open water, where a few lily pads may be floating.

Buttonbush, which often stands with its feet in the water, has summer flowers that grow in heads somewhat reminiscent of the spiked mines sown in harbors during wartime. The image is fair enough, for the seeds will produce new shrubs to tie up perhaps another yard of marshland farther out next year. Sedges ring the shrub base with tough, slender blades that can make fine slashes in your skin as you walk through. It is often easy to tell them from the round-stemmed grasses by their solid triangular stems—sedges are wedges. Their seeds may be one of the last foods of the marsh bank to be tasted by waterfowl before *they* depart, and the last wetland cover for marsh hawks. While the hawks are still around, though, it is worth a few minutes' time to watch for adults giving their young target practice in the air by dropping mice.

This edge where land crosses into water has a famous history as a transition zone. I need only mention the evolution of gilled fish into lunged amphibians during the Devonian period. Possibly even earlier, primitive terrestrial scorpions evolved from aquatic euripterids. At any rate, we can be certain that the peculiar air-breathing gills called book lungs, now found in both scorpions and many spiders, came into being along such a boundary, which may have differed only in being brackish and lacking flowering plants—these last did not evolve until the Cretaceous period.

A marsh may be totally obscured from the side by one reed that forms its own thicket and grows to a height of twelve feet or more. Giant reed, often so well known that people use the generic name, *Phragmites*, appears in marshes, along canals and rivers, and even in quite brackish waters around the world. A high water table next to a thruway may be identified from a mile or so down the road by these tall grasses with brushy tops. They are also one of the largest plants to grow within reach of the highest tides, the storm-fed ones of autumn and winter. In autumn their squeaking stalks and heads gone tawny indicate that the swimming season is past for most of us. As a hedge *Phragmites* attracts many roosting birds, though it produces too few seeds to bring in birds solely for feeding. As far as many airport managers are concerned, however, too many birds find these grasses attractive. The swirling bird populations that roost in the grasses beside runways that are near wetlands may interfere with aircraft of all sizes. Occasionally we read in the newspapers about broken windows and body dents caused when a bird plunges against an airplane; I don't imagine there is much left of an individual that has hurtled through a jet engine.

My most distinctly useful acquaintance with a *Phragmites* stand occurred during one of the worst snowstorms of the year. It was Washington's Birthday, and I had been forced off a northern thruway by winds, snow, and ice that threatened to claim my car part by part if not as a whole choice morsel. After pulling into a garage for respite and repairs, I left the automobile poised high over the grease pit while I did some investigating out back. Sure enough, buried up to its long skinny throat in a snowbank, *Phragmites* was giving the only near touch of color to a landscape that was fast disappearing under curtains of snow.

I broke off four or five stems and tossed them into the descending car. The shop owner made a comment, and I said something about living-room decorations. Then I asked him how his garage drainage was. The question socked home. He said it was always soggy in back, that when the ground was wet anywhere else *his* place seemed likely to wash right off the hill. I also gathered that the concrete floors had cracked and run. Eventually, he came around to inquiring what had made me ask. So I told him, "The table decorations. They grow only where it's wet all the time, and your back yard is full of them—probably where a spring lets out. I think the guy who built this place goofed and didn't have the soil tested, or ignored what he was told." When he asked me where I had learned *that* stuff, I felt as if I had scored one for nature interpreters across the country.

A tall golden bulrush called wool grass can be easily confused with *Phragmites* along a marsh edge, but its richly seeded head is usually tossed over, like girls' hair when thrown forward in the sun to dry. *Phragmites* more resembles a soft feather duster set on end. When back-lit its autumn heads often have a silver shine, while wool grass glows orange, as though hot within. The very furry wool grass seeds cluster on finely divided sprays of the drooping heads.

A thin zone, or sometimes just a gardenlike patch, of flowers often lightens the shadows thrown by these two tall grasses. Three of the major marsh flowers are a curious collection: blue flag iris, sweet flag, and arrowhead. During May blue flag iris spreads its striking blossoms wide, each bloom radiating three bee traps. The bee must push its way into a tube that divides in two and then clamps shut like an alligator's mouth. Once inside, the insect is brushed free of some of the pollen it may already be carrying and then is dusted by the flag's own pollen. Farthest in is the nectar. Sweet flag flowers, on the other hand, have no pretenses, but are grouped tightly on fingerlike projections, each called a spadix. This name may be familiar from jack-in-the-pulpit, which is in the same family. The sweet flag spadices are on the sides of the stems, however, where they somewhat suggest yellowish insect galls. Because the blossoms are so small, June flowering can pass unnoticed. Actually no blossoms will appear at all if water does not cover the roots most of the year. Sweet flag's slender blades rather resemble those of the blue flag iris. Bending, they each act like flags.

In July, dragonflies and damselflies pause among the white-petaled, yellow-faced flowers of arrowhead, which are often a spray of flowers standing out in the marsh. First to open on any one stalk are the female blossoms, commonly the lower ones. Not only do insects fertilize them, but so also do aquatic snails, which are really visiting to chew up the petals. The male blossoms come later, usually too late to dust ripe pollen down onto their sibling female flowers but in time to pass it along to others. Not surprisingly, the leaves resemble arrowheads, and some of the narrower-leaved types suggest fanciful spaceships. None of the leaves retain water very well, however. As a result, arrowheads can be dangerous to other marsh plants during summer droughts because they release so much water into the air. When the arrowheads themselves go, ducks may be the first to miss them. These birds yank their tubers up out of the mud to eat, as did Indians. Thus another name for this flower, which is known best for its leaves, is duck potato.

The final arbiter between marsh and upland remains our familiar cattails. Most marshes simply do not seem worthy of the title unless they have at least one cluster of these in the shallows. That lake I spoke of earlier was more a marsh by virtue of its great swaths of cattails, and I appreciated it as such. Now our greatest appreciation of marshes threatens to be their uses after an attack on them by draining. More than 30 percent of our heritage in marshes, swamps, and general wetlands has been eliminated in this way. As a result, the most constant remaining relationship with cattails may be that of muskrats, which still maintain colonies in out-of-the-way places.

Muskrats lack the appeal of beavers. After all, they are only large water rats closely related to pack rats. But muskrat ecology, if not the beasts themselves, will be missed when we have done-in our larger marshes.

Their houses of plastered cattails are the most familiar hints that muskrats are around, but actually they often come and go with or without building any. When I was a boy, friends of ours had a pond that attracted houseless muskrats, and also trappers. Coves a foot deep along a far steep shore provided the answer. The muskrats had gone underwater and dug in there, constructing tunnels that led up to dry underground rooms beneath the bank. Further holes appeared under untended shrubbery nearby. Occasionally one of the entrances would announce itself by collapsing under me as I walked beside the pond. Such tunneling is common along rivers whose strong current would drag a house away, so it is wise to be especially alert when striding on *those* banks.

Dome-style muskrat houses may not do well under conditions of deep or flowing water, but a hurricane now and then can be a real benefit. In his *North with the Spring*, Teale says that on Mississippi River delta marshes hurricanes have saved muskrats from, of all enemies, ants! Down there

> These insects breed in astronomical numbers. . . . They oftentimes nest in the vegetable masses of the muskrat houses and the skeletons of young rats have been found picked clean by the swarming insects.
>
> Hurricanes come to the rescue of the water rats. They sweep away the infested houses and the decaying logs where the ants are breeding.

Also, Teale notes, hurricanes flush salt water into the marshes, making them inhospitable to saw grass but a better environment for other plants. Saw grass has almost no food value for muskrats, whereas "the best food plants for both the rats and for overwintering waterfowl demand brackish water."

Muskrat housing and cattail survival are not just an on-and-off proposition, though. Commonly a cycle occurs that drags all kinds of life with it, like a great net hauling in not only the intended catch but everything else besides. As cattails begin to fill a marsh, muskrats find in them food and the necessary building materials for their houses. At first the domes stand out, but eventually cattails fence them in, and an outsider may find it easier to look for muskrat trails instead. As the houses multiply, however, the cost to the marsh goes up in terms of cattail roots that are eaten or else drowned as the stems are nipped off, the roots suffocating from lack of oxygen.

While the marsh is still deep, fish wander freely. If it is deep enough, you will see kingfishers hunting there. This is getting to be a rare situation, though, since runoff from farms and housing developments is so great. As a marsh matures, silting up and thus providing more shallow places for cattails to stand in, fish may congregate near the muskrat houses. They do this especially along trails where the owner has cut a "lead-in" from deeper water to the dwelling. Now fishing birds nest beside the lead-ins and feed on fish coming up them. With luck, the secretive sora rail might be found here, together with its lively precocial young. Coots, or mud hens, are worth seeing if for no other reason than to examine the wavy flanges of the feet—which remind me of the leaves of winged sumac. The first thing many people notice is their red-furred young. Then again there is that mixed bird the common gallinule, which clucks like a hen and has an outrageously red beak and facial plate. Finally, as long as they can find room, grebes will be building their floating nests. These are made from cattails which the birds yank out; they are attached to the living reeds and so do not float off. When the birds are going to be away from the nest they give it an unmade-bed appearance by covering it with cattail blades.

A well-balanced marsh would have muskrats, cattails, and birds keeping each other company in a rather small community of mutual support and dependence. Actually, of course, the advantage swings now this way and now that. If the cattails do too well and thatch over the marsh, the birds will leave. Muskrats help keep the birds around by clearing out excessive cattails. A very productive marsh can serve muskrats well, but it can also trip off a muskrat population boom.

At that point one of two disasters can depose the rats. They can ravage their own habitat, starving themselves and destroying all the cover, so that most birds can no longer nest in the balding marsh either. A really thundering overpopulation, with hundreds of muskrats per acre, can build up and shear acres and acres of cattails. This can lead to internecine battles, incidentally, even with populations less than one tenth this size. Equally disastrous, vast numbers can bring on minks, predators that will finally clean out all the muskrats. This gives the cattails and birds a chance to come back.

Man himself is no mean factor in marsh ecology. The problem does not begin with cash crops—growers probably could establish a balance between plant and harvest—but, rather, with runoff. This comes not only from farms but also from housing developments, shopping centers, and other building activities. We can divide the attack into two phases. The first is the silting in of the marsh as water flowing off the land carries away exposed soil. The second is the flooding of marshes as highways, streets, driveways, parking lots, and other concrete and asphalt "lids" on the land reject water and force builders to pipe it away—and a convenient final trap often turns out to be a low marshy area. Here high water builds up, causing a massive die-off of cattails as the stems are flooded and the roots suffocate. Duckweed and underwater algae may then become the dominant plants. With very high water, dead cattails break loose from the bottom, and we have islands of floating cattails. Here again, birds are eliminated and won't return. Ironically, these thick drifting mats become new ground for fresh cattails and perhaps mallard nests. Black terns prefer old ones. Least bitterns may escape all but the worst inundations, for they build their nests high enough on the cattails so that water fluctuations won't ordinarily swamp them.

Deeper water may signal the limits of cattail, but it introduces a whole new world. Great pan-shaped water lilies bump each other like full-skirted dancers in slow motion. Duckweeds not only float everywhere but even get blown out of the water and slapped onto tree trunks a foot or so up. In autumn the sugars in their leaves change to starch, as in the roots of trees and many prairie weeds and grasses. The leaves, becoming denser than their environment, sink to the bottom, where the plants overwinter. Spring sunlight and warmth revive the plants, which convert the starch back to the lighter-weight sugars, and soon they are bobbing on top of the wavelets again.

Duckweed *is* consumed by ducks. I have even seen mallards with green mustaches. The plant also seems to have a peculiar sort of strife with the water chestnut. During the 1950's, water chestnut trees in New York State failed rather badly along Mohawk River backwaters, where duckweed was a prominent growth; in quiet places where water chestnut had been taken away, duckweed moved right in.

There are four duckweed genera, and most of us who have visited marshes have seen at least three of them (the fourth is pretty much limited to the eastern United States). The tiniest, watermeal, has a maximum diameter of about 1.5 millimeters. It is probably our smallest flowering plant and is likely to go unnoticed. Just a smattering of green dots. Water birds eat all four, though the one called common duckweed seems to be preferred by far. Undoubtedly duckweeds help draw down to the marsh those calls that Aldo Leopold knew and loved so well. In *A Sand County Almanac*, he wrote that from the birds' cries in the early morning he could just about count them and tell where they were.

> To arrive too early in the marsh is an adventure in pure listening; the ear roams at will among the noises of the night, without let or hindrance from hand or eye. When you hear a mallard being audibly enthusiastic about his soup, you are free to picture a score guzzling among the duckweeds. When one widgeon squeals, you may postulate a squadron without fear of visual contradiction. And when a flock of bluebills, pitching pondward, tears the dark silk of heaven in one long rending nose-dive, you catch your breath at the sound, but there is nothing to see except stars.

When dabbling ducks topple over and work the marsh bottom, exposing their rumps to bob above like fluffy markers, you can guess that they are not only nuzzling through the mud but nibbling at one or another of the submerged plants. Two of the most common of these are waterweed, or water celery, and naiad. Waterweed, often better known as *Elodea* or *Anacharis*, is familiar to most keepers of indoor aquariums. Biology classes raise it to demonstrate the easily seen cyclic travels of green chloroplasts within the cells of leaves. But birds have simpler aims —eating leaves and fruits. The stomach of one dissected redhead bay duck bore six hundred fruits. Naiad is such a favorite that all except the root is consumed. I have seen these weeds massed so thickly that they were throttling life in a small pond. The only openings were black channels that had been parted by muskrats.

The first large-scale marsh in which I ever spent much time lies like a broad platter within the terminal moraines of glacial drift, a place that is also the home of several species of oaks. Roughly fifteen acres of open water still remain in the center, surrounded by a slowly contracting soggy rim that varies between 100 and 450 feet in width. This adds up to approximately twenty-three acres, if we assume the marshland area to be a perfect circle—which it almost is.

Mallards, black ducks, blue-winged teals, and coots are among the birds that slip in to plunge near the edge for arrowhead roots, waterweed, and other food. They cannot nest out in the open water, of course, though after the nesting season is over and the feeding pressure has been lifted, arrowheads rise to add broad expanses of heavy cover where formerly there was none. In some places, to make a study by boat practically requires a machete.

The center can be lost from sight for long periods if one is plodding toward it through some of the wider rims of growth. At the edge, bur oak leaves cloud the view. Pushing aside the twigs is no easy job, for the corky growth on them, which made this species resistant to prairie fires, continues as a sleeve right out to the twig tips. Beyond the oaks, hedges of gray dogwood and white spiraea, in some places anchored beside short American elms, are strung here and there. When I last visited the marsh, early one spring, spiraea blossoms were attracting little green-and-black solitary bees that climbed over and through the massed blossoms like tiny kittens. Walking through the sedges, bur reeds, bulrushes, horsetails, sweet flags, and others, I touched and came away with the foul odor of hound's-tongue, then in clustered leafy rosette form. I missed seeing the full-grown white marsh asters. In August they can tower well over a man's head. Perhaps this loss was made up for by the birthday-cake heads of pink-and-white milkweed blossoms I had seen in June the year before.

I remember, on the more recent trip, getting as far as the cattails, where I squatted until my knees stiffened and ached. That was what came of trying to entice a curious long-billed marsh wren in closer. The bird, a male, had been darting about this particular area for some time, jumping around within a radius of ten to twenty yards. I presume he had been laying claim to his territory by setting out dummy nests—reverse decoys which would keep other males at a respectful distance. Like grassland or prairie birds, these inhabitants of the wetter meadows sing while flying. Edward H. Forbush relates warmly, in *A Natural History of American Birds,* his experience of their singing:

> . . . In the still and peaceful night, when the full moon of June rose grandly over the river marshes and the full chorus of the wrens was at its flood, sounding from far and near, I have listened with much pleasure to the sound. They often sing from the rushes or cattails, sometimes from the water brush, and frequently rise in brief flight straight up into the air for six to twelve feet, singing as they flutter down. The male cannot resist the urgent impulse to sing while on his way to the nest with a billful of cattail down for the lining. He sometimes sings two or three times on the way, thus losing his down and having to pick it all up again.

Such huge amphitheaters as river marshes and twenty-three-acre impoundments lend an appropriately majestic backdrop to any chorus. Frogs' complaints of bellyaches, insectlike screeches, and rhythmical belling tones rule the dusk air. In between this vocal range may be heard the passing bark of a black-crowned night heron. And, far later than might be expected, the whistle and rattle of cicadas rises from reeds and drives down from tall oaks. No jungle sounds we might know or imagine should let us forget the notes that can fill the night close at hand; some of the best stage settings may be only a short distance from one's own door.

Far away from the large marsh and late in June, morning freshness had been captured down in the lowest part of an oak-hickory forest when

I passed by the dark leaves of spicebushes and stood suddenly beside one of the smallest woodland marshes I have ever seen. I couldn't spit across it, but my father could have. Of course, he had been brought up in a day when long-range expectorating was a sign of power that is now seen only in vestigial roles in Western movies. Anyway, its diameter can best be judged by the green frog that gave a sharp yelp, leaped in, and hit near dead center on the fly.

Perhaps it was its minuteness, as marshes go, that gave me the chance to see more of its denizens over the next several months. For instance, in June I was rewarded by the sight of green bulging submarines that every so often glided along for short distances. These turned out to be green frog tadpoles, huge fellows that were about two years old and would soon gain their legs. As with other frogs, the left arm appears first, poking past a flap of skin on the side of the head. If the water were still high later on, the adults would probably mate here. The female attaches the firm jelly of her egg mass to sunken twigs; a dry spell can leave the eggs hanging juicily exposed to the hot blasts of summer.

In July the marsh did recede. Down it went, the water sucked out by roots of oaks, hickories, black cherries, and the surrounding sedges and rushes. Air-breathing pond snails congregated in pockets all across the bottom, often more than two dozen to the square inch. The mud became dry enough for tiger swallowtails to pause for a drink out near the middle. Eventually the duckweeds lay ironed out and ivory-colored upon a green felt of algae.

I was amazed to find here dragonflies, damselflies, and other insects that spend a large part of their lives as nymphs underwater. How they managed to survive the yearly drought is a mystery yet. In midsummer I dug a foot down into the dried black muck in several places and came up without a single nymph. Possibly the adults did find their way from fields and ponds elsewhere, though it must have taken some wandering to find this cup of water. Still, the knotweeds and jumpseeds here were favorite landing places for two species in particular, the large white-tailed skimmer dragonfly and the blue or green-and-black forktail damselfly.

This latter I have had occasion to trail around a larger, tree-shrouded marshy pond for several months, learning what I could about the ways in which males recognize females. It was a mildly complicated study, in which I learned that male forktail damselflies can distinguish between orange immature females and blue mature ones. Even more than that, they will try to mate with colored paper that has been cut to resemble a female damselfly. But there is more to this story of a day in June that began in maple and elm shadows overhanging the water:

At the edge of the woods night remained past eight o'clock. The damp pebbled leaves of cove pondweed dried soon after the sun rose over the far rim of maple and elm, however, and night simply became morning.

Eight-thirty, and the damselflies unhooked tiny claws from stem and leaf, lifted legs slow to move in the cool shadows, flicked one wing and finally all four into blurred motion. The insects had hung from weed and grass all night, swinging pendulously as though tacked up to dry. Now, by ones and twos, they fled down dark corridors among the weeds and into the yellow day.

Tiny gnats were jittering above the water. When they landed they often disappeared amid the leaves and pollen on the speckled surface. Where one embankment was backed for nearly twenty yards by an open slope, the morning breeze slid off the shore and tended to drive pollen, leaves, and insects into open waters. The return of some insects after a brief drift suggested the release from tension of a stretched rubber band.

By midmorning dozens of damselflies had begun to weave among the weeds and grass and to glide in small and great arcs out into the shallow cove, trapping insects that flew over the still visible bottom. One green-and-black male steered slowly along the shore. His pioneering deliberateness made me think he was storing the weed and muck contours in memory. I was watching most closely when he slipped out toward the end of a long projecting stick. There he paused, vibrating as though tethered from all sides, and hovering a few inches above a strip of orange paper on the stick. Suddenly, the insect hurled itself at the painted stripe.

All along this shoreline damselflies were weaving intangible paths over leaves, around jutting granite rocks, down streams of faint wind. Sometimes a chain of two or three of the green males would file slowly by. Such companions resembled friends walking together, each engrossed in a newspaper. The insects became individuals, solitary hunters, however, when they came upon an adult female of their species. It was this strong attraction that had apparently driven the male toward the orange paper. Though mature females of this species, *Ischnura verticalis*, are grayish blue and younger, immature ones orange, even the phantom on the stick was able to serve as a stimulus. That paper image was for me the last experiment in a long series undertaken to find out what characteristics drew damselflies to other damselflies and, incidentally, male to female.

I had begun several months before with the youngest winged form. The days were just beginning to turn hot and dry when I glued a first dead immature female to a length of branch and pushed the pale orange body out over the pond. From the shadows cast by towering Chinese elms I was reaching into an insect-strewn airway drawn from a cluster of blue flag to a low range of smartweed sprawling several feet into the shallows. Flies crawled in the sweat behind my ears. Once a black swallowtail came and fluttered in one of the iris heads; its rapid departure made me feel I was intruding. A few male damselflies drifted by almost dreamily.

By the end of the second hour my eyes seemed to be focusing only on the sun buried in the water a yard away.

Nearly two weeks later I was able to make some sort of reckoning. It was a thin show for the hours spent. Out of fifty-three males that had flown to within four inches of the stiff specimens I offered, one had made a nearly complete circle about the bait, fourteen had merely slowed down, and thirty-eight had appeared to ignore the sun-baked odonates. In time I would find that wings alone drew nearly the same range of behavior, while only five males out of forty-two paused near a wingless body.

Searching for the most favored territories of the species, I had moved first to an open sandy beach, then to a clearing where a woodland path punched through to the pond between woody blackberry bushes. On several occasions I had sat at the tip of a sere peninsula, a pebbly spot where damselflies touched down on spare filaments of grass but then were rushed off in unpredictable gusts.

Finally I had poised four of the translucent insects at two-inch intervals near the tip of a six-foot pole. They struck poses of life, but I thought of them as dancers frozen at the height of the crescendo. One male *Ischnura* flew upon this stilled scene. Slowly he moved down the examples of death. Then he turned away. I, too, became convinced by this dumb show and abandoned these "assorted characters of death and blight."

The next morning I fell under the spell of literature's pathetic fallacy at nearly every step. I saw depression in the drooping willow I had regularly camped under while marking insects. Here were ten thousand snares in the morning dew, quicksand to minute flies. And when I shouldered my way out of a thicket, morning shadows drawn in stripes stretched away like the many paths I knew might lead only to deeper darkness. I turned almost without hope toward the pond. The shoreline here was narrow, a rugged embankment guarding it from human visitors. As I gazed down the stony slope, despairing of working where my back would part a set of thimbleberry bushes, a yellow damselfly, smaller than the average crane fly, sailed up past my feet and disappeared over an abandoned lawn. Watching its flight, I caught another movement. It was an orange damselfly.

As if for the first time, I noticed the insect life around the furrowed grass, the low chicory, the two small deserts of hardpan clay. Without moving, I saw half a dozen immature females of *Ischnura verticalis* nosing restlessly through their natural habitat. I had seen them on earlier occasions fly in off gently sloping banks, wander onto the grass, perch on distant clover, wing out of sight in the shadows of sumacs. Now it was clear that the pale, freshly molted females rested at first near the place where the larvae emerged. Then, hardened to a deep orange, the still immature insects retreated to these nearly windless spots. Later, dark blue and robust, they would slip back to the pond. Males have the same wanderlust, but I often saw them return.

To answer the question of how many of the same individuals I encountered on successive days, I marked the wings of over 2,000 during the summer. Using a simple code and keeping a record book, I could identify any of the marked insects. In the course of the summer I recovered 56 of 875 males, 46 of 849 females, and only 5 of 281 immature females. That figured out to 6.40, 5.42, and 1.78 percent respectively. Very few insects were caught a third time.

Where did they go? How was it that never did I net the same marked orange insect in its later color? Immature ants fall to pillaging raiders; honeybee colonies sicken and die when stricken with foulbrood; natural virus infection may leave thousands of tent caterpillars rotting like old catkins over acre after acre of infestation. City streets have been turned into driving hazards by the crushed bodies of hordes of dead mayflies. But rarely does death strew large numbers of damselflies about their natural haunts. These conspicuous creatures, which appear to spend hours of their adult lives frequenting the water's edge, evidently have extensive territories.

The only dead male I noticed during these early weeks was an individual downed on the pond's surface. His four gauzy wings were outspread and lying flat like those of a specimen in a Riker mount. It was easy to imagine the end of many newly emerged insects, however. Early one cloudy, humid morning, when I was marking damselflies, I saw a wrinkled young *Ischnura* female laboring up the willow trunk I often sat against. She tilted precariously on the ridges like a sailboat caught on high waves and carrying too much sheet. Her useless wings clasped each other at the tips like crinkled tin foil. She fluttered weakly as passing ants climbed over her. Before she could become a prize to be tugged at and finally hauled away by victorious ants, I transferred her, on the tip of my pen, to a weed. There, with two pieces of dried grass, I pried the slowly hardening wings apart. The last I saw of her, she was hanging from a leaf petiole, nearly transparent in sunlight reflected from the pond.

In the shadows of murder contemplated by Macbeth and Lady Macbeth there are greater shadows. Here the blind fellow Misunderstanding sits dumbly. Greed stretches insolently before the fire calling for more logs. But Death, it will be proved, comes hidden even when the sun is shining, for its shadow is so fine. So at the pond, in the dusk above the water, at high noon in goldenrod's harsh shade, or in the open mirrored heights between two boulders, crisscrossing gossamer may mean the last flight for many insects. The sticky strands of large stringy spiders, members of genus *Tetragnatha*, linked chicory head to pondweed, rock to leaf. Tough timothy stalks, leaning far out over the brown wrack the female damselflies so love to cling to in egg laying, were curled down by semiorb webs. Often these scimitarlike nets were speckled black with immense numbers of tiny flies, plant lice, and other insects strained from the air. Some spiders dangled under the leaves, like collapsed balloons swinging by their own ropes. Others stretched riblike under grass blades. All had armlike chelicerae, the appendages near the mouth that are used for seizing prey.

One dark cove, where the prevailing breezes swept inland from the pond, was a natural graveyard of floating debris and, consequently, the home of countless damselfly eggs. Here shingles of bark, willow leaves twisted like long warped canoes, crane flies lying on their backs with legs akimbo in a weird six-sparred embrace, and dead half-submerged pondweed drifted and eventually made anchor. One peninsula with its trapped debris had become the base for dozens of female damselflies, who were landing on the half-submerged pieces to lay their eggs.

When a female oviposits she may attach as many as four hundred eggs to one bit of dead plant. So constant was the activity over this cove that on a single palm-sized float of scum two or three females might be jockeying simultaneously, like small planes maneuvering in the wind on a crowded field. Ultimately, thousands of damselfly nymphs might depend on the survival of that float. Lifted too high by the gases evolved in pond rot, it might dry up at a spot where eggs had been inserted. Wind might push it ashore. A wading dog might drive it into soft ooze only a few inches below.

It was in this rich scene of life and death that I made my first experiment involving dead mature *Ischnura* females. I was soon able to see most of the normal male mating behavior through attempted matings with them.

In the normal mating procedure a male will clasp a female by the back of her head or the front of her prothoracic area, using appendages at his tail end. Both insects will then depart in tandem, the female flying behind and below, in much the same position as an airplane being re-fueled in mid-air. The insects copulate aloft. The whole act of clasping and copulating I refer to as mating, out of convenience. If clasping sounds better as "courtship," it is rapid, violent, and almost irresistible.

Initially a male would tend to make a partial or complete circle above an "alighted" female of my experiments. Then he would land on top of her thorax and head, eventually curving his abdomen so that his posterior claspers could grasp her on or just behind the neck. Once in this position, he would usually attempt to fly away, towing her at the tip of his abdomen! For the most part, however, the male went through the complete behavior pattern with a dead female only when the offering was a whole insect. Females lacking abdomens, for instance, evidently convinced males that they were worth landing on, but they often proved unconvincing partners for the complete act.

Thunderheads were piling up in the west late one afternoon when I made what then seemed to me the ultimate test of my damselflies' credulity. For days I had noticed the way the males would dive on resting insects. A male passing a stem where an aphid clung drinking would turn like a compass needle tracking a magnet that was being brought closer. Suddenly, as though the behavior pattern had been switched from one set of nerves to another, the male would spurt toward the prey. Having captured it, the hunter dined in leisure. It appeared to me that winged insects were more likely to draw a reaction. So, as the leaves of distant cottonwoods turned silver and the depths of the pool became dun, I began gluing sets of front wings to sticks. Before the first raindrops hit I had obtained enough information to convince me that this was another type of experiment to be worked into my series over the next weeks. Eventually I recorded that nine insects out of forty-five, or 20 percent, attempted to grasp the wing bases, while another twenty-five turned in flight and hovered above or to one side "inspecting"—I presumed. Only eleven, or 24.44 percent, of the passing males gave no indication of interest in the bits of tissue.

Further experiments indicated that wingless torsos drew considerably less attention. Out of 72 males passing such dead and dismembered females, two landed and appeared to attach their claspers and try to fly away, while twenty-two landed and seemed to make an effort at attachment. Thirteen males hovered or otherwise seemed to pause and take note, but then went on. Thirty-five simply passed over the bodies or within two or three inches of the stick tip, but made no other observable change in behavior. So about 33 percent were truly attracted, that is, seemed to be interested in a female with which they could copulate, though with difficulty.

I imagine that the winged forms are more easily perceived; thus the male damselfly may well be attracted first by the wings. Once contact has been made, mating or even realistic attempted mating can only occur with a torso, and the more complete the better. Other experiments with wings appeared to support the idea of their general attractiveness. For instance, an attack on prey and a premating dive on a presumed sexual partner may appear to be similar at onset. Twelve of fifty-nine males appeared to try to grasp a single wing, but twenty-nine of them darted by seemingly unaware. So in life at the pool smaller insects may escape attack altogether. The same is probably true of wingless insects and those with dark or covered wings. When I put out a head-and-thorax combination, only two of forty-two males even circled it. An intriguing question: Would any *Ischnura* males have attempted to mate had they landed?

During these trials, incidentally, I occasionally set out orange females that were darker and therefore probably older than my original specimens of the first weeks. Few males even slowed near the head-and-thorax bait, while a wingless individual and even one solitary wing were more "attractive." Strangely enough, damselflies without abdomens, even those with a pair of front wings alone, drew stronger responses than complete insects. Again, I suspect that the males were lured by the wings. Probably something about the body, perhaps color, is a signal that the female is sexually immature.

So it came to my mind, as a similar thought had to others before me, that the reactions of the insects might be tied to particular stimuli or combinations of stimuli which could be synthesized. Since paper models have achieved a fair reputation for solving the riddles of suggestion, I read up about models and copied a few. In the end I designed some of my own. This opened a door to all kinds of experiments, and I soon began offering models feverishly. When *Ischnura* males were scarce in one spot I tried another. By noon I had usually located the spot where most of the insects were gathered that day, and here I might use several models at a time on separate sticks. In this way I could run several experiments for brief periods during a single day.

The days seemed to grow shorter far more rapidly than the swift weeks could admit. I was getting up and going out earlier and staying later simply to test that last lone male still drifting along a shoreline. In the waning hours of the afternoon, however, as occasional lisps of a cone-headed grasshopper came more often from nearby reeds, the damselflies would disappear from their small flyways. I would rise, usually rather stiff-kneed, and go home, there to restock my library of manikins. Outside in the cooling night air beetles soon rose from the turf and thumped against my window screen. Moths whirled whitely around our front-door light. Both insects followed beams which had been designed by man long after the insect species evolved. Inside, I set other traps for insects of the daylight.

Using cellophane for wings and strips cut from three-by-five cards for bodies, I began to work my way through forms which I considered parts of the damselfly "vocabulary." No optical instruments were available to measure the many facets of color, unfortunately, but possibly it was easier to estimate what *shape* the insects recorded. Constructing several examples of each design, I eventually had about me several dozen flat, flightless gliders.

One style, with a body twice as wide as that of a normal *Ischnura*, reminded me of the old B-24 Liberator bomber of World War II. Another had a spatula-like abdomen. If insects used words, doubtless they would have nicknamed this one something like "Dum-Dum." One model, resembling one of man's early attempts at flight, had wings twice the usual breadth. Perhaps my favorite was a giant I dubbed "Gorgo." Double the species' wing and body dimensions, it was an ennui-inducing prototype which seemed unlikely ever to evolve in damselfly natural history.

At the pond people seemed better able to understand what I was doing when they saw the models on the stick. Before, passers-by had often asked, "What you using for bait?" Without a word about fishing, I had promptly answered, "Bugs!" But every so often someone would notice that I had no line, and a few, possibly the more startled, brought this to my attention. Almost no one questioned the bits of paper on my "rod," however. I imagine I went down as "that guy with the worst tangled line I *ever* saw!"

Yet these shadows of the species, these cold stars, these cutouts, joined the damselfly community and were accepted to an extraordinary degree. Blue individuals approximating the size of mature *Ischnura* females proved nearly as compelling as the dead orange insects. However, as with the single wings of the mature damselflies, the males grasped the models but never successfully pinched their claspers about them. Perhaps it was impossible.

The whining of a deer fly against the inside of an automobile windshield has always seemed to me a personal call of distress. I, who have tried to tug open a tight drawer and have pulled off the knob, hold a ready sympathy for the bumblebee struggling loudly to open the floret in my honeysuckles. Yet when male damselflies inspected my models, when some actually attempted to clasp the cardboard, the spitting buzz their wings made was a most pleasurable sound. Arched into tense bows, they often appeared to be wrestling the glued object. Some males would suddenly leap away into the air as though violently frustrated. A few, after hurling upward, darted back and tried again. When I used specimens painted orange I was surprised to find males reacting nearly as strongly. Green-painted models? Well, that is a later story.

During September the damselflies came later and later to the pond. By ten o'clock only two or three might be flying where formerly there had been a dozen. On the day of my last visit to the cove an unusually large male *Ischnura* was plowing back and forth along a shoreline deserted by his kind. I didn't even set out my specimen models. We had conversed enough for one season at the neighborhood pond.

6 | *Swamp Forest:*
A Habitat in Foreclosure

Separate the branches of a honeysuckle and lilac, grown together almost as Baucis and Philemon of Greek mythology, and follow a well-worn path downhill past alfalfa, goldenrod, and sumacs. A spray of stems you will first see from about twenty yards away is a young willow, and it marks the far bank of a creek. Angle left sharply now, away from the path, crunch strawberries and orchard grass underfoot, slide for two or three steps down a slaty knoll, and you stand beside a gigantic American elm.

Only a few dozen pages ago you listened to katydids here. Before you trickles the creek that the insects called across, and a few steps beyond sleeps Snake Pond. Grassy banks invite you to mis-step and toboggan in. Arrowheads may be ganging up even as far out as dead center. Willows are closing off one cove, but we never go there. You can stand near the point of a spur of land jutting out a yard or so and get a glimpse of woodland aquatic life of dozens of varieties.

The water is too shallow to allow much catching—almost every attempt roils the bottom so badly that everything for feet around is clouded. Water striders jerk across the surface. They are unaccustomed to having anyone so gigantic get close, or at least are warily against it.

Small shadows speed toward the bottom and dive headlong into rotting leaves and twigs. During winter it is possible to get a better view by chopping away ice and lowering a waterscope, a box with a plate-glass window and a flashlight shining down into the pond. But at no time are you likely to find snakes. Then why the name Snake Pond? Probably that slight tinge of fear lingering around dark places.

I don't know what I would call the place now. The scene is as I remember that part of a woods back home when I was a boy. Perhaps by now the marsh, as Snake Pond was then, has gained a buttonbush and a willow in the center and thus become a swamp. Doubtless the overlording trees that shaded it from morning till dusk have done their best to drain it dry. One Saturday afternoon a friend and I labored for hours to break a drought there by spading out a trench between the pond and the creek and then damming the creek. Whistles came from our homes late in the afternoon just as we patted in the last gravel on the dam. I could hardly wait to get up the next morning and see how we had done. And so it was . . . that a Sunday was never more glorious. The arrowhead leaves were once again sailing over the water like deeply keeled ships.

Now all that world may be gone. The snakes of Snake Pond that never were. The shadows that might eventually be resolved as beetles and tadpoles. The pond that was a marsh but that has probably allowed water-loving trees and shrubs to replace the island of arrowheads. And does even that scene survive? Or is its size now only as large as my memory has kept it?

In contrast, a few months ago I was walking through a swamp which was so huge that four hours passed before I made my way out. But even this one was threatening to sink into a forest floor. In one place I could walk not more than two dozen steps and see dramatic changes. On my right lingered a pocket of cattails, an example of a marsh habitat. Every year their dead stalks added soil to the debris here, and so gradually they were creating the kind of land that shrubs and trees can survive on, making the swamp type of habitat. Then, no more than fifty feet away, a section of the true swamp was similarly killing itself under piled leaves as it changed to a wet forest. Typical swamp hummocks of sedges, mosses, and ferns had become colonized as usual by shrubs and trees, but many of the hummocks were already being obliterated by the accumulating dead foliage of successive autumns. Slowly but surely that brown blanket was rising above the local water table to build a fairly dry forest.

This process is the natural succession a marsh, and then a swamp, is likely to take. You could set the process back by starting a fire during fall. Nature has been starting them for eons. But unless the heat grew so intense that it destroyed even the roots of cattails out in the water, a good blaze would be simply a brief holocaust through the canopy of shrubs and trees, sweeping up the drier debris but leaving behind a blanket of cattails. The real aquatic plants survive such a bonfire while everything else is bowled over the horizon as a black cloud.

Most difficult to hold in true form is the swamp. It is a habitat in foreclosure, with its trees its own worst enemy. The trees dry out the soil too easily. I have seen water in one small woods drop nearly three feet during the two weeks of spring when most of the tree leaves were opening. Dozens of small ponds there were completely swallowed up by the demanding roots, as though their bottoms had dropped out beneath them. A carelessly discarded cigarette butt, not completely extinguished, could easily have ignited the highly combustible crisp leaves underfoot and turned the woods into a roaring oven.

A large swamp like the one I recently walked in is outstanding simply on the basis of the variety of animal life it supports. During winter great numbers of white-tailed deer are willing to risk a skid on ice to get at the young red buds and twigs of red or swamp maple. At other times they stand quietly out in the ooze and water chewing on the hummocks and leaves of the shrubby understory. One of the most popular dishes there is greenbrier, or catbrier, which forms tight thickets.

This thorny vine can render a swamp forest almost impenetrable to humans and thus an excellent hiding place for deer. Most of us are probably familiar with greenbrier as a reasonably low vine that is no more of an impediment in the woods than raspberry or the invading Asiatic bush multiflora rose. Peter Kalm evidently found it quite a bit worse in the old forests. In the spring, with the leaves filling out, he noted that greenbrier

> occasions a deep shade in the woods, by crossing from tree to tree so often. This forces you to stoop, and even to creep on all fours through the little passages which are left close to the ground, and then you cannot be careful enough to prevent a snake (of which there are large numbers here) from darting into your face.

Well above the greenbriers in my path I could often hear the drilling of woodpeckers as they chopped out roosting and nesting holes. And what a range of habitats these birds represented: yellow-shafted flickers from broad fields where large trees are close at hand; yellow-bellied sapsuckers, which are familiar to many of us for the rows of holes they drill in apple trees; downy woodpeckers, equally at home in orchards or suburbs and in woods; and, finally, the hairy and pileated woodpeckers, which really prefer the deeper, older woods. The many woodpeckers were immediate evidence that trees were dying all about the swamp. Their shallow roots allow them to be blown over more easily, and excessively dry or wet times kill specimens along the border. Soon the weak or lifeless wood attracts hordes of wood-boring insects, some of which can grind out enough sawdust to make anyone sorry for pulling off a particular piece of bark. A number of insects attack the living tissue, of course; the larvae of long-horned beetles dive right away for the sapwood, where they may stay for several years. The arrival of woodpeckers signals that a tree has reached its last stages of deterioration. The birds' pockmarks come too late to save the wood at hand, but they may retard further invasion. In one place out in the swamp stood a tall tree that had snapped almost clean through its trunk about five feet up. Hundreds of dark exit holes for beetles were visible in a belt where the bark had been ripped away; a few gouges that had been drilled by woodpeckers were scattered among them, revealing the tawny sapwood inside. It occurred to me that the birds were likely to take the blame because their blasting pits were so large, dwarfing the beetle holes.

Another visitor to this swamp from far realms was the goldfinch. A bird more commonly seen dipping over fields, it seems to be fond of the seeds of smooth alders here, which it wrenches from the erect woody cones, or strobiles, of last year. These are female equivalents of the male catkins, those soft-drooping tassels that become laden with pollen first thing in the spring. Possibly the down from cattails in deeper water, as well as that from thistles in the meadows, provides the goldfinches with lining for their nests.

Many swamps are redoubts for extensive colonies of those hold-overs from the past the mosses and ferns, and this one was no exception. Both common haircap moss and peat moss make pads a yard or so wide in places, which sometimes resemble rugs underlain by toys. The fringed haircap is the former neck of the female reproductive organ, which the spore-carrying capsule lifts loose as its tall stalk grows upward during spring.

Haircap moss has a life history which is typical of most mosses. Its eggs are borne in rather flask-shaped female organs that crown some of the leafy green plants, one egg to a flask. To these swim the sperm cells, which have a pair of whiplike hairs that enable these microscopic beings to climb the spirally arranged leaves as if they were going up a staircase and fertilize the eggs. Apparently chemicals liberated by cells in the flask's neck attract the sperms. The sight is worthy of notice, and can be studied under a stereomicroscope.

Subsequent divisions of the egg soon produce a many-celled em-bryo, which continues to be protected by the flask, or archegonium. The retaining of the vulnerable young form in this manner was probably ex-tremely important for the evolution of land plants from aquatic algae. The embryo soon elongates into a stalk and capsule. In spring the capsule will doff its green cap and free huge numbers of dustlike spores. From these arise the first green threads and shoots of the next generation.

Peat moss, or *Sphagnum*, has a similar growing pattern, but with enough exceptions to make it worth looking up. While mosses in general signify to most of us a life history in the haircap style, peat moss really has its best-known place in just plain history as the familiar and age-old "peat." A typical bog, marsh, or swamp-forest plant, it thrives in acid waters. Such places are so resistant to decay that they have proved very fine graveyards; archeology has a long-standing debt here. Peat bogs can be quite deep, since the moss of one year grows right on top of the old plants of previous ones and can form a mat a foot deep in one hundred years. Cut and dried, peat has been a major fuel in Europe for heaven knows how long. The heat given off may be double that of most kinds of wood. Peat also has long been useful as a packing material, especially for live matter, because of its ability to absorb moisture from the air and store it in specialized cells of its leaves. The dry moss can absorb as much as twenty-five times its own weight in water—some say two hundred times, which I think more likely but will have to experiment on first. Alive or dead, the plant gives up its water easily, however. So white are dead ones during winter that you may overlook a tuft or so which the snow has missed.

While swamp mosses are perhaps best scouted out in spring, when their stalks and capped capsules often show as golden needles above green fur, ferns are well worth the trouble even in midwinter. Sensitive ferns stand out by their chocolate-colored reproductive stalks. The tops have beadlike spore cases clustered along half a dozen or so erect branches, and could be mistaken for seed spikes of one of the docks. These fertile spires appear late in the summer and can last through several winters. As the spore cases are buffeted against each other in spring, wispy mists of spores curl away.

The brown, fertile stalks of cinnamon fern also contrast attractively against snow. Their spore cases often turn a nearly luminescent cinnamon color at season's end. One winter I dug down through the usual cover of litter and brought sunlight upon one of next year's fronds. A curled fuzzy head was all that showed at the time, but the woody tufts will probably remain intact at the base of the frond throughout its life in the swamp.

Fern reproduction puzzled people for centuries—no one could find flowers or seeds. As a result, some conjectured that it took place at night; others gave it a mysterious magical quality. Popular superstition in Shakespeare's time held that fern seeds were visible only on Saint John's Eve, June 23. Using the appropriate rites when you collected them then would make you invisible. So we find in *Henry IV, Part 1* (II; i; 86–7), the line ". . . we have the receipt of fern-seed, we walk invisible."

Less ancient in their relationships than mosses or ferns are the mound builder ants, which pile up rather conspicuous hills. A fairly representative mound would be nearly two feet high and a couple of yards in diameter. Some of the ants are said to live for fifteen years, which gives an individual plenty of time to contribute its load to the top. A pair of scientists actually risked the herculean labor of counting the ants in one mound. They arrived at the eye-watering figure of 237,103 ants, 1,407 of which were queens!

One smaller swamp, which I have investigated primarily for the animals that could survive there, has a life that each year flickers on and off like a lamp with a short circuit. Here a curving bank of buttonbushes and swamp mallows, and finally ashes, honey locusts, willows, and red maples, is closing down on a shallow pond of cattails, pondweeds, pickerel weeds, and an immense number of frogs, insects, and other hardy inhabitants.

I say "hardy" because each summer the swamp becomes a damp meadow at best and is revived only by rains, primarily in the spring. Unfortunately, the drying periods become longer each year. If left alone, or "preserved," the temporary pond a hundred years hence might be a damp woodland of ash. Even now these trees with the flaking bark dominate the rim. Their journey began perhaps seventeen thousand years ago, when the glacier left this kettle and kame country and meltwater settled into the parched water table, and aquatic and semiaquatic plants and animals began gathering.

When I was there one April, tiny gray copepods chugged over the leaf-strewn forest floor. Their red eyes were conspicuous even from my standing position in the flood. They suggested elfin lanterns in a lilliputian mob scene. Below them, on water-logged leaves, lay hundreds of snails. I made a count and found that right-handed pond snails (whose opening is to your right if you hold a shell with the opening toward you and the tip upward) outnumbered left-handed individuals by more than a dozen to one. Most species of snails are right-handed; very few species include both kinds. I also noticed that ramshorn snails, *Helisoma trivolvis,* occurred in various sizes, suggesting different broods in the changeable habitat. Fluctuations in snail populations could be reflections of aspects of the spring phenology here. The situation should someday be compared on different dates.

As a matter of conjecture on the future, slim red maples appearing spottily among the ashes were already competing for a role in the canopy. They were earning another of their names—swamp maple—for here the water varied from four to twelve inches in depth. How long, I wondered, could the ash trees remain dominant?

The culminating adventures of spring were already playing themselves out on the bark of one dead ash. The gray surface was erupting with shelf fungi. I snapped open one of the clam-shaped fruiting bodies, and a pack of darkling beetles fell into my palm from the shafts they had dug while eating. From a few pockets motionless, shiny blue-green sap beetles stared out as though transfixed in place. They had probably been rendered immobile by the sudden light. After consuming the better part of the meat of the fungus, the beetles would, I presumed, move on, carrying spores to new wastelands.

The swamp forest ended abruptly with a hedge of willows. Beyond lay a small and very temporary brown lake in which tall pondweeds wavered a few inches below the surface. Perennial bluets spread their leaves, which were still green, but the lilac blossoms lay closed in rotting buds.

An offshore breeze rushed ever-changing surface riders over this sunken garden. Spiders trotted daintily past me, high-stepping on their eight arched legs. Pausing to sail with the wind, they gave the appearance of something one might call a "hemispindle." A soldier fly maggot with black and yellow stripes hurried passively by, suggesting a gay flat-bottomed boat torn loose from its moorings and now off and away on its own. Only a dusky green liverwort, almost a yard down, seemed realistically attuned to the swamp cycle. Such primitive bryophytes as this would doubtless outlast most of the smaller land plants now sunken in this temporary abode. Liverworts have long made their living with one foot in water and the other on land.

A colony of buttonbush, a shrubby relative of the bluets, entered from the willows and extended as a living jetty thirty or more feet out into the depths, where it met a half-acre crop of cattails. Normally preceded in their advance to deeper water by water lily, spatterdock, and other emergents, the cattails stood alone at the limit of their range. They are an edge phenomenon and here marked the swamp's usual shoreline.

On one blade, snapped and lying flat on the water, a small antlike insect stood fiddling with its antennae like a castaway signaling for help. Later, under the microscope, the voyager proved likely to have had an adventurous morning, for it was wingless. I was surprised to find that it was an ichneumon, a parasitic wasp. The insect looked out on the world as a rarity, for most adult members of its family have four wings. The chances that it would reproduce its kind looked very slim.

The summer droughts this swamp was prone to were indicated by the *high* populations of aquatic insects and other invertebrates. Water boatmen, backswimmers, water striders, aquatic sow bugs, and even leeches fell prey to my net. For the first time I saw a leech swim, when one undulated rapidly past like a bit of black shoelace. Seasonal drying prevented fish, crayfish, or other large predators from being permanent natural residents. Only species that flew in and out or that entered resistant stages could survive. Such a situation makes for a food pyramid, or web, in which a high percentage of the relationships are dependent upon age groups. "Who feeds on whom" depends more on how old and large

poison sumac   *blueberry*   *downy woodpecker*

fiddlehead fern   *cinnamon fern*   *spotted salamander*   *catbrier*   *red maple*

the predator is than on what species it happens to be—just as a cub wolf is overmatched when faced with an adult fox.

Northern, or at least cooler, moist climates have a very distinct sort of swamp called a bog. Dank and often the tone of tea, such places are graveyards of decay. They give the feeling that the leftovers of a picnic lunch can be tossed into the acid depths and they will be digested, as it were, in a matter of minutes. A white handkerchief dampened in bog water may instantly acquire a rusty stain that spreads over the cloth. The hummock you rest on belongs to the half-revealed roots of tamaracks and perhaps black spruces, doubtless overlain by a greatcoat of peat or sphagnum moss. Naturally there is every chance of getting up soaked to the skin and cold to the marrow.

Once, while kneeling beneath tamaracks to photograph sphagnum —I had been impressed by the way it grew both under water and out of it—I experienced a series of ground swells that made focusing increasingly difficult. At first I thought I had settled on a turtle. It proved to be only a nearby tamarack buffeted by spring winds and pulling at its anchor.

Tamaracks are apt to fall prey to the larvae of a wasp, the larch sawfly. In the early 1880's many tamaracks, or larches, in New England suddenly became conspicuous skeletons after having been completely defoliated. Tamaracks are unusual among pines for shedding all their needles each winter, but these trees never came back from the insect attack. Worms of a rather pretty black sawfly with a bright orange band about the abdomen had chewed up millions of the trees in a series of outbreaks that spread, within thirty years, from the Atlantic seaboard to Minnesota. An examination of tree rings on older tamaracks showed that such depredations had raged even earlier, especially around 1840. This business of dying has its advantages, however. Death makes room for new tamaracks. Presumably the departing ones were less fit for survival, and perhaps some of the replacements were more fit. As a result we can say that death is important to evolution. Certainly our world was set upon a very particular course of possibilities when death of each individual organism was written into every life as a necessity. This is true of all but the most primitive species, whose individuals live on and on, simply dividing now and again.

Walking toward the open water of a bog can be quite unsettling. The shrubs there are hardly any more stable than the trees were. They may even be spreading out on a shelf of organic peat which rocks or quakes underfoot. This is a difficult habitat and often includes at least two shrubs not familiar to most of us: dwarf birch and poison sumac. In the eastern states the latter was prolific back in the days of vast swamp grounds. Peter Kalm referred to it as "swamp sumach" and wrote at some length on its poisonous qualities. For some people it was and is well-nigh deadly.

> I have known of old people who were more afraid of this tree than of a viper, and I was acquainted with a person who merely by the noxious exhalations of it was swelled to such a degree that he was as stiff as a log of wood and could only be turned about in sheets.

Most of the shrubs, though, are evergreen heaths. The nodding flowers of bog rosemary and leatherleaf may attract us out, in spring, to get a closer look. Some, such as blueberries and cranberries, can lure us even farther, to places where we are sure to get wet—perhaps just after the first nip of autumn. These heaths are certainly worth examining, how-ever, if for no other reason than to see their waxy, thick leathery leaves that are rolled up, apparently to conserve water. I won't hazard a guess at why this characteristic developed, but I like the idea that this is a tough environment and these are characteristics that often occur in other some-what barren places.

How can a bog be barren in the midst of so much decay? Peat can be seen almost everywhere, as well as felt in that mattress underfoot. The empty cells of peat, which can serve for water storage, act as floaters and also have an affinity for mineral salts. They draw in nutrients dissolved in the water and store them, thus making a bog a physiological desert.

And so we find along the bog's tremulous edge not only sphagnum but also plants that derive a large proportion of their food directly from *living* animal flesh. Sundews attract insects with their pearllike globules, which soon snare the visitors as if in airplane glue, to digest them at leisure. Early pioneers among these insectivorous plants are the long-leaved sundews, followed by the round-leaved species. Yellow bladder-wort has compressed bladders that snap open at a touch and suck in minute animals such as fairy shrimps and young insect larvae; once inside, the beast is absorbed by minute hairs within perhaps twenty minutes.

The most famous trap is the red jug of pitcher plant. Downward-pointing hairs on the inside make exit difficult for snoopers that attempt to walk out; the slender neck is a likely rebuff to those that might choose to fly up and away; spider webs down inside are often the only saving nets for unplucky souls that tumble back; and, last but hardly least, the limpid pool at the bottom has enzymes which do a considerable amount of their digesting right out in the open. A friend of mine has poured as much as a tablespoonful of insect heads and wings from a large dried pitcher. Evidently in the past at least one sort of fly managed to survive, however, an insectan Ulysses. Only a mosquito, this individual, or more probably its eggs, and subsequent innumerable generations remained and made a good thing of it all. Its descendants are sometimes found—truly flies in the soup—mosquitoes that can withstand pitcher plant enzymes. I have had another surprise in connection with the pitcher plant. That was when I read in Thoreau's *Journal* his admission that he had had a rather blundering and unfortunate encounter with a few of these pots of water by *sitting* on them!

All these bog plants, to which can be added wild calla and white pipewort, create their own flooring as they literally float out toward deeper water. The base is a bog peculiarity, floating organic mud. And out beyond this, in many cases, the plants have been preceded by those first-class experts at knitting: the wire grass sedges. The sedges may be accompanied by water willow, with both exploring distant realms by means of horizontal stems, or stolons. Dr. James H. Zimmerman, of the University of Wisconsin Arboretum, says that truly "sedges make a bog what it is; sphagnum makes a bog what it isn't."

Come autumn, we could follow one species of bird from its spring and summer nesting and breeding sites in northern forests and bogs to its winter residence in the south, where again we are in bogs, or at least bog-like swamps. None of the bird's field marks are quite as true as the white throat patch which identifies it as the white-throated sparrow. More fun is watching its way of feeding on seeds, larvae, and other bits of life in the soil under autumn leaves stiff as parchment. From yards away it can be heard scratching the fallen foliage aside with both feet, then taking a break and rummaging through with its beak. Its song, coming from a field weed, seems to whistle "Ol' Sam Peabody Peabody Peabody." Dr. Zimmerman says the birds speak out more frequently in the rain and at dusk because they are responding to an atmosphere that is like their summer home up north in spruce forests. Then, on one October evening, they will bid their farewell. If you are lucky, you will have already taken the opportunity that Cornell naturalist E. Lawrence Palmer said, in his *Fieldbook of Natural History*, should not be missed: "A 'white throat singin' in the rain' is worth getting up in the morning to see and hear."

Southern bogs can be called simply swamps if they are developing into deciduous rather than coniferous forests. By whatever name, though, some of them have their own fame, one aspect of which is the prevalence of northern plants in waters that are cut off from similar habitats. Possibly one of the best theories looks at these as isolated pockets left behind by the glacier. For me, one of the more interesting trees found in such bogs is Atlantic white cedar, which has been dignified by having one of the swamps in which it occurs placed under state protection, up north on Cape Cod. Cedar swamps often act as refuges for odd species of birds, such as the more boreal, or northern, brown creeper, red-breasted nuthatch, and Canada warbler, which collect in these cool swamp forests of Massachusetts.

Atlantic white cedars once were used frequently in and on houses.

The door in an office I once had was made twenty years ago of cedar and veneered with gum (which we will meet again before this chapter ends). A new lock system had to be installed, and the carpenter gave me the cylinder of wood he had drilled out. It smells even now quite a bit like honey. Peter Kalm has many things to say on this timber, which was admired for its lightness combined with durability. I will string some of his comments together for a view of a part of our heritage that has largely evaporated with the massive draining of our wetlands. The wood made excellent roofs, which could last half a century, and therefore was much used. But herein lay a problem, for in Philadelphia

> many people already begin to fear that these roofs will in time be looked upon as having been very detrimental to the city. For being so very light, most people who have built their houses of stone or bricks have been led to make their walls extremely thin . . . violent hurricanes sometimes make the brick gable ends vibrate perceptibly. . . . At present this kind of wood is almost entirely gone. Whenever, therefore, in process of time these roofs decay, the people will be obliged to have recourse to the heavier materials of tiles or the like, which the walls will not be strong enough to bear.

Lightness and resistance to rot were not the only attractive qualities of white cedar, of course. A third aspect was its value during fires. You can see, in this passage of Kalm's, the respect with which people at the time regarded urban fires:

> When fires break out it is less dangerous to go under or along the roofs, because the shingles being very light can do little hurt by falling. They suck the water, being somewhat spongy, so that the roofs can easily be wetted in case of fire. On the other hand, their oiliness prevents the water from damaging them, for it evaporates easily. When they burn and are carried about by the wind, they constitute what is commonly called a dead coal, which does not easily set fire where it

alights. . . . All churches, and the houses of the more substantial inhabitants of the towns, have shingle roofs.

The final swamp or bog we should consider is one which, again, appeals to some of us because of its wood. Many people collect and display driftwood, but in only a few homes will you discover a polished, varnished-appearing stalagmite of wood that is as prized as cathedral spire wreathed in antiquity. You hold it lightly and admiringly in your hands. I have one such piece, a cypress "knee." As I work my fingers along its flanks, I recall a trip of nearly one thousand miles to a lake hidden at the end of a sandy road. The name did not belie its nature: Singletary Lake.

The tracks of a small mammal led from a log at the lake's edge across hard-packed sand and into irregular currents of the soft upper beach. There the sand no longer held the imprint. From the marks, however, I could imagine the rest—the beast's leaping into the shoreline duff after briefly stitching water to land, the dark shallows of Singletary Lake at his back, the pick-up-sticks ground cover of the Southeast Evergreen Forest underfoot. Shortly afterward I was observing and speculating on the longer history of this coastal plain, these Carolina bays, this cypress bog.

The coastal plain from the Piedmont uplands near Raleigh, North Carolina, eastward to the Atlantic beach glides down a half-dozen or so ancient terraces. During the Tertiary period this plain emerged and submerged as the continent shifted and ocean depths varied. Even now the ocean is reoccupying the peripheral terrace. Repeated glaciations during the Pleistocene have led to irregular invasions of this fringe by certain northern plant species.

Geologic structure alone sets aside the coastal plain as a distinct territory. The low relief extends out under waves that come in over a shallow shelf; a slight uplift increases the land area considerably. Unusual inland waters, typified by Singletary Lake, are scattered from New Jersey to Florida. Dug out of a sand substrate, these shallow lakes are fed slowly by springs. Tannic acid from cypress and duff lends a dark color to the fresh water, which is characteristically low in silt. The soil around is relatively sterile; the low calcium content yields plants that are high in fiber.

Perhaps the least likely explanation for the creation of these Carolina bays and others of their type is the theory that they were swept into their rather neatly oval form by the movement of large schools of fish. More acceptable is the argument involving complex underground drainage patterns. It has been suggested that the underlying limestone base has cracks oriented to the peculiarly uniform northwest-southeast axis shown by the lakes and that the sands have been washed down as in great sinkholes. Countering this theory is the claim that the lakes show no correlation with the underground geology.

Appropriate to the theory held most widely today, the uniformity of these lakes was apparently first noticed by aerial observation. A flier is said to have commented that they appeared to be the work of meteorites, resembling the marks of flying objects plowing into white mashed potato —*phud!* Although no meteorites have been found and there is no evidence of recrystallization of soil minerals, the lakes are generally deepest toward the southeast end. Here the highest sand rim rises and the magnetic field is strongest.

The lakes appear to have been smashed out 250,000 or 300,000 years ago. Perhaps for at least a brief time a fiery curtain was drawn across the earth, leaving, like half-shut eyes into the past, the dark lakes down the eastern coast of the United States.

If each of these bays has been indeed created in one relatively brief moment, it is ironic that most are found in a place where, in a later day, time was to be reckoned as steps between flashes of lightning. Apparently fire controls the dominant plant species that identify this region as the Southeast Evergreen Forest Formation. Longleaf pine is considered to be merely a fire climax species, which dominates the dry coarse sands between the bays in this area only as long as fires occur fairly regularly. Some ecologists contend, however, that oak and hickory would replace it even during the intervals between natural forest fires except that man's interference has kept the natural reinvasion burned back.

The white sand near Singletary Lake glares out through irregular patches of a low "ground pine," *Selaginella.* It is not really a pine, of course, but a club moss. A tougher ground cover is formed by wire grass, which waves gently in the wind and ground heat. The first large shadows fall beneath the numerous turkey oaks here in their local northern edge of range. Young turkey oaks almost invariably have their leaves oriented vertically; this apparently allows them to receive more light under the fairly dense canopy. Longleaf pine rises high over full-grown turkey oak, the leaves of which have long since turned to the more familiar horizontal plane.

A number of other trees dominate the scene closer to the small lake. Red maple, myrtle, and white cedar generally are the most prosperous. White cedar in this area has achieved a certain fame for its use in barrel staves. In season, the hardy flower of *Tradescantia,* or spiderwort, appears here and there as a liquid blue spot against the hot sand. Its thick stems and viscous sap have enabled it to succeed also in a distant but broader belt, the midwestern prairie.

I knelt and ran my fingers around a low knob that projected through a ground cover of pine needles. Its even contours suggested the top of a bedpost, implying a submerged bed. It was, in fact, a cypress knee, which is the aerial projection of a swamp cypress root. Apparently, the knees conduct air to the tissues underwater. These pneumatophores can be boiled, the bark peeled away, and the very light pieces of wood used as ornaments. The trunk itself makes fine timber; the past two hundred years have seen considerable logging here. The tree is not to be confused, however, with the cypress of the Mediterranean or with our cypress of the genus *Cupressus,* neither of which is related to it.

Young cypresses grow best where the water table is fairly low. Mature trees prefer swamps; these bald cypresses give these lakes the name "cypress swamps." Like religious symbols from a lost culture, the trees are staked out in the lakes. Spanish moss—not a true moss but an epiphytic flowering plant related to the pineapple—drips tantalizingly from the branches like something just about to drop. A fine central black fiber in each strand helps make the wait almost interminable, however.

In some places cypress is associated with broad-leaved gum trees, *Nyssa*. Both have bases which are buttressed broadly, apparently a characteristic of trees occupying water habitats, for even elm, beech, and other trees will enlarge in this way. Gum needs more drainage than bald cypress, which will come in only on land that is at least occasionally drained. So cypress-gum swamps can occur where water is low and sometimes absent. These swamp forests suggest dumps, collecting everything from knots of algae and a fine coat of pollen to cottonmouth moccasins and dragonflies.

As I followed a tan, scuffed road out of one of these swamps I was preceded by a silver-bodied dragonfly, a male white-tailed skimmer. The broad dark band across its wings blended with sodden black leaves and sunken alga-coated perches. I thought of swamps of the Carboniferous age, when dragonflies were giants. Many of these places had long ago become coal deposits.

7 | Lowland Streams: A Long, Slow Autumn

October had spread its yellow hand upon the land and the songs of late summer, sunken low, were few and far between. Yet in an alder I heard high notes holding out above the frosted ground. They came from perhaps the last crickets of the year, insects that had settled down in the shadows of leaves which hung throughout the day in warm sunlight where a woodland brook opened and nearly became a swamp.

While deeper in the woods the stream splashed down shale bedrock in a broken descent, here it slipped sluggishly under pin oaks, alders, sumacs, honeysuckles, and the straight shrubby branching of jewelweed. Where the latter leaned dead over the stream, long past their days of attracting hummingbirds, they thatched it like a roof. Old skunk cabbages lay limply out to sun; undisturbed hoods of a few had earlier been nesting places for yellowthroat warblers raising their first broods. The solitary voices of the crickets, trilling at noon but gone by two o'clock, intimated that life here was slowing down to its last grinding.

During spring this swampy flat had swelled out like a great pool of molasses, spreading brown and viscous with mud over matted sedges and grass. Then, in summer retreat, it had left a tan stucco of silt widely on both banks. Bird tracks mingled before being dumped aside by grass and sedges lifting up again. So far, this autumn had had too little definition of its own, such as the hearty storms that often pass through, rolling over everything in their paths. The slow creek in the flatlands had stayed passive. It became even more than usual a collecting place for autumn leaves (their tannins made the water darker), brittle stalks, and crickets in their final days. An oily slick of dead plant and animal matter formed an iridescent surface that hinted of the decay here.

This creek was re-enacting a scene familiar to many flatland streams. Their pace is slow, and they tend to bring life around them to a standstill. Often they are old themselves, traveling in wide beds which now cut only slowly into the earth, having done most of that eons ago, while young. Today very much at rest and in semiretirement, such streams are apt to wander from side to side across that wide swath they sculpted in their prime, like an old person meandering in his spacious thoughts.

No matter what the normal life around it contains, a bottomland like this holds steadily to its own ways. It has a kind of familiar sameness, no matter what the uplands. If you come downhill from prairie, old field, shrub thicket, or ancient forest, you may find a scene that recalls another you saw years ago elsewhere.

The key is moisture. Should you descend from an exposed hilltop of white oak and hickory, you would perhaps first enter a long slope which picks up whatever water has not soaked in above. Now chestnut and red oak replace the old dry forest; red maple and black birch fill in an understory which, above, was sweet gum that was gracefully dying out in the shade. Behind are the uppermost rock-defended ridges, while underfoot is the most ancient wandering stream bed, which may be a mile or more across from wall to wall. This is the first terrace, a benchlike flat with rounded contours where sharp features have been blurred by age.

The next cliff down may be even softer, hiding the solidness of the second bank, which gently curves onto the second bed. These sidewalls have been weakened enough, by a warmer wet-humid environment, to lose their crisp angles. The cliffs are apt to be rhythmically scalloped where the meandering stream once snaked across its alluvial terrace.

Here, in moist silts that flow down from above, black oak may dominate a forest that includes beech, basswood, and hemlock, with tulip trees dying out in the understory.

The final pitch ends on the flood plain of the present stream. Here the land is subjugated by the whims of the stream, and species gather in an environment that is quite independent of the regional climate. Pin oaks and American elm rule, with river birch beneath. That is about as clean-cut an edaphic, or soil-determined, forest as there can be. And the key is obviously soil moisture, here more than normal for the region as a whole. Some authors have called this final scene a mixed hydrophytic forest association—a mixed stand of various water-loving species.

Walking close to the river itself, one may suddenly step down into a narrow slough or perhaps an oxbow, separated from the river by a dike or levee. This may once have been a channel of the river, or perhaps was the short cut taken across a bend during flood time. At any rate, it was abandoned and now is being slowly undercut as the main path shifts away and takes the water table with it. At this moment in the river's history, however, the slough is generally waterlogged, and occasionally is inundated when the stream leaps the low levee. Because it has a silty base of fine, clogging clays the slough drains poorly; in fact, it is half bog. Oaks are the so-called water oaks—pin, willow, and black.

Ahead, on that well-drained alluvial dike, American elms and silver maples rise over hackberries. A few steps farther down the bank to the stream itself lies a slick of the most recent silt deposition. Here is a hangout of willows, cottonwoods, and their companions.

Have you recognized more of the trees than you might have expected? Some of these riverbank species now line many city streets. They grow quickly, or else they might be swept away during floodings while still small; developers prefer trees that attain large size rapidly. Their root systems lie close to the ground surface, where they can more readily obtain oxygen in the swampy woods; for city architects this means that the trees can be moved easily. Finally, they can take the dry conditions of street life, where sidewalks and streets surround them with concrete and asphalt, and where people press the remaining loose soil around them into platy layers. Trees in the city suffer from drought due to runoff, whereas down along the river their drought comes from seasonal lows when their roots are left high above the ground-water level.

Slow-moving streams have very definite characteristics. In general they are old and tend to ramble within wide floodplains they have laid down over thousands or even millions of years. The silt shard along the bank is typical evidence. Being shallow with the amount of muck it has allowed to accumulate in its bed, the stream fills easily to an overbank condition after a rain and regularly leaps across the lower levees. Thus its waters have a very marked influence on the riparian soils. One is likely to need boots to walk even several hundred yards away in the woods.

Shallow waters such as these are usually warmed by the sun quickly and deep down. Their dark base receives most of the available light, rather than having it reflected away, and changes its energy to heat. The same sort of thing would happen to a black blanket left on the beach in the sun. So the fish doing best in such streams are the warm-water pan-fish, the bass groups, including walleyed pike in intermediate-to-swift currents. Smallmouth and largemouth bass and some carp are able to take this sort of silt, an enemy to other fish, which get their gills plastered with it and then suffocate. A catfish in the net is about as clear an indication of stream sluggishness as any other story you could take home.

Warm water does not hold as much oxygen as cool—"boiling" it away under the noonday sun—and so the fish in these slow streams do with less. They are especially deprived when the day is hot but overcast, so that algae can't produce as much oxygen. Thus a gar, one of the trash fish—as are carp and catfish, or bullhead—uses the air reserve in its swim bladder when not enough oxygen comes in via its gills. On a particularly hot day these and other kinds of fish can be seen popping the surface for oxygen.

Mud banks attract their own little communities, and so otter and mink trails cross here. Otters, like raccoons and muskrats—which are found not only along the mainstream but also in backwaters—help clear out fresh-water mussels, leaving mounds of shells up on the banks. Minks can cause trouble among the herons, wood ducks, black ducks, and mallards here. Kingfishers are safer where they have found a really steep bluff on one of the floodplain terraces.

One of the worst aspects of slow streams for the people who live near them is the prevalence of mosquitoes. They breed in great numbers in the shallower places where fish cannot swim easily or find it too hot. Still, probably one of the worst enemies of mosquito larvae is the killifish. The mouth of this predator is formed so that the lips open widest at the *top* front of the skull. Thus this "top minnow" can glide just below the surface in shallow places and pick off mosquito wrigglers while hardly raising its head. Aside from that, though, mosquitoes have a fairly good life. Not even drought can dislodge them, for many lay eggs that *require* a dry period before they will hatch.

Down along a coastal plain, a group of us entered one of these hydrophytic forests on a misty morning late in October. The air was truly cold and clammy, but this only slowed down anything small trying to escape and gave us more opportunity to see the natives. The woods which had dropped anchor here had done so at a far different stage than the adjoining oak-pine uplands. We decided not to be satisfied with enumerating the fresh species, but to see if we couldn't establish some "whys" for the two forests' being so different.

We began, and perhaps ended, appropriately with the soils. The deepest underpinnings were an ancient sea bed and whatever that might be lying on. Therefore, here were no rocky terraces and their variances in drainage to contend with. Thus our answers as to why we found two distinct forests abutting on each other did not lie deep in the ground but at a more superficial level. We got out shovels and our cold hands, and began to paw and dig.

The first layer was leaves and minor debris, of course. But this was remarkably thin as compared to that under the oaks and pines farther up. Evidently this was at best a few years' accumulation. We hypothesized that the river had flooded the place on and off not too many years ago. If we had taken the time for a hike, we might have found branches and leaves still lodged in tree crotches farther up the slope, where the overflow had crested. But we stayed where we were and put our faith in the shovels.

Cutting into the first true soil—"dirt," with all its inappropriate connotations—we uncovered a granular dark-brown layer that was curiously lacking in pieces of decaying bark, leaves, twigs, and so on. This went down about three inches. Then we recalled the high-cresting river and gave up looking for a top layer of coarse organic humus such as we had been familiar with. It had all been swept away again and again.

Down through the next six inches of spading, the soil became lighter in color. Granules were more massive individual chunks of mud on fingers. They had definite oblique angles, which indicated adequate spaces for water to percolate down. Thus flood and rain and melted snow water could sink at least nine inches into the ground, and hope to find exit. Some roots and occasional earthworms showed that the soil was indeed reasonably well aerated; the species we found could not live underwater very long without drowning.

Then a shovel plucked up on its tip a new brownish soil. It had a few mottled reddish spots. And the next *thunk* into the hole hoisted up a gray soil in which clay was very liberally sprinkled with red, partially oxidized iron, as though it had measles. This was a gley layer in which oxidation was poor. We counted roots and earthworms and came up with zero. The gray gley zone had such poor drainage and terrible aeration that it was the terminal layer, into which no roots or worms could penetrate. And this material persisted for a total of twenty-three inches. Below that we found bits of mica and then clay of undetermined depth. A granite stream bed was hinted at by the mica, in this case meaning that the river had reached the same rock base which made up the coastal mountains nearby.

Thus the whole forest around us was resting on a useful soil only nine inches deep. Taproots would be of no use here and probably would never develop fully. Though basket and pin oaks shared the overhead scene with red maples and sweet gum, we knew from past histories that the last two were fading. Along with them would depart the better-than-occasional tulip poplars and some beeches. These latter rode on mounds, as though afraid to get their feet wet. This was indeed the case, for American beech needs a well-aerated root zone.

Our understory gave us plenty of room to step around in, but I counted at least eight species of trees jostling for dominance. Neither they nor the canopy giants had produced enough shade to keep out the grasses, however. By their abundance I would guess that summer in this woods must be a warm experience with dappled green glades. One would have to be careful about touching anything else when reclining against a tree trunk, though, for the vines were only once in a while grape but very often poison ivy. In some cases the ivy was nothing more than russet rootlets sewn on in stemless parallel threads. I have acquired very swollen fingers from pressing against such hairy bark.

Some animals of the woods we could identify only by their signatures, others by their voices. Signatures included pellets and hoofprints of white-tailed deer and runs made here and there by white-footed mice. Mouse droppings were missing, so probably the mice had been driven out, most likely by inundations. We heard many blue jays clamoring for attention, probably ours as we intruded among their acorns and beechnuts. Chickadees tempted several of us to imitate their *fee-bee* whistle. Someone was lucky enough to pick out through this the high *see see* notes of a golden-crowned kinglet. Very likely the kinglets were merely visiting from pine woods above. On western mountains, they might at this time be moving down the slopes, following October's descent.

The smaller, more active ground-dwelling predators had camped here in considerable numbers. A tree toad had wedged itself into mosses at the knobby base of a beech tree. We could have increased our catch of woodland salamanders by filtering through more damp leaves. Spiders and salamanders were so frequent that I was reminded of the *beginnings* of ponds I have studied—the predators seemed to arrive in force there before their prey.

Woolly aphids dressed in white fluff drifted here and there in the air, while froghoppers made valiant last stands on beech twigs in the open. But perhaps no insect reached the abundance of the minute gray springtails that shot away to right and left on the forest floor. Their ability to walk takes second place to this catapulting style, wherein the tail is held under the abdomen and then released with a snap that fires the beast many times its own length. They sometimes appear on warm winter days as dark flecks on the snow, where their behavior has given them the name of "snow flea." Our discomfort in this wooded dampness was evidence that the place was their insect heaven-on-earth. Rotting leaves were their steaks. I note that *An Introduction to the Study of Insects*, by Drs. Borror and DeLong, says that springtail populations in some woods have been calculated to run as high as 10 to 15 million individuals to the acre. We could only have concurred.

Far less active, though, lay the clamped shells of field clams. These were "fingernail clams," measuring on the average slightly over one-quarter of an inch in length. Perhaps they had been thrown up here during the spring floods. During such wetter times the thin, almost translucent white valves would be slightly parted, allowing a fleshy foot to emerge and perhaps drag the beast at a slow creep over leaves and grass. As a rule, the clams avoid clay or rock substrates. They are the annuals of the bivalve world, generally living only a year or two.

In another part of the woods, where the water was so deep that we needed at least low boots, we shuffled into a nearly pure stand of ironwood. A few tulip poplars and sweet gums had entered, however, and were beginning to overshadow the ironwoods, or American hornbeams. As is commonly the case, though, trees of lesser importance were already hinting at the real direction development was likely to take. Here and there we could see evidence that the swampy condition was only temporary, that from scattered beeches, red maples, big-toothed aspens—trees that were likely to shade out the others eventually—a mixed association might one day arise. Dead river birches pointed backward at the sort of woods that had gone before.

The forest showed signs of being just a first jump away from man's control. Most of the trees were only an inch to an inch and a half in diameter, probably about ten years old. We encountered a bridge on which we warmed ourselves in sunlight, it being nearly the only break in the young, tightly knit canopy and close-growing trunks. It was flaking and needed a good sweeping. We could legitimately classify it as a ruin. Underneath flowed a creek that had to shove its way past tumbled heads of trees, loose sedgy hummocks, leaf jams, and temporary mud bars.

I spotted a lean reddish dragonfly which had begun to circle the bridge trusses. Finally it found a patch of suitable sunlight on one of the slanting planks, dropped down, and landed. I could imagine something like its engines being switched off and gears being engaged to lock it in place as the insect's wings ceased vibrating and its shoulders hunched forward. With its wings depressed to the bridge, the dragonfly was clearly tied down against any ground loops due to untoward gusts. I could see now that it was one of the common skimmers whose nymphs inhabit marshes. The adults come out late in the summer season. Low woods provide about as even a temperature as can be found, and this had been a long, slow autumn. Mostly I was impressed with the information rendered by the *Sympetrum* dragonfly that this stream closely resembled a marsh or swamp habitat, since no other ponded situation existed nearby. Slow streams often have this aspect, possibly best illustrated on a large scale by the broad, phlegmatic flow of the Florida Everglades.

Perhaps the slow woodland stream that is most familiar to many of us is the one that cuts its way through old, tree-filled suburbs, demarks the boundary of a township park, and then exits for Lord knows where, its life enriched by lubricating oil, beer cans, soft-drink bottles, paper, and tinsel from a Christmas tree that was too much of a drag to be carried but which could nevertheless contribute. I once traced such a stream from its apparent headwaters to its dumping into a major river some miles away. I began with maps that showed the changes that had occurred in a southern city over nearly a century.

In 1877 the origins of Timber Branch Creek were obscured on the earliest map I was offered in the town library. At that time the city limits to the north ended slightly above the meeting point of Duke, Commerce, and Peyton streets, while the stream arrived from the neighboring county to the north. By 1907, however, the metropolitan area encompassed the necessary upland springs in a dissected oak and pine woods. Timber Branch could be seen to arise in the watershed of Jefferson District (the district also issues tributaries to Four Mile Run Creek, on the other side of a dividing ridge), which empties into the coastal river.

When I searched outdoors for the origins of Timber Branch, one wintry Sunday in November, my journey ended at a hillside pipe which opened at the foot of a long, undulating incline, now a series of housing developments called Heights. Mountain laurel and privet, native and import respectively, mushroomed from the banks above me. By mid-April the stream flanks would be aflame with the pale-pink flowers of azaleas, which a recent or even pioneer homeowner might have brought down from the Appalachian Mountains. Two centuries ago this would have been for their elegant beauty alone. In our time he would have doubtless done so to bury the pipe orifice and the sludgy deposits at its lip. The charm of a hillside colonial brick house that overlooked the somewhat meandering waters still had a flavor of the Old South. Seen through the slats of a weathering fence on the street above, the carefully cast shrubbery gave no clue to the modernity of the flowered park. Of such azaleas, naturalist Peter Kalm had written in the mid 1700's that they belonged in every flower garden.

Driving back and forth through the Heights with my younger daughter, who had become interested in a developing story, I could pick up the disturbed birthplaces of the creek. A damp lawn here, chickweed clustered in soft sod there, some grassed rivulets in a lawn (they reminded me of the grassed waterways the Soil Conservation Service often advises to carry away excess water and prevent erosion, but here they merely provided a minor ripple in the path of a lawn mower), and the dozens of street entries to storm sewers—all now indicated the old watershed, and a tale of the present.

Some of the more recent contributions to the stream could be identified at the mouth of the concrete pipe. Oil and algae mingled on the surface as automobile drippings and lawn fertilizers embraced after their competition for the land above. Tissue paper lingered, promising to depart after spring rains flushed it through. A raft of leaves had jammed into one embayment and now threatened to choke even the spring discharge.

City engineers had evidently wisely seen that the creek could hardly be expected to survive on storm-sewer offal alone, and so tile pipes from the surrounding hillsides also opened here, in the faces of retaining walls. One curious ten-inch-diameter tiling emerged from under the road and added a rather wicked-looking orange liquid to the already colorful waters.

These, of course, are the sorts of problems we have come to expect from breaking into natural drainage patterns. Springs still erupt, only now on lawns; rain water still joins the underground stream, only now in pipes; the contents of the soil still color our streams, but now the color is a stain on the land. Timber Branch is a rather mild creek, however, and its gentle fall leads it among rocks and pools which allow many of the heavier and stringier contents to drop out. Only a few yards downstream we could again walk the old brown bed and the loaves of early snow that rose nearly level with the low banks.

We walked first in a flat open park where a few oaks and river birches had scattered their curled leaves like boats on smooth water. The ground was thickly grassed, and it seemed likely that buttonbushes, willows, and their natural companions had been uprooted to turn the wide terrace into a suburban playground. I could not blame the landscape architects who saw it thus. It was still a lovely spot. So we investigated to see if they had *added* anything. And they had. Here were two conifers, adding diversity under a cold autumn sun that was fading now. Norway pines, which prefer dry sandy places, they led us to suspect we could thank tiling there. The pines looked to be about forty years old and doubtless had a certain northern elegance after one of the rare heavy snowfalls. "Norway," reputedly, is false advertising, the word having been added by a dealer in Norway, Maine, who presumably used the name to get a higher price for inferior wood—as though better timber came from northern Europe. Donald Culross Peattie, in *A Natural History of Trees*, however, contends that the tree had been so named before the town was. The resins of Norway pine stick to the saw, and the scientific name *Pinus resinosa* is certainly appropriate.

Here also was a copse of red maples. Probably they came in by themselves, and surely have a parent or so lurking along the wooded slope to the east. These swamp maples added our third season of outstanding color to the new origins of Timber Branch: pink and white of azaleas in spring, winter green of Norway pine along with red from its bark (which also gives it the name of red pine), and now scarlet and yellow of maple for autumn. The mixed plantings seemed to promise much for our hike.

Before continuing downstream, though, it was worth a minute to look at a modern map and read some of the local street names. We were, to no one's surprise, on Valley Drive. Edgehill Terrace, hardly an imaginative choice of name but a descriptive one, leads past many of the dwellings where the wellsprings still flow. Ridge Road and Crest Street are laid out along higher elevations. Quincy, Cleveland, and Roosevelt show a tendency to name things after ourselves; the Indians named their things and themselves after parts of nature. Osage Street reminds us of the Osage-orange, transported here from the Missouri-through-Texas west, perhaps to be used as fencing for cattle in colonial days. Peach Street indicates a local industry of present and past, while Fern Street recalls a past that lingers only as a memory—ferns are no longer common here. Farm Road tells us of the humble background out of which all this development grew. I could still cross certain lawns here and on about every fifth one find a tumbledown apple tree that is a remnant of an orchard.

I wonder sometimes if humans as a species have taken the "right" route or the "only" route. When we build a city on the bones of our farms, having buried them, are we acting in the only way man can act? In *The*

Immense Journey, Loren Eiseley notes the self-confidence of frogs, who as a species have lived for millions of years *as* frogs:

> Every spring in the wet meadows and ditches I hear a little shrilling chorus which sounds for all the world like an endlessly reiterated "We're here, we're here, we're here." And so they are, the frogs, of course.

And so *we* must appear in our remolded vales, our Timber Branches, as *humans.* But we have a knowledge of what was here when we first came and for long eons before. This could guide us, if nothing else could, so that we could live in the ancient ways, as do the frogs, rather than reconstructing the natural world. Certainly Fern and Farm are reminders enough to say that we do respect and appreciate the wilderness.

Timber Branch was enough of a name to tell me what people here once had *wanted* to have recorded. So my daughter and I went farther with the very quiet waters of late autumn and did some more recording of our own about the effects of man on land and vice versa.

We came next to a wide valley where the stream was taking a swifter short cut. I suspect that it had been boosted out of its natural sluggishness by the runoff from asphalt-covered slopes. New shallow riffles were so cold that the small animals living here would have burrowed out of sight much earlier than before. My daughter picked up a small stone wearing a white ice cap. She bit off the cap, thus partaking of probably the cleanest open water within miles. We could see that trees of this flood plain regularly stood in wedges of silt, but the forking of red oaks near the ground indicated that the overflow conditions were not quite right for them. Evidently in spring the storm sewers bring violent floods to the lowlands.

Only a few hundred yards farther, the creek had been forced to constrict itself at the concrete sphincter of a tunnel under Timber Branch Parkway. Some of the water would sweep through peacefully; some would try to blast the culvert down. Over the years a few molecules had succeeded in getting at the underpinnings, for my older daughter on another day pointed out that the thing had a decided tilt. Concrete blocks jumbled in the pool at the culvert exit told us that other stream control efforts had also failed and that their products had gone down in irretrievable disarray.

We soon entered an oak woods. Cardinals jumped from weeds on the bank. The culvert under a second street loomed ahead—we were getting too thick with civilization, so we decided to leave. On the opposite side again appeared concrete blocks and a pool. Actually, these deep spots slowed the current. A few yards farther city engineers, obviously doing the same thing in their own way, had recently built a dam out of rocks and macadam. Such an impoundment can become a natural haven for minnows and other forms of life unable to risk being hurled downstream after every freshet. But only snails and a yellow-green filamentous alga were in evidence on this day—the day autumn slowly ended, on perhaps the coldest note ever.

8 | *Upland Streams of the Woods*

The continuous downward-cutting curve of a stream, its long profile, may flatten out into something that wriggles mostly from side to side, like a snake. But so long as the stream retains its youth the uplands will be sharp and precipitous and full of white water. Such cascades come in all sizes. Mountain streams with their scoured walls, cold water, sudden deep pools, and multiple falls are a part of the memories that many of us have, for they actually occur not only up where the towering cataracts are quarried but in miniature on simpler slopes as well. Most of our barren-bottom stony creeks come under this category.

While trees and shrubs along slower streams are allowed to infiltrate where they can, they must enter more openly here and may be exposed at any time. The clutch their roots have on rocks resembles old fingers hanging on. Thoreau once pictured them doing better than that, even managing to throw the rocks aside. It is a curious scene he paints:

> I see where trees have spread themselves over the rocks in a scanty
> covering of soil, been undermined by the brook, then blown over and,
> as they fell, lifted and carried over with them all the soil, together with

considerable rocks. So from time to time, by these natural levers, rocks are removed from the middle of the stream to the shore.

I happen to know a part of one woods, however, where the reverse is true. The pitch of the escarpment is steep here, and the channel is strewn widely with boulders whose diameters are occasionally as much as nine feet from corner to corner. So little soil has accumulated between the rocks that roots cannot dig in. This boulder field shows its peculiar weakness after storms by the number of blown-down trees. They do not pry the rocks free that I have seen but rather ride on them as a ball-and-socket joint. In such a scene of wild giganticism one can give in to fancy for a moment and imagine a menagerie of the worst sort lying in wait underneath.

Where we have to settle for stones rather than boulders, or pebbles rather than stones, however, great events must come in small packages. Probing the bottom is still an adventure, though, and when you look under a rock all sorts of beasts which it would be a crime to miss may go racing downstream. It is handy to jam a net into the current on the lee side when collecting aquatic specimens in a swift stream. This leaves a moment or so for examining the underside of the stone.

One of the more interesting inhabitants of such a stream is often another set of stones—packed together by something that gathers bits of stones. Caddisfly nymphs, whose adults look like hairy butterflies or moths and are, indeed, fairly closely related to them, are apt to create homes of sandy gravel. One style of case suggests a quarter-inch-diameter snail shell. The gravel helps weight the larva down to the stream floor, where it feeds. When the insect is preparing to pupate, it hoists the coils onto the underside of a large stone, often preferably in the company of others. Numbers of caddisfly larvae seem to enjoy each other's presence in this way. Of those that are lone wolves, many weave fine nets which seine food from the current. Some of these larvae live apart from their webs, among piles of rocks nearby, while others do their net tending from within the tubular snares themselves. One of the best ways to find one of these is by using a flashlight and hand lens, for the nets collapse when lifted. Trout have an easy time devouring the caseless larvae, to say nothing of the pupae when these slit their way out of the cases and swim to the surface, where the adults emerge. If you open a trout's digestive tract, though, you may still find pebbles and sticks from the cases, which the fish has not been too fastidious to eat along with the home builder.

Caddisfly nymphs are dependent for food upon other things that live in the stream. It has been said that case builders are browsers on plant material, while fishers and naked nymphs are carnivorous. But some of the less recognized supports of this whole population are the leaves that fall from the forest above. The herbivores chew on them directly; the carnivores devour smaller leaf eaters. Stream headwaters are particularly likely to be rich in leaves, since they often speed through forests and collect vast quantities in their narrow V-shaped defiles.

While caddisfly nymphs can provide for themselves the necessary ballast to walk on the bottom and the silk to stick themselves onto rocks, other inhabitants have done very well using a variety of methods. I'll leave these for later, but it is worth mentioning now that those who live in rapids have generally had to find means of hanging on. It is a characteristic of swift-water species. Caddisflies illustrate it by their tendency to build rock homes rather than log cabins.

One of the beauties of life among the rapids is that the water is usually quite highly saturated with oxygen. Not only does turbulence drive it in, but cool water holds oxygen and most other gases better than does warm water. A stream that slows down and bakes in the sun can lose so much oxygen as to asphyxiate many of its larger animals. The heat alone can kill. Heat and lack of oxygen are both aspects of thermal pollution. Floodwater-retarding dams have actually wiped out trout in a stream below by releasing only water that has been drawn from the top of a pond, which is relatively warmer and deficient in oxygen. If the water runs freely without impoundment at other times, this stream may experience longish runs of cool water interrupted by hot blasts. As a result, neither trout nor warm-water fish do well, and fishermen may call these "trout or nothing" streams. The best answer seems to be always to draw the water from down near the pond bottom.

I once heard a story about a trout fisherman who did his fishing almost naked every spring in a Maine woods. Friends of mine who occupied a nearby camp each year used to suffer bites from black flies day after day, but they managed fairly well by trying to limit the amount of skin revealed and the degree of exposure. The other fellow, nevertheless, would open his trout season by striding to the stream clad in nothing but shorts and tennis sneakers. He lasted one day. Then he howled in bed for another three while his welts rose and subsided like a pickle in prime and decline. After that siege he rose from his pallet and rejoined everyone while the fishing was still approaching its apex. Others fled, the camp slowly died, but he continued into the height of the trout, and certainly of the black fly, season apparently now temporarily immune to the insect scourge.

My own more recent experiences with black flies have been limited to attacks beside a small woodside brook that develops thousands of the larvae under its rocks. The fat little brown bags swing there like algae, but they are straining out microscopic organisms just as fast as they can. Turn over one of these stones and place it in a water-filled pan, and the larvae will soon make it look like a medusa—a face full of tentacles. Children sometimes call the flies "Fat Alberts," after a story character created by humorist Bill Cosby. They might also be called something less endearing, by game managers and farmers who are familiar with the black fly's ability to infect both domestic and wild ducks and other poultry with a leucocytozoan parasite. In tropical areas of North and South America and of Africa some species carry a filarial worm that can cause obnoxious tumors under the skin, and even blindness. Other kinds of filarial worms passed on by the fly do great damage to cattle.

One of my favorite rapid streams traverses a steep south slope, starting from a ridge of hard traprock (diabase) and crossing weaker shale, where its bed widens by more than 200 percent. From the nearest parking area you enter this shale portion through a cluster of wetland pin oaks. They lend a certain drama, with their curtain of lower limbs that veil much of this lower forest dominated by big trees. A botanist might see another theme, though, that of change in prospect. *Young* pin oaks seem to have gained almost no admission, while sapling sweet gums, red maples, and white ashes sprout all about. Evidently the future belongs to these rather than to pin oak, indicating that the lowland here is gradually drying out. Even black haw, spicebush, arrowwood, witch hazel, and highbush blueberry—never more than tall shrubs—seem to have more promise. The ground is regularly damp rather than wet, and during mid-autumn you can catch a musty odor of prime black haw leaves. As the season becomes drier, seed capsules of the preceding year's witch hazel flowers split and fire their seeds, making small popping sounds followed by the plunk of seeds on leaves a dozen or so yards away.

During August and September here, the huge triple leaves of jack-in-the-pulpit stand out. Tropical and oily, they add a lush giganticism to the low growth. Too soon they pitch over in a golden tan, as lightly luminescent as the old leaves of their occasional companions the day flowers. Where sunlight breaks through regularly, the famous striped hood lacks good color; in a dark regime it attains a more royal purple, attesting to the fact that jack-in-the-pulpit truly prefers shade. Farther uphill and deeper in the woods, partridgeberry replaces the jacks. It is a comparatively Spartan substitute that is, however, more fitting to the cooler environment. Both plants have scarlet to red berries that soon are likely to fall to those who eat in the "wildewood." We humans can eat the fruit of partridgeberry, too, but horror will quickly cross the face of the one who tastes the ringing sting of jack fruit that has not been boiled before he eats it.

My stream cuts a clean path through both lowlands and highlands, for the weak shale beneath forms little more than a flight of steps which direct water off the upland flanks. A large number of the loose stones have little depressions on the underside, and now and then you can find in these cups the larvae of strange beetles called water pennies. The larvae resemble certain flatish, domed spider egg masses, only in this case the glossy top is a living backside, a plated cap bending over six agitated legs. Adult water pennies evidently have better things to do than crawl about with the hope that their stream-living will purchase them safety— they move out and can often be found clinging to plant stems nearby. At this point they may be picked off by one of the green frogs which I have seen sitting absolutely still on the rocks here.

With their eyes mounted on the sides of the head, green and other frogs can watch, defensively as well as hungrily, in almost any direction. They stand as classical examples of prey animals, ever in danger of being eaten themselves. Furthermore, like many aquatic types their urine has a high content of ammonia, which is quickly flushed away in swift streams. The classic submerged predators in this kind of stream, however, are the crayfish, which nestle under ledges and peer out with their eyes on stalks. In this woods, they are the brown of oak leaves, or sometimes the blue-green of shale with a thin coating of algae.

Variety in upland forested streams has perhaps been best caught by the travels of one creek I know, which cuts through glacial moraines made up of till high in limy clay. The Silurian dolomite and Devonian limestone of the stream bed are liberally sprinkled with jingling drift that was dropped more than ten thousand years ago. I am most familiar with this north/south-running creek in a place where swift waters divide sharply under the trees of a box elder woods.

The west branch begins with a fat pool that bulges to the side and probably picks up much of the spring overflow, thus acting as a safety valve. Then the channel cuts deeper, forming a run of smooth water. Finally, it rises onto pebbly shallows, called riffles, and bends back to the right. The east branch, narrower, flows over a riffle run and then races in a slight arc to its reunion with the main stream. In early May, at the tip of an island, its riffles gleam with silvery choppy water; the island's canopy will shade over the creek from late spring until leaf fall in autumn.

The change from day to night is little noticed at the bottom of a run. Olive crayfish walk shadowless. Blunt-nosed minnows wind sinuously upstream, pause, drift back, swivel about, and then repeat their hunt. Toys and cans find runs natural graveyards, while silt rests in the deepest parts, where the current flows most slowly. If any nutrients fall in, they soon support a scum of bacteria, fungi, and blue-green algae. All these demand oxygen. Even the most attractive stream may have its places of oxygen deficiency.

Silt in the form of mud is the pantry of a minute aquatic relative of the earthworm, however. The red torsos of *Tubifex* worms, buried headfirst like arrows bereft of most of the shaft, are variously scattered or massed over the bottom muck. The crimson blood seems only bare cheer against the stream's foreboding unstable bottom, but the hemoglobins that give this color to the blood of *Tubifex*, and also to earthworms, midge larvae, vertebrates, and a wide range of distantly related species, can mean dominion in some places, because hemoglobin has such a strong affinity for oxygen. If the run goes stagnant during a drought, *Tubifex* may extend ten to twelve times its usual length. Eventually the waving tail reverts to corkscrewing, which draws down fresher water. Finally, the available oxygen depleted, *Tubifex* collapses. Perhaps someday the graduated extensions of the lowly worm will be used as an indicator of stream pollution. In bad times it might be said, "*Tubifex* is up today."

Almost everywhere in the overflow pool, life is adapted to an even slower pace. Near the bottom a few stonecats scull deliberately as they guard their nests, while dimpled shadows of wind-blown water striders glide stealthily along the bottom. A lassitude seems to descend from the forest. Now and again a grayback dragonfly flickers into view momentarily as it flies to another tree trunk. There it adjusts its wings much like a golfer loosening his shoulders before he attempts a long drive, and the brownish body vanishes as it mimics ridges in the bark. The sounds of birds are magnified above the rhythm of water flowing over stones a few yards away. At the pool I have learned more by watching than by catching.

Under water, flat giant water bugs often hang face down from erect water-logged sticks. They could be leaves. Their watchful eyes bulge like glands on leaf petioles as the insects tilt toward the bottom, in position to lunge swiftly at passing food. I keep hoping to see one of the more nimble water bugs turn around and launch itself Polaris-like into the sky. If not interrupted these powerful fellows can wait for hours in leaflike mimicry, breathing through a short retractable snorkel that projects from the posterior into the open air. A powerful water bug, such as the droning electric-light bugs that often batter at street lamps on warm nights, can easily handle a fish an inch or two long. One unimpressible insect can wipe out an aquarium full of shiners within a few days. One time we tried such a mixed population in our living-room-window aquarium. The insect soon reduced the gay bodies of the fish to skeletons that drew my attention by looking like small strips of raw bacon fat on the bottom. The beak of one rather small but nervous bug once stung my index finger with what felt like the wallop of a fair-sized hornet. The jolt given fish, tadpoles, and other insects must be a corker.

The few water bugs in this pond doubtless took some of the killifish that snipped moquito larvae and pupae here and there along the water's surface. So predator and prey were in a balance, there being more killifish than water bugs and more mosquitoes than either. The welts I got from the adult flies one spring were my contribution for the right to be a watcher at the pond. Another was the shock I received upon finding I had knelt almost on top of a young water snake. It lay right along the pond edge, like any twig banded with woodland shadows, and it might well have plummeted down from a shrub on my arrival some time before. Now the stocky fellow stared up unblinking, mouth open in a lunging gape, but the jaws were parted by a fish.

Curiously, then, my view of this sideslip pond was one that hardly implied much of a future for many individuals. Doubtless the minute *Daphnia* and *Cyclops* types of crustacean, as well as countless smaller species, formed a column of food which supported some of the larger organisms. Part of their function in ecological economics is to reproduce as fast as possible before disappearing into the dark gullets moving upstairs and down. And so it is that a dozen or so female *Cyclops* in one small embayment can hatch in one breeding season more than twenty-four hundred young, which may themselves mature to adults within a week.

In the end, though, the most successful beast of the dun depths was probably a fuzzy-looking mussel. Coated with debris, but holding its valves ajar like lips pursed on words unspoken, the creature blended neatly with the pool floor. Long after the other large clams were plucked out by raccoons, this one would likely remain, in excellent health, feeding and breathing at no great expense to the pond resources. Later, out in one of the riffles, I found wedged among the rocks another species of mussel that likewise summed up the world about it. The shell was wavy from ridges of marl. This had been deposited by algae, which had withdrawn calcium and carbon dioxide from the cool water and precipitated them as calcium carbonate onto the mussel.

Mussels are usually either male or female. Males release their sperm into the water, where they are sucked in by females through the same siphon that brings in food. Fertilization and eventual development of the larva takes place in the female's gills, which soon puff up and feel a bit like dough. A large female may incubate three million or more young ones at the same time. The mature larva, or glochidium, has a hinged set of shells, or valves, like the adult's. When their time comes, the glochidia are exhaled and left on the bottom. With luck, a fish bumps into them or even sucks them in, whereupon the valves clamp down on fish flesh and remain there. If no fish appear within a few days, the young will die. Once in place, though, the larva becomes covered by a cystlike skin of tissue that its host grows over it. Fishermen are familiar with these lumps when they are external or on the gills. Usually within a few weeks the parasite drops off and becomes a "juvenile," which burrows down into the bottom. After one year, or sometimes as many as eight, the juvenile develops sexually and can be called an adult, at which time it begins contributing to future generations. Since I turned up only a few of the mussels in this pond, I could see that the losses in the immature stages were terrific. But stream particles were being changed into flesh, represented by the sperm and glochidia, and these were probably better food for other inhabitants. Thoreau says, in *A Natural History of Massachusetts*, that adult mussels have also served as food, for the

> common mussel . . . left in the spring by the muskrat upon rocks and stumps, appears to have been an important article of food with the Indians. In one place, where they are said to have feasted, they are found in large quantities, at an elevation of thirty feet above the river, filling the soil to the depth of a foot, and mingled with ashes and Indian remains.

In the crook of one bend of the brook a stumpy backwash cuts into the island loam. At the mouth of this heavily silted jog, crayfish patrol in the shade. Their presence is a first hint that the animals in this place are probably larger types, as a whole, than those in the pool. From what I have seen, crayfish are now the top, or dominant, predators here, feeding even on darters and hog suckers that wander in from the stream rapids. Such stream fish are apt to take refuge in slow cutbacks but to feed at the base of rapids. In this way they link pool and rapids communities.

Pouting lips identify the bottom-dwelling sucker. In the spring these fish would probably be on their way upstream to spawn. At the pool they may have sucked up smaller crayfish or perhaps clubtail dragonfly larvae sunken in the mud. This takes work. Some of the insect prey can burrow out of sight in a matter of seconds, leaving only bulging eyes and the breathing tip of the abdomen exposed.

Fish and crayfish also dominate the riffle run of the east branch, at the point where the stream splits to form the island. Here the water varies from several inches to several feet deep. Johnny darters spread their long, broad pectoral fins to brace themselves among the glacially deposited rocks, where shallow water flows too swiftly. Six or more crayfish may occupy each square yard of bottom in the deeper sections. By using a seine, several friends and I once picked up some lobsterlike specimens that were at least six inches long. We turned the bottom with an ordinary garden rake, and fish and crayfish literally poured into the net. Pond populations of crayfish have on occasion hit one thousand pounds of the crustaceans per acre. Stream populations tend to average somewhat less, though the record to date may still be a haul of 1,176 pounds.

Along with the more common *Cambarus* species, the rusty-streaked crayfish *Orconectes rusticus* lives here. *Orconectes* seems to have evolved around the junctions of the Ohio and Missouri rivers with the Mississippi. From there the species radiated to the Gulf States, Colorado, Lake Superior, the St. Lawrence River Valley, and points between. A few of the creatures even crossed the divide and wandered into Atlantic coast watersheds. *Cambarus* probably originated in the Ozark and southern Appalachian Mountains. Its first migrations went off toward the northeast, traveling at high altitudes. Some species, however, later clambered into the lowlands, spreading out in all directions and wandering far and wide. How long it might have taken *Cambarus* and *Orconectes* to reach their present wide distribution may be suggested by studies made on another group of crayfish. Individuals were found to wander less than one hundred feet from their home base over a lifetime of several years.

Across the bubbling waters of the riffle runs minnows and shiners feed in great numbers. Female trout nest in the riffle gravel. To increase the trout population of a stream, wildlife-management ecologists lay stone bedding along places in the channel that seem to have food and shelter for more fish than are presently there. They estimate what is known as the carrying capacity of the waters and try to meet that potential, stocking the stream where necessary. For example, such an effort might be especially valuable after a particularly disastrous flood has not only hurled the fish downstream but also silted over their breeding grounds.

One October morning, above Iowa City, Wisconsin, I got a closer look at one of these man-made nests. A wildlife biologist of the Soil

Conservation Service took me to a spot along Trout Creek where he and members of the Wisconsin Department of Natural Resources had been stocking fish. Pushing through a thick, tangled hedge of chicory and wild sunflowers, we worked our way down the bank to a quiet crook. Just out from the ten-o'clock shadows of bur oaks we could see the new floor. Here the creek had been dredged. Then a foot-deep layer of large rocks had been sunk in and overlain with two feet of gravelly pebbles.

Filaments of matted watercress sprouted on the downstream point of a mud bar. Their small white blossoms added to the stream's brightness. But when I tried to get closer my feet began to dive into the ooze. We kept our distance that day, the cress and I. The plant was originally introduced from Europe, and the ones here were contributing to the production of fresh-water shrimp, water sow bugs, and other potential trout food. Stringing farther out with the current were massed, flexible stems of water buttercup, some of the plants over a foot long. Largely submerged, the finely divided leaves trailing downstream like girls' hair, this colony gave cover to a nearly uncountable supply of prey for the fish that even that morning were being lowered into the creek. It also offered protection to the trout themselves, which are often preyed on here by belted kingfishers. Actually, these diving birds do more damage among the slower chubs and suckers. In *North with the Spring*, Edwin Way Teale gives one good reason, besides identifying their catch, for watching these predators closely as they leave the stream:

> A nesting kingfisher, for example, can be recognized by the way it carries a fish in its bill. The bird always swallows a fish headfirst. But when it is carrying its catch to the nest it holds the fish reversed, head out, so that it will slip easily down the throat of a fledgling.

The secret of the death of trout streams is that too often man is the *worst* intruder. Soil washing off his furrowed hills of corn or soybeans, soil cascading down the bared banks of new highways, soil running in a thin soup from housing-construction sites—all of it can end as silt that clogs the fish breeding grounds. It buries their eggs, or even the rocks before egg-laying time. Fine particles coat their gills, and the fish suffocate. Trout prefer cold water. Silt raises the stream bottoms and slows their flow, with the result that the water becomes warmer, and trout will no longer enter these streams. So the silted creek in the shade of old bur oaks sinks into a dying stupor as far as trout and other cool-water fish are concerned.

Riffles of a swift woodland stream sometimes form natural dams that accumulate all kinds of trash and the resultant silt, thus changing the temperature and oxygen capacity of the water in their own fashion. However, they usually purge themselves before wiping out the indigenous populations. As a boy, I used to enlarge and destroy dams in the creek behind our house, creating wide flat reservoirs and instantaneous floods. In spring flood time the natural self-pruning material from trees overhead often supported dikes that formed, swelled, and burst in one smooth motion. There was one outside corner of the stream where orchard grass of a neighboring bushy meadow lay bent over in wavelike hummocks, its ripples still retaining the rhythm of the spring flood.

Every autumn the surface of one creek I know disappears beneath a bric-a-brac of twigs and patchwork of colorful leaves. The current slows. Silken algae stream from exposed rocks of the riffles. Only repeated September thunderstorms save the creek from choking to death in summer's end. Spring torrents clean out the winter debris, but more dramatically.

Snaking as a gentle two-by-four through pleasant residential neighborhoods, beneath a woods where Civil War bunkers still look off down the slopes, the brook is acknowledged to be a pleasant wader for small children. That is, until mid-June. Then, one afternoon, the sky falls in—actually! What has been a gentle rain suddenly crashes through the trees, drums on the roof, pours out of the overhead eaves into a shallow hardpan depression just off the back steps. The house immediately fills up with children shaking like animated wet sheets.

Just as swiftly it is finished. And everyone rushes down the street to the underpass. The crested creek is now rushing like blood from a cut jugular. Like the dark eye of a reptile or amphibian that shuts from below, the culvert entrance closes as the stream rises. Brown water overleaps the banks, lacing neighbors' lawns and ripping out unpaved driveways. Fortunately, a downstream plug of branches eventually gives way, and the whole flash flood collapses as though punctured. Immediately after one such storm, my younger daughter went walking on what had been a driveway half an hour before and promptly lost a sneaker. It was simply sucked off her foot, and we never saw it again.

The banks along that woodland creek up among the glacial moraines also showed the work of spring torrents. Often the sides were steep and wore shocks of grass that had dropped in from being undercut too far. The variety of life was curiously recorded in the mayfly nymph population, which was high and helped feed the trout. In shoreline deltas, burrowing nymphs had plowed molelike burrows in which front and rear openings not only provided for easy escape and rapid elimination of wastes but also allowed the current to pass through, bringing in oxygen and carrying away carbon dioxide. I have read of some sloping banks that were mined with several hundred such cells. Other mayfly nymphs, attractively colored like sequins, dashed about in the rapids like darter fish. Finally, one sort of mayfly larva, living more or less in the open, was spreading its bristly front legs among the pebbles as a net to snare food that was being carried downstream.

In some ways the greatest threat to the brook stood overhead. Box elder, a tree of waterways, frequently loses limbs to heavy snows and ices of winter. Dead branches, cracked but still holding on—loggers call them "widow-makers"—posed bleakly above, like old snags in the spring. Trash of the winterkills constantly drops into the water. When I think how spindly the ground cover was on the island I wonder if it might be better if all the trees were to die, letting in more light so that grass could grow thick and hold the silt in place.

But if the black giants fell and grass came, jewelweeds along the bank might be lost. The creek would lose the private hum that rises from bumblebees riding out summer breezes on their bucking orange blossoms. Maybe the darkness over the creek is all that protects it from becoming another pasture stream, perhaps another suburban wader.

9 | *Ravines and Hollows: Where Time Stands Still*

A narrow, deep valley is a scene of capture and slow farewell, an old envelope that holds a letter which was never destroyed. The piece remains, a living treasure from the past, as though time were standing still. The steep V-shaped ravine and the sunken bowl known as a hollow may similarly hold in place a green and dark world. Change here may be reckoned in terms of thousands of years, rather than hundreds.

Slow streams overleap their banks and change course during a single flood, a matter of hours or, at most, days. Fields mature into young woods during one person's lifetime. But in enclosed ravines and hollows the parting with the past may be so slow that for us as individuals it might never take place at all.

Many of our deepest valley clefts were born as the Wisconsin glacier retreated. Overflowing upland ponds and lakes emptied through narrow defiles that have remained active to this day. Springs, rain, and snow continue to feed such hidden places, where April torrents are heard only by birds and other wild things at the bottom of a rugged gorge. Other valleys, especially hollows, have been the work of streams that plucked away at weak spots in the floor and burrowed down until they again met resistant rock. The result may be either a sort of wide cave standing on end or simply a sunken bowl where frosts gather early and stay late. Farmers avoid such places lest their crops get frost-nipped. In wilder days bobcats or even pumas may have paused here at dusk to catch the odors of prey, the scents being brought down by the cooling heavier air that flows from the rounded knolls above. Foxes do so often enough that I know of at least two places named Fox Hollow.

Stream beds wear away so little in some gorges that the water is strikingly clear. Spring floods, which double the velocity of the current, increase its carrying power sixty-four times, and almost anything that falls in is rushed away as though a social reprobate. Down beside a stream in its July condition of quiet, old ferns and sedges may have a neatly combed appearance where the last high water was recorded. Brush piles are few, except where caught in a slender pass between sharp boulders, like bits of celery trapped between teeth.

Trees on the valley floor may rise to stupendous heights as they go up after light. Who would ever bother to come down to cut out these few specimens, even for the hundreds of board feet offered by their thick straight trunks, even though they are practically branchless for several dozen feet? Having little soil to dig in, roots travel great distances, and their backs are often exposed on the rocks like serpents winding slowly past. The local name Rooty Hollow identifies one such captured forest.

Shade cast here can be so dense that an oppressive mood settles over the scene. Stories begin to filter out, often in the past peopled with demons and goblins, and in some few the hint of a real event that may have been just as entertaining without the enchantment of apparitions. Washington Irving's "The Legend of Sleepy Hollow" seems likely to have had its foundations in some village tomfoolery. Irving begins by putting the small-town folk, and our doubts, to sleep:

> From the listless repose of this place and the peculiar character of its inhabitants, who are descendants from the original Dutch settlers, this sequestered glen has long been known by the name of Sleepy Hollow, and its rustic lads are called the Sleepy Hollow Boys throughout all

the neighboring country. A drowsy dreamy influence seems to hang over the land, and to pervade the very atmosphere. . . . Certain it is, the place still continues under the sway of some witching power, that holds a spell over the minds of the good people causing them to walk in a continual reverie.

All the elements for his story are here, real and unreal. He need only bring us down later from the rich farmlands that both Ichabod Crane and Brom Bones coveted to the innermost part of the dell. The concluding horseplay will take place there:

> Over a deep black part of the stream, not far from the church, was formerly thrown a wooden bridge; the road that led to it, and the bridge itself, were thickly shaded by overhanging trees, which cast a gloom about it, even in the daytime, but occasioned a fearful darkness at night.

Irving does not mention it, but to this account should doubtless be added a mist that pulls itself together in the darkest hollows and deep-set ravines. Dampness exuded by leaves and spray thrown aloft from cascades contribute heavily to the mist. Breezes are enjoined from clearing the atmosphere. Here we find liverworts, mosses, horsetails, and ferns, all of which need moisture to provide their sperm a suitable soup to swim in. Edible rock tripe moss, tufts or even swaths of *Mnium cuspidatum* and other mosses, together with half a dozen kinds of liverworts and blue-green algae, lie slack against the steepest dripping walls.

Irving could not have been expected to toss those all in, but he did a very creditable job of logging in other recognizable inhabitants, such as a giant single tulip tree, oaks (especially pin oaks, I presume), chestnuts, alders, and cattails. To these he might have added hemlock, yellow birch, American elm, sugar and red maple, American beech, spicebush, ironwood, witch hazel, hobblebush, Dutchman's-breeches, giant trillium, wood sorrel, wintergreen, trailing arbutus, and countless others that enrich our gorges. In Irving's hollows no birds sing, but *we* can often expect to find phoebes in places where banks are rocky. Before we put up bridges and buildings nearby, phoebe nests were commonly found perched on shingled ledges beside the water, where the birds could bathe and also collect mud and mosses for their nests.

One hollow I once came to early in spring, before the leaves were out, resounded with the shrieks of chorus frogs singing in shrill synchrony. Their sounding board was the entrance "hallway," which was choked with small trees, most of them having diameters of only two inches or so at my chest height. They appeared to be crowding around to march into the hollow. I found the air growing noticeably cooler as I walked from the gangs of straight trunks outside to swishing boughs of hemlock a dozen or so yards inside. Spring had been retarded in this chilly conifer microclimate. A few solitary bees were having to travel yards to find infrequent spring beauties, while *Hepatica* had not yet opened. I was amused to note that the first large boulder to bring my path down to a one-horse trail, so typical of hollows, wore a scalp not only of mosses but rock-cap ferns (*Polypodium virginianum*).

Perhaps the most violent of the defiles I have investigated required a tall climb through mountain forests to get to. Once there, I found it all too easy to slide down toward the stream on sheets of maple leaves and hemlock needles. The soaring current made shouting the normal conversation as it plunged into a series of arcs, curving down one sluice after another and kicking off into spraying spume at the bottom of each. I find it even now the wildest thing I have ever come upon. It brings to mind all the racing mountain streams I have known, especially those named Mad, Wild, and Swift. The season was autumn, and coming and going I passed between a couple of witch hazel trees in bloom. They are amenable to dry ridges and wet lowlands alike, true vagabonds of the woods. Here their yellow spidery blossoms were small lamps lit to see the passage both in and out.

Perhaps my most memorable visit to a ravine began on the crest of a lofty hill during the first week of February. All of winter's progress had been brought to a standstill that year by a long period of cold that was reaching deep into a snowless ground. December and January had passed, almost nameless without snow, and now every day was setting a new record in the state. I could see where, in another winter, hemlocks at the bottom of the ravine would have been sweeping the white banks and rocks with their lower branches. I could imagine curl spots where deer had lain protected from blizzards. But that day, on the crest of a long ridge, I crunched the leaves of black oaks underfoot, snapped the revealed brown and white teeth of ground ice, and headed down toward the dark band of ice winding below at the dictates of hard diabase walls.

My descent would be similar to a hike up the North American continent. I would be traveling from a region of comparative warmth on the ridge to an end point of noticeably chillier temperatures by the stream, from oak leaves to hemlock needles. Deep ravines can locally reverse the usual rule about climbing upward to achieve colder climates —the taller a mountain, the more northerly in aspect will be its plants. Ordinarily, a rise of one thousand feet in elevation is equal to traveling about six hundred miles up the map. Each ravine has its own individual ratios, but certainly I crossed several zones here, for I went from the environment of our great oak forests of the midcontinent into the hemlock-hardwoods of the north. Fortunately, the ravine telescoped not only distance but time.

It has been said that if you scratch an American, underneath you will find a farmer. The uplands on the ridge were no exception. Farmers had preceded me in this place as well as in my ancestry. (When I was a boy I was shown one day an ancient family graveyard of tumbled-down slabs that went back well before the Deerfield, Massachusetts, massacre. Now, under a grove of white pines, it reflected the ponderous names of my forebears who had harvested there: Abraham, Ezekiel, Moses, and others.) Up here some hardy souls had been practicing the upper level of two-story agriculture of ridge top, ridge, and valley.

The last farm had died not too long ago, for red cedars were still pressing their bent, arthritic backs up against the hardwood canopy.

Their lower branches were all hardened and dead, though. Over them on all sides towered white ash and black oak, which early in the forest growth had taken advantage of plentiful light and grown as fast as any potential competitors might. Relatively infertile soil and a dearth of moisture had pretty much reduced the struggle among giants to this attempt to gain the upper hand in a reach for light. Their trunks showed bodies pared to the minimum. They rose straight and limbless as though stacked upright. Branches in the shade had died and been pruned off, leaving under the bark what would be minor knots in the board feet.

One lofty black oak stood out among its kind like a domineering patriarch. Sometime in the far past it had been declared lord of the territory and allowed to grow in the open, unhindered by neighbors and unchecked by human landlords. Perhaps its shadow gave cows relief on hot summer days. Maybe its crooked branches and massive trunk, with typical deeply furrowed bark, gave the west side of a house or barn more and more protection each year from wintry blasts. Other trees born the same year had been dragged away in the service of their growing nation, for whose sake they became ceiling beams in courthouses, king posts, chords in long bridges, and even ornamental furniture. Down the brow of the slope, in damper soil, a red oak still wore a broad blaze near the base of its trunk as a memento of the lumbering operations. A broad grassy ditch passing by was evidently a former logging road, and the red oak had been grazed by logs every so often. Tulip trees here were also reminders of logging, for they had come into the old forest where openings had been created by ax and saw. Anyone interested in evolution should take a look at a tulip tree leaf. It has remained a very faithful copy of those that first appeared back in Cretaceous days, about 100 million years ago.

A few chestnut saplings clinging to the rocky escarpment had less favorable prospects than the tulip trees. Their apparent health belied the fungus disease which even then was doubtless killing them all. Soon patches of dead bark would be speckled with the orange sporulating heads of the blight. One type of the fruiting bodies gives off similar spores which have a special coating of ooze that makes them stick to insects or anything else passing by, to be distributed onto chestnuts far and wide. This destroyer was first written up in 1904 by Herman Morke, chief forester of New York City's Zoological Park. Since then the disease has spread throughout the American chestnut's range. The fungus was a visitor native to China and Japan that, like so many introduced pests, found better pickings away from home, and few or no natural checks. In this case, the immigrant swept the field in less than half a century. Old roots still send up suckers like these saplings, but so far they are only ghosts. Even if they produce flowers, pollination is unlikely, for the pollen must come from another tree.

Though large chestnut trees were absent here, the species had had a favored position in our past. It provided prized lumber and was also the prime local source of tannin, which is used in preparing leather. The tree's demise was a smashing blow to American tanners. I myself remember chiefly the chestnuts, freshly roasted in the cart of the man hawking them, which for a while were sold in warm paper bags on many streets. Even these, of course, had an enemy of their own in the form of two weevils that laid their eggs in the nuts—which soon became more insect than plant meat. Maurice Brooks, in *The Appalachians,* recounts how

> my father once collected a measured bushel of chestnuts, all of which had unbroken shells when he assembled them. He hung them in burlap sacks above sheet metal that trapped the worms as they dropped out. In a period of five weeks he collected 3600 worms from his bushel of nuts. This may explain why the chestnut season in cities was a short one.

Brooks points out that bobwhite quail were satisfied with chestnuts in either pure or wormy condition, since the bird liked both nut and larva. I imagine that this is one of the advantages a countryman once had over

a city dweller: even as his edible nut crop ran low, the quail crop pros-
pered.

Down the ravine slope I passed from oaks and chestnuts into a
narrow zone of beeches. All along the valley at this level beech trees stood
out—they still held their golden leaves, on branches that are among the
most resilient of all under burdens of snow and ice. In most cases some
of the leaves from each tree could drop away and roll down boughs of
small hemlocks that intermeshed with the base of the beech line. On a
snowy winter day these young hemlocks must remind one of Christmas
trees.

Sprinkled sparsely among both beeches and hemlocks were springy
striped and mountain maples. Normally these are strangers to the area,
doing much better in New England and Canada, but then the descent into
this ravine is a northward journey. The large squarish leaves, five or six
inches on a side, often remind me of Halloween cats' faces. Their bright
yellows illuminate the understory of many cool woods during autumn.
Carolina wrens can be heard among them there in almost any decent
weather. Their secretive nests, in brush piles, are not necessarily wasted
after the first year. One in these woods had had at least two successive
years of occupancy.

Climbing downward from the beech canopy into one that was
primarily hemlocks, I entered a world of unquestioned giants. Beeches
now were fading old fellows, though often three feet or more in diameter
at chest height. Soaring, glossy hemlocks averaged from one to two feet,
while tulip trees, which became more frequent as I stepped from the slope
onto the valley floor, came to slightly more than that. I would guess that
the latter tree, also called yellow poplar (in reality it happens to be a
member of the ancient magnolia family, rather than of either the tulip
flower or poplar families), will not continue in the final forest here, since
there were so few younger ones. The tulip trees also ran a high risk of
losing their seeds to small animals that eat here, often leaving only piles
of the wings that had brought the seeds spinning softly down.

Beside one fallen hemlock trunk lay a midden of seeds that was no less than two feet long by six inches wide, and four inches high at some points. It spoke wonders about a favorite dining place, and perhaps about a social life of long standing. I was soon glad I had paused nearby. While I watched entranced, a beam of sunlight turned momentarily green on a tiny forest of mosses; for seven months of the year, their fresh cool odor is a major spirit of many ravines. Then, at the base of another supine giant, I noticed a shelf fungus the size of a dinner plate. The weathered top was still darkly shiny as though especially glazed, and it appropriately bears the name of varnish conk.

Hemlocks almost touched others across the ravine's brook, which was about thirty feet broad where I came down. The trees, having shallow roots in a thin soil, leaned out dangerously. Bedrock was close to the surface all down the ravine wall and across the floor, except where it was actually bared by the stream. Few small plants were living here which might add to the litter; three months later I noticed that almost all the trout lilies emerging had but single leaves, a sign that they had not taken in enough nourishment to put out another leaf and the blossom that usually follows. Hemlock roots lay exposed like huge ribs. Among them, down on the rocks, sycamore roots, spare but large, caught my attention for having flaked bark just as the trunk does. I expect that the hemlocks will outlast all other trees in these deeps, for no matter what the fate of the old ones, younger trees were doing very well in their shade. Across the way, on a north-facing slope, these trees were so intertwined that they excluded almost everything else. Maples and beeches may appear in such habitats, but harsh frosts of May and June soon show why oaks, hickories, sycamores, and others usually keep out. Their leaves become "burned," and the trees may even be stripped of all foliage for nearly a month.

Masses of matured and bronze hemlock cones often remind me of ornaments. Closed hemlock cones belong to the first autumn. By October the fertilized female reproductive organs inside have matured into ripened fruit, but the cones stay closed all winter. They open during the following growing season, but are highly sensitive to moisture. Given a spate of rain or snow or even a rise in humidity, scales of open cones will close again.

The cascading seeds, averaging two hundred thousand to the pound, sometimes find their best rooting along fallen relatives—dead hemlock trunks that stretch out as twenty or more yards of moldering fertilizer. Thus a string of hemlock seedlings may rise from one of these "nursery logs" and grow in a straight line among randomly dispersed companions. During one especially cold year, cones on trees farther north were such poor feeding that the trees down here became a noisy pantry for dozens of red crossbills. Suddenly, the boughs were full of them, and seeds were thrown wildly to left and right.

Ravines and hollows are among the best places to look for winter when you miss it in the fields and roadside woods. The ice caught Thoreau's attention:

> The sun, shining down a gorge over the woods at Brister's Hill, reveals a wonderfully brilliant as well as seemingly solid and diversified region in the air. The ice is from an eighth to a quarter of an inch thick about the twigs and pine needles, only half as thick commonly on one side. Their heads are bowed; their plumes and needles are stiff, as if preserved under glass for the inspection of posterity.

I once found the only ice crystals around in a hole at the bottom of a similarly frigid ravine. Down beside the creek a burrow entrance was crisscrossed by half a dozen grass stems. Just inside, the owner had been poised close to the openings and had left his warm moist breath recorded on the straws as white spikes of hoarfrost. He had gone, but they held true as a nature note.

10 | *A Land of Oaks*

From Minnesota to Maine, down to Florida, across a portion of Texas, and finally up the Mississippi-Missouri drainage system to Minnesota again—with aspen outposts in eastern North Dakota—a broadleaved forest dominates the eastern North American scene. Green by summer, an almost legendary variety of colors in most places during autumn, and increasingly leafless as we go north in winter, this forest is about as characteristic of the United States as any single element we might choose. Wherever one travels in this huge formation he is likely to find oaks, maples, beeches, and basswoods (or lindens). Lucy Braun, who has put together the most comprehensive view of this land of deciduous trees in her *Deciduous Forests of Eastern North America,* sees in these four species a strong thread of unity—which we will also find through forests of this and the succeeding chapters.

In Europe a second massive deciduous formation was long ago partially denuded of trees by man and then crushed between glacial ice and southern mountain ranges like a stack of toothpicks caught between a hammer and anvil. Asia still retains its forest, though the tones are said to be more muted. The colorful autumn display is mostly an American phenomenon.

After the Tertiary period, the glacial masses of a new time, the Pleistocene epoch, swept down over America from Canada and either destroyed our deciduous forest or drove it south. For a million years or more, ice sheets threatened its existence this way. But certainly since the last one, the Wisconsin glacier, whose lobes began to depart about fifteen thousand years ago, the deciduous forest has been rebounding. Various species in different combinations have spearheaded its advance, which still appears to be continuing, possibly under the influence of a warming trend. A central point of distribution may have been the forested Cumberland Plateau and southwestern parts of the Allegheny Plateau, or this area may simply have a concentration of reasonably untouched Tertiary forest that is hanging on in Appalachian coves as a lucky remnant. Conifer forests and some deciduous trees may actually have ridden on top of the trailing edge of the glacier, having taken root in the soil that had been laid down there by pollen and other dust and then by hardy small plants. Possibly early Americans even hunted in these woods, unaware of the mile-or-so-deep icecap flowing beneath them. In the end, forests dominated by oaks and various of their companions went off in many directions at the glacier's retreat, while they also managed to hold on to at least some of the territory they had occupied during cooler times.

Thus many of the same kinds of oaks flourish up the Mississippi River, over in Tennessee and Rhode Island, and down south through the Appalachians. But diversity has also enhanced their movement, for various species may rule in different localities, such as post oak in the oak-hickory forests of Texas. The over-all ability of oaks to withstand difficult conditions, extreme cold excepted, made them dangerous flags to follow when the pioneers from Europe came over and looked for favorable routes west. In the hands of unscrupulous land speculators, oaks became perhaps the cockroaches of the botanical world. Their presence merely indicated that they could survive as a genus (*Quercus*) even on sand, marshy lowlands, and craggy cliffs.

Oak is in our blood today, and there is reason to think that for many Americans it was there long before their ancestors arrived from

Europe 350 and more years ago. When the Pilgrims landed at Plymouth Rock and Sir Walter Raleigh's expedition went ashore in the present Jamestown coastal fringe, they were entering a land not wholly different from their own. Short sessile oaks frequently dominate upland woods of northern and western Britain, while the taller pedunculate oak is the main oak of southeastern England and parts of Europe across the channel. In 1616, Captain John Smith was doubtless pleased to report, in his *A Description of New England,* that oak was the chief timber. As far back as 1016 the English king Canute the Dane had set judicial officers over the oak, beech, and holly Forest of Dean, down near the Welsh border. These "verderers" may have held court primarily to ensure that deer hunting was reserved to the king and his followers, but doubtless they also defended the woods against being encroached upon by farms. Robin Hood's legendary adventures, early mentioned in the fourteenth-century poem *The Vision of William concerning Piers the Plowman,* took place among the oaks of Sherwood Forest. One tree standing there now, Major Oak, is held (lightly) to have been perhaps a special hiding place for the elusive outlaw. Finally, Shakespeare made much of oaks, referring to them freely through his plays, such as "Jove's stout oak" of *The Tempest* (V; i; 45) and, in *The Tragedy of Troilus and Cressida,* the lines "The splitting wind makes flexible the knees of knotted oaks" (I; iii; 49–50). Evidently the trees of Birnam that marched against Macbeth were oaks and sycamores, if we are to judge by two behemoths alive today that seem to be the sole survivors of Birnam Wood. Many of the ancient forests exist now only as secondary or tertiary growth at best. They fell victim in their time and became the ships of Elizabeth's navy, fuel for furnaces of the Industrial Revolution, and, finally, the raw material of housing booms.

In America our original oak forests have largely fallen into similar hands, and the products of today's timbers are weaker than those made earlier, from trees that were often centuries old. It is doubtful that a trunnel from a modern oak could hold up against one from a patriarch of the old primary forest. How rapidly a forest might be disposed of today is told, with at least a grim sense of humor, by Professor Maurice Brooks of the University of West Virginia, when he writes in *The Appalachians* about the remarkable fate of just one tree. It was during the early darkness of World War II, when Nazi submarines were torpedoing Allied ships on the high seas and then coming in closer to mine harbors and shipping lanes freely. The mines could be cleared away, but only by minesweepers with wooden hulls, which circumvented the detectors on the new magnetic mines. White oak was the preferred timber, and Appalachian coves provided the most usable stands. Brooks and fellow foresters helped whisk some out of a prime stand in Doddridge County, West Virginia. For the particular tree, he tells the story this way:

> One morning a magnificent old white oak was felled, and from its trunk a 42-foot log was cut. It was skidded to a landing, loaded on a special truck, and that afternoon moved to Parkersburg to the only mill in the region with facilities to shape and saw it. The sawing was done, and an oversized truck was used to move the squared timber, all 42 feet of it, to Ashtabula, Ohio. Here the stick was placed in an accelerated-action dry kiln, given a quick seasoning, and used in the construction of a United States Navy minesweeper. Eight days from the time it was growing on a Doddridge County hill it was afloat on Lake Erie.

Ohio, as a matter of fact, provides a good measuring stick for the depredations on our timber. This easternmost of the midwestern states is considered to have been 95 percent forest in 1788. By 1853 this had shrunk to 54 percent, and within comparatively recent times—1940—the over-all coverage has been rated at only 14 percent.

However cut up our oak forests are, though, both large and small woods have an abundance of life that is staggering. Fortunately, the scene is a layered one in which even the casual visitor can pick out a dominating canopy, an understory of smaller trees, a shrub and vine layer, and a ground cover that is owned mostly by herbaceous low plants. This arrangement makes it possible for us to concentrate on one horizontal zone at a time.

The forest canopy keeps the internal temperature down and the humidity up. Thus the leaves below can expand into fine sheets without danger of drying or being burned by the sun. The thinness of the leaves allows some light to pass through and be used more completely by chlorophyll on both sides. Also, the leaves grow out more or less horizontally and thus gain to the fullest extent from direct and incidental light, with the lower ones arranged so that no leaf is directly above another. Broad leaves give the deciduous forest its characteristic lively green during summer and are responsible for the great changes that occur during fall and winter. The wide, shallow leaf form cannot withstand freezes as the needle style can (and also lacks the necessary thick resins). Therefore most of these leaves, such as those of oaks, seem to need to translocate their food out of the blades come autumn. They also develop an abscission layer of tissue which allows, even helps, the leaf to break away.

Both oaks and pines reabsorb so much of their leaves' mineral content into the branches and trunk, removing it before the leaves drop, that dead November foliage is almost pure cellulose. Bacteria, molds, mushrooms, earthworms, and other growth that might normally digest the leaves abstain now because the diet is so one-sided. As a result, forest floors fill with this undecomposed mattress. Discarded paper is a similar substance, and lingers around on the ground for months for many of the same reasons. Bacteria living in oak and pine forests have to get their food elsewhere while they act slowly on the leaves, and so they may strip the soil, especially choosing accessible nitrogen. In this sense, farms that come in after oak-pine dominion are facing a progressively more impoverished situation. The leaves themselves are, in a way, negative assets chemically. Incompletely broken-down organic material—the worst offender being pine needles, which are notoriously lacking in lime—yields many acids. In oak woods these include a huge supply of dark tannic acids that give dead oak leaves their familiar chocolate-brown color. The acids depress the activity of decomposers like bacteria and fungi and increase the leaching of soil.

Soil acids can hardly be considered wholly damaging, of course. Many plants are physiologically adapted to them. In addition, they promote the development of mycorrhizal fungi—fungi which have no disease aspect but, rather, a favorably symbiotic or co-operative behavior. Their threads invade actively growing and absorbing roots and pass soil nutrients into them, adding to what they get from the microscopic root hairs alone. The fungi benefit from this relationship by using carbohydrates and other materials from the root cells. Oak litter does carry chemicals that inhibit mycorrhizal fungi, but possibly the chemicals affect only the fungi of other trees, not the strands that are favorable to oaks, since mycorrhizae are usually specific as to the genus of tree they will affect. It is worth plucking a few oak root tips out of the soil and examining their surface for the characteristic web. Oaks, hickories, beeches, birches, pines, and other trees develop a thick mycelium, or mass, of fungal threads there. Maples, tulip trees, apples, heaths, and most shrubs are among those that acquire a mycelium whose threads are less dense over the root's surface.

One of the effects of a thick leaf litter is the retention of water in the soil. As a result, roots can remain closer to the surface. This can mean trouble, in that there is an increased danger of wind-throw and roots are bared quickly when erosion occurs and are more vulnerable to even a fairly rapid forest fire. On the other hand, the trees do not have to expend so much of their supply of carbohydrates on sending their roots deep in search of water; also, the mycorrhizae which affect oaks and some other trees are most concentrated within the top several inches of soil. Mushrooms that poke through the soil and litter show where the fungi have invaded successfully.

Aldo Leopold found that another type of fungal or viral infection in oaks actually increased the number of grouse visiting a woods in autumn and during winter blusters. With the advent of the snowy season a grouse's toes grow comblike scales to each side, becoming effective snowshoes until the fringes are shed in spring. Leopold says, in *A Sand County Almanac:*

> My woods houses a dozen ruffed grouse, but during periods of deep snow my grouse shift to my neighbor's woods, where there is better cover. However, I always retain as many grouse as I have oaks windthrown by summer storms. These summer windfalls keep their dried leaves and during snows each such windfall harbors a grouse. The droppings show that each grouse roosts, feeds, and loafs for the duration of the storm. . . . The cured oak leaves not only serve as cover but . . . are relished as food by the grouse.
>
> These oak windfalls are, of course, diseased trees. Without disease, few oaks would break off, and hence few grouse would have down tops to hide in.

The lasting nature of oak leaves makes it almost impossible to depart from a cleared trail without announcing every move in crushed cellulose. Along the woodland edge a brown thrasher may reveal himself this way as he thrashes among the leaves for grubs. Snakes sometimes also make a scraping sound when dodging along in autumn, heading over crinkled leaves toward some burrow across a land that no longer can be flushed for beetles or young mice. Eastern kingsnakes are among the more common, though last October I was chasing mostly garters, including a pair that stayed nearly parallel to each other like a set of sled runners. In spring their mudded skins indicate the sort of place they chose for hibernation. One way to make a tally of woodland snake species that may have been heard but never seen is to find crested flycatchers' nests. These are often in old tree holes, and it is worth climbing to see what skin or skins have been woven into the nest.

Oak leaves so control the forest ground cover that finding a large number of herbaceous plants there is a sign of erosion rather than well-being. Erosion removes leaves and allows seedlings to get started. Many really small seeds have no choice but to avoid litter altogether. White avens, for instance, prefers shade, but it has trouble getting going in more productive oak woods. Look for its foot or so of stem with very cut-up, ferny leaves. Throughout most of the summer at least one of the plants will be surmounted by little white flowers. From August on, its minute hooked seeds ride with you after you stride through a patch of the little burs. The ride may be as much as the seeds will ever get out of life, however, unless they detach over bare and reasonably moist ground. Small seeds like these cannot produce enough root to drive through thick leaf litter, and sometimes even a thin litter dries out so quickly that the root dies on its way down—especially likely in a sunny oak woods. Avens and its sort really need freshly bared ground to start on. I look for a story where it flourishes, even as simple a story as that a dog went nosing after moles there.

White snakeroot has about the same ecology as avens. Historically it has also helped point out a lesson in land use and abuse. During the depression of the 1920's many farmers allowed their cattle to browse in scrabbly woodland ground cover. The beasts soon ate this away and left the land bare, open for erosion. Along with the subsequent gully washes came disturbance indicators like white avens and white snakeroot. As luck would have it, the conspicuous leaves and stems of snakeroot carry the poisonous alcohol tremetol, which not only sickens cattle but can be passed on in their milk to people. Farmers who saw their animals stumbling about before they were milked were the lucky ones.

Oak woods lack the rich profusion of spring flowering plants that arise and fall just after winter has left and before the shade of foliage becomes fullest. The woods are comparatively so sunny during summer that many shrubs and weeds do well, and the competition for nutrients and water eliminates most of the delicate spring types, such as bloodroot and Dutchman's-breeches. These spring ephermerals are far more characteristic of dark, shrubless maple woods. Among oaks, even in places that look about right, the ground is probably so smothered by old leaves that none of them could begin to poke through.

maple-leaved viburnum   ruffed grouse and young   spice bush   white snakeroot

white avens   *white oak*   *king snake*   *burdock*   *blackberry*

Thus oak woods have a close affinity to fields. Red cedars survive longer in these woods. And it does not take much of an opening to acquire a colony of burdocks. These, incidentally, develop a microscopic structure that gives a strong hint as to the nature of their habitat. A cross section of a woodland burdock leaf compared with that of one grown in a sunny field would show that the waxy cuticle coat is thinner on the woodland leaf. Perhaps the leaf in the woods is so much more protected from rain, wind, and other rugged elements than the one in an open field that it can dispense with the protective layer. Plants growing near the ocean edge, such as seaside goldenrod, are famous for their *thick* cuticle, apparently a raincoat against salt-water spray. Therefore we might expect to find less covering on shielded plants. A thinner cuticle might also let in more light, important in the woods. In addition, woodland burdocks develop longer palisade cells, which contain the chlorophyll, and not so many layers of them. So it might be that light is more likely to reach all the cells when they are not piled deeply.

Blackberries also turn up very quickly in oak openings. During winter the canes can be identified easily by their squarish fluted contours, and summer and autumn of wet years will find even those in deeper shade loaded with black tasty globes. Fruit-eating birds carry blackberries into new woodland openings rapidly, for the species that live in such places tend to travel directly from one clearing to another. Indigo buntings are well known for contributing this way to the success of blackberries and then nesting among the canes. Don't listen for their song from down below, though. The canarylike chirps may begin on the lower branches, but they definitely end up coming from high in the trees. On a larger scale, I can see a definite significance in this bird's arrival. While most of the indigo bunting's close relatives (genus *Passerina*) are tropically oriented, this species, like the oak and maple forests of the east, may actually be moving northward in postglacial times.

Few birds of any kind nest in the upper stories of the woods. Half the nests seem to occur within six feet of the forest floor, while more than a third may be within the first two feet. Thus openings and open woods can be among the most attractive sites for expected woodland birds, and even for such exotics as brown thrashers.

Shrubs and small trees can make an oak woods a showcase of associates. Spicebush, maple-leaved viburnum, hawthorn, black haw, and multiflora rose may completely fill the lower zones of woods less than sixty years old. A special unkempt look among their limbs is worth hunting for. A number of these types are susceptible to a fungus which produces misshapen growths along the branches. Those on cherry may appear as spriggy sprays, which unmistakably identify them under their name of witches'-broom. Other witches'-brooms suggest the curling of a French horn or the loop of a playground ring. The fungus that attacks hackberry, among others, is carried by *Eriophyes* mites. Hackberry is usually attractive, even with witches'-brooms, and it has found plenty of service outside the woods. Early settlers planted it as hedges, and it was only later that its name was corrupted to "hackberry" from "hedgeberry." Mature plants were used as corner trees by the surveyors of the Virginia–North Carolina state line. It was popular enough in colonial times to be sent back to England as early as 1656.

Thicket growth in the woods, if not too dense, attracts deer. Their winter paths show up in splintered twig tips. Deer rip the last several inches off, leaving brushy ends where they have shorn them between toothless upper jaws and well-chiseled lower ones. In a tough year deer will stand up higher and higher against a young tree and eventually ride it to the ground like beefy tacklers in a football game. A tree that has been punished in this way will be browsed far above any normal line. And deer not only nip off twigs but may even strip trunk bark. They peel it upward and leave it hanging in strips, which characteristically narrow toward the top. Long vertical slashes on the trunks of large trees are another matter. These are usually territorial marks raked by bears, using either teeth or claws.

When the woods are filled with deep snow, deer are apt to gang up in "yards," where they tromp drifts into submission. The yards are not so often swaths but, rather, crisscrossing trails. In *Wandering Through*

Winter, Edwin Way Teale tells of asking the game warden of a Maine forest what was the biggest deer yard he had ever seen. The man recalled a trampled area that "was three miles long. It covered about one and a half square miles of woods."

Rabbits in the woods leave sharply incised twig ends as their chewing marks; it is as though someone had crawled along using a knife to blaze the path. Teale says they also are known to peel open Cecropia moth cocoons for the pupae, which, like the rabbits, will be more prevalent where low cover has a foothold. Shrubbery covered with Japanese honeysuckle, catbrier, and bittersweet provides continuous hutches and is one of the most attractive territories to them. Deer come in here, too. Leopold writes: "I like the bittersweet because my father did, and because the deer, on the first of July of each year, begin suddenly to eat the new leaves, and I have learned to predict this event to my guests. I cannot dislike a plant that enables me, a mere professor, to blossom forth annually as a successful seer and prophet."

In the understory of oak forests are a number of trees that indicate either the future of the forest or its previous status. White ash, for instance, speaks of the past, when the woods were young and sunny. The tree grows swiftly and attains full height before the oaks. Shade, however, kills off both full-grown ashes and their saplings. In the olden days farmers cut out these trees before they died and sold their wood to be used in barrel hoops, furniture, tool handles, and the like, as a valuable cash crop. Young oaks, on the other hand, usually tell of the future, that the present oak woods will continue to develop in the same way, though their shade is often their own worst enemy.

Dead leaves held after autumn by young oaks have proven to be a real boon to overwintering birds, though. On several occasions, one observer saw two hundred or more evening grosbeaks roosting for the night among heavily foliaged branches. Oak leaves on the ground in spring can give young oaks a head start since they reduce competition by preventing plants with small seeds from gaining a foothold. Acorns, of course, have little trouble turning into seedlings, as anyone can believe who has left a few to grow in a home terrarium. They get around the leaf-litter problem by carrying plenty of food, enough to produce a good-sized root and stem before it is used up.

During a snowy winter, oak leaves give the woods a warm color that would otherwise be lacking; without them black sticks would stand out too starkly against white snow. In maple woods young beech trees provide the same effect. I can interchange one tree for the other when reading Robert Frost's lines from his poem "Reluctance," which show how well acquainted he was with the woods at this time of year:

> The leaves are all dead on the ground,
>   Save those that the oak is keeping
> To ravel them one by one
>   And let them go scraping and creeping
> Out over the crusted snow,
>   When others are sleeping.

11 | *Oak Forests in a Varied Land: Four Sides of a Many-sided Figure*

Oak woods differ somewhat from place to place, but I know of four that illustrate four major points of view. The first is on ground that is recovering from having been farmed some six to eight decades ago. The second consists of a series of steps up a rocky gradient over a half mile long. Two parts make up the third, a young and a mature oak-chestnut woods. And the fourth consists of an oak-hickory forest which has been saved by one of the better-known conservation associations.

Old farmland that has been allowed to revert to woods does not simply take one long, steady successional route but proceeds at different rates in different places. Hiking one of the old paths worn by farmers and their children can be an excellent way of turning up some of the more historical spots, such as a springhouse and its associated marsh. After a few times over the trail, one can see that a certain organization has begun to assert itself along the way. The entry point, for instance, will show various edge-of-the-field phenomena, such as tree crickets that concentrate in the banks of shrubs, making the night mellow with their pulsing song. Deeper inside, the woods becomes darker and less crowded. Shy birds become curious about what is happening on the ground below.

Voices are more important here and the birds are apt to react readily to imitative calls.

So I consider it only appropriate that the stony path into this woods that was once a farm should pass by a few tall bunches of Indian grass and enter through dozens of nodding May apples just inside. I am actually near the end of a long, sloping field at this point, and all the hillside wash that could do so has swept through here spring after spring and fall after fall. Cows had destroyed most of the nutritious tall grass by cropping it to within about half a foot of the ground. Too much soil was bared. Each spring for years now, the twisted foliage of May apples has drilled up through the thin litter, and each August a few people have had the temerity to try the lemony-sweet apples growing underneath the umbrella-like leaves. Only plants with paired fronds, rather than just one, produce a flower and its subsequent large, fleshy berry.

The woodland path turns sharply left through the May apples and glides gradually downhill at a slight angle off the horizontal, as though someone had laid it out by rolling a ball across the slope. Shortly after sunrise one morning, five of us walking here had progressed about fifteen yards when we turned to look back at the low rays of sunlight breaking in at tree-trunk level. In the door to the woods stood two fawns, immobile as though irresolute. Then we heard a snort and a brief stomping noise in the leaves several dozen yards off to the left. Evidently the parents, which we now saw, were signaling. One fawn turned and bounded off in that direction. The other held its ground; then it turned and trotted out into the field, and into a moment in the sun that could have been its last.

Occasionally, walking this trail, you may hear white-tailed deer crashing away through undergrowth, but usually the dominant sounds of disturbance belong to gray squirrels. Generally it's the smaller animals that make the greater noise. Those fawns appeared to be twins, incidentally. A doe will, given the opportunity, hide them in separate places. Deer populations here, as in many woods, boomed as Europeans spread their civilization, with the resultant lumbering and burning. Tall forests fell and were replaced by more open grassy and weedy places, increased sprouting from stumps, and more seedling trees. This resulted in mounting leafy food and cover for the white-tails.

To what degree do trees control the passage of rain water in the woods? Tall trees that reach the canopy overhead can give a hint. In a storm, more than three-quarters of the trunks of many of these will be black with water. Thus rain water, falling brokenly from leaves and sliding down trunks, strikes the woodland path with a broken force. That is just as well, for the ground here lacks the protective weaving that grass roots provide; a heavy rain can rip a wooded slope apart. On the other hand, woodland soil, with its thick mattress of leaves and humus, stores water quite well. Therefore forests are often cited as necessary natural reservoirs.

I rarely think of rain as causing much damage to live leaves, but it does leach enough nutrients from them, on the average, to keep a fair supply coming back to the forest soil throughout the growing season. The total phosphorus and potassium returned in this way may just about equal that regained in autumn, when the whole leaves drop. Thus a short mineral cycle occurs within the larger, better-known one.

Fairly damp woods like this are good places to search for mushrooms, shelf fungi, and puffballs. Many of the trees doubtless have mycorrhizal fungi associated with them. Their spore-producing heads occasionally appear above ground as variously shaped fungi loosely encircling or radiating from the tree. One less than essential fungus, however, is the kind that collects as black tips on leaves and fills the vein indentations. It may be especially prominent on leaves of the understory where "honeydew" secreted by aphids and other insects has splattered and concentrated as a sugary base.

Black haws, their wiry branches arching over a dark part of the trail near the field (along which they might once have marked a fence line), reveal here perhaps the blackest fungus-coated leaves of any. They look just plain filthy. More picturesque is the foliage of spicebush farther down the trail. Its leaves are a waxy green and range in size from some of the smallest to largest single blades in the shrub layer. All of them appear to have been dipped in India ink. Undoubtedly a good deal of this added color comes from bits of airborne debris from the woods itself, as well as from soot of nearby towns and highways. Rub a hand on the gray bark of even a "clean" beech tree in a deep forest and see how much black powder comes off. An odor as of old closets pervades this part of the woods after the middle of autumn. It comes mostly from the black haw leaves which lie damp and moldering on the ground.

There are few beeches here to sprinkle their golden leaves on the ground or to rub, I am sorry to say. And these trees are reproducing only by root suckers rather than seedlings. Farther north and along mountain crests, where beech is a climax, or final, member of massive beech-birch-maple forests, it succeeds itself regularly, growing from sweet nuts that are enclosed as pairs in spiny burs.

Along the trail just beyond the haws there does stand one lofty beech that must have been deliberately left by several generations of farmers. They may have been adding to the monetary value of their property the intangible gain of having wildlife feed on the piles of nuts that poured down around the base each autumn. I have looked in vain around this beech many times for an amber-brown twiggy growth coming up from the general root area. It suggests a witches'-broom and, like it, is a parasite. But this one, beechdrops, is a flowering plant with tubular white flowers that appear late in summer. The lower flowers are less showy and pollinate themselves, as do the hidden lower flowers of most violets. Beechdrops are worthy companions to beech trees because they are stiff and almost woody, very like root suckers.

Farther across the crest of the hill I find eastern hop hornbeam coming in. Its autumn seed pods suggest hops. The uninitiated may think at first that these are small elms, but their leaves are not lopsided as are those of elm. The gray-brown bark peels off in small rectangular slabs, giving a look of being poked off from inside like caps. The wood is exceptionally hard and heavy, giving the tree the epithet "ironwood." It makes these trees a mainstay of woods that, winter after winter, are tested by snow and ice storms. Hop hornbeams, here as elsewhere, are typically spaced widely through the woods, notably where the rocky brow is showing.

But this is primarily an oak forest, as are so many of our most familiar woods. Some of the largest specimens are white oaks growing on uplands that were last mowed more than a hundred years ago. An occasional really old soldier stands out where generations of farmers left it as a marker or perhaps as a relic of open-land elegance, which has since then passed in favor of small, heavily used plots. Most of the trees in the same place, however, have a uniform trunk diameter, having grown up together after the same cutting or burning. The white oak trunks in this woods are noticeable for being quite free of branches, which is typical of trees that are "close grown," or raised in a crowd.

We see fewer white than red or black oaks in here and generally throughout the east. Possibly this reflects the tastiness of white oak acorns and the bitterness of the others. Animals eat fewer of the reds and blacks, and thus they survive to become trees. Black and red acorns take two years to mature, which means that at least some will probably be dropped every year, thereby keeping the oak population as a whole going through poor years—and the animals as well. Identification of the acorns is fairly easy. Those of white oaks may grow to about an inch long and are topped by a short lumpy cap. Acorns of red oaks are likely to be a little longer, with flat shallow caps, while those of the black oaks are generally the shortest, appearing to be about half cap and half nipple. The flavorful acorns of white oak were even ground into a flour by Indians. Today a typical oak stand will contain about ten times as many black and red oaks as white.

Hickories, mostly shagbark but also pignut, appear about half as frequently as oaks here. Probably chestnuts were once as common, but the chestnut blight destroyed most of the large trees in the east, and hickory has supplanted them on this soil. Both oak and hickory are nut-making trees and seem to be quite dependent on squirrels for seeding. The artist-naturalist Ernest Thompson Seton felt that the spread of white oaks absolutely depended on there being a flourishing population of squirrels to plant seeds. Acorn nuts may freeze if not buried; then, too, moisture in the ground will weaken the shells and thus make it easier for them to open later. Burying also gets around the hazard that some seeds face in that they may die because their roots cannot penetrate the deepest forest litter. Hickory nuts contain such a large supply of food, though, that they can often remain on top of the fallen leaves, where even acorns fail, and still send their taproots into the ground—with enough food left over for the seedling to rise above competing weeds.

White oak leaves themselves have stories to tell here. They vary from broad, flat, almost tissuey blades to deeply notched, rather thick ones. Leaves in the top of the oak crown tend to be the latter. Perhaps the notches let cooling breezes in more easily, like Venetian blinds, and thus reduce solar heat. Hold your hand closed, facing the sun, and then open it and see if this isn't true. Inner leaves need all the light they can get, and so billow out like jib sails. Many smaller woodland plants similarly betray their shaded residence by leaves that are considerably larger than those of the same species growing out in the open. I have, incidentally, a photograph of two white oak leaves that are over eighteen inches long and a half dozen wide—even with the tips (at least an inch more for each) missing!

On and off through the years hay-scented ferns have appeared along the path where it winds downward below the hop hornbeams. They come in, as guests during a disturbance, on exposed soil where dead leaves have been kicked aside or even washed away. Their spores do not store much food, and so the young plant dies when trying to grow on fresh forest litter. The more decomposed the leaves are, the better, for then they become humus soil. Where litter piles up rapidly, though, such spore-producing green plants as mosses, ground pines, and ferns quickly die out.

Once hay-scented ferns do get in, they spread rapidly by their roots and may be difficult to get out. They seem to be equally at home in such widely divergent places as shady woods and open fields. In some pastures they can become a large carpet, unusual for the "lowly" ferns. Rubbing your fingers along the stipe (the lower part of the stem) will produce the hay scent, which is given off by wax secreted by hairs there. It is a mellow scent, and I wonder that someone has not synthesized the substance and sold it for use in men's after-shave lotion. In the field, old hay-scented fern can be identified, at least tentatively, by the tendency of the blades to turn toward sunlight. For me, the final identification test is to cut a frond directly across. The vascular tissue, or main vein, is distinctly Ω-shaped, like the upside-down cross section of a roof gutter.

After passing these ferns, the path down the slope comes to rest abruptly at the bank of a stream. This is the most distinctive opening down the trail so far. A catbird nested in one of the smaller streamside red maples this past spring. Roots with their tributary rootlets snake in and out of twigs and leaves of the nest. These slate-gray birds prefer shadows within dense shrubbery, and so they have followed where forests have been cut. Down here the familiar call is a reminder that this woods is not the sort of dark and fearsome place that Robert Frost found so often. Catbirds are native Americans and have remained, for the most part, on our continent, though a few accidental guests have made their way to Europe. Doubtless they enjoy civilization there as much as they do over here.

A coolness descends in evening, especially under a cloudless sky. As the moist air chills, it becomes heavier and slips into low places. A ribbon of fog may hang over stretches of the stream, thicker in narrows, where breezes cannot enter easily and damper air has been captured. In spring and fall, the gathering cold can frost-kill plants that would not be injured farther up the bank.

One kind of tree here, the pin oak, often looks as though it has been injured, perhaps from being overburdened with snow and ice. As a matter of fact, it is the oak that suffers the most this way. Dead branches droop around its base like unkempt hair. Actually, however, they are not necessarily a sign of poor health but rather of lack of sunlight as the tree grew up and shaded itself and was shaded by companions. This is the beginning of self-pruning, for many of the branches eventually will drop off, a common phenomenon among woodland trees. Pin oaks have such a distinctive shaggy appearance that they are easy to recognize at a glance, even looking in from the roadside.

During warm weather, when this area is sprinkled by at least one rainstorm each week, the brook tumbles over a red shale bed and attracts two-lined salamanders, green frogs, small fish, crayfish, and even dragonflies. The bed is broad and its current generally easily paced. Most of the time water purls along on either one side or the other. It is the sort of stream where biddy dragonflies wander slowly up and down following the contours and flying a foot or so in the air. Once in a while aquatic animals do get trapped in a slough—a bend in the creek that is left behind to dry up after the current takes a short cut during a flood and leaves a small crescent "lake" that will probably die slowly.

Across the stream the forest floor flattens out for several dozen yards. This part of the woods was farmland sixty or so years ago. Undergrowth here is very noticeably denser than on the other side. There it was possible to see clearly perhaps fifty yards in any direction; here it is usually ten yards at best. Shrubbery and low plants of this understory have not yet been eliminated by shade or root competition from the forest trees. And so every spring the understory threatens to choke out the old path.

One of the major companions along the way is the damp-ground-loving weed or herb called jumpseed. It is related to the knotweeds and tear-thumbs so common in wet lowlands and at the edge of ponds, marshes, and swamps, and is well named for the actions of its awl-shaped seeds, which in late summer leap off the spike stem as you run your fingers up the stalk. By the middle of October they have been known to hit people in the face.

This woods is said to be dominated by oaks and hickories. Between the two, their foliage certainly occupies over 90 percent of the top canopy. That is only one concept of dominance, however, and does not take into account the lowest growth. Along this path and others, jumpseed takes up so much territory with its many individuals and their broad fleshy leaves that it should also be called a "dominant" in a sense. Compared with its herbaceous neighbors, it surely rules, in the sense of having the most leaf surface and in apparently enforcing a bare-ground regime below. I could further measure the dominance of jumpseed by estimating its productivity. If I were to collect all the herbaceous plants (those that are not woody, as are trees and shrubs) in an area and dry them out and then take their dry weights, the heaviest would be those which have been producing the most tissue. They would thus be dominant in *that* sense. I think I know who would win.

One curious little flower found here grows large enough so that it could dominate other plants within its own tight patches, and yet "dominate" again becomes a strange word. The flower is that pale white seed-bearing plant which lacks chlorophyll: the Indian pipe. Until the seeds are complete, its blossom hangs over self-effacingly at the end of the fleshy stalk like a shepherd's crook. As summer wanes, the bloom, which has become even darker as it matured, turns rather erect. The fat ovary at this point often suggests a crudely scalloped goblet on the end of a long, scaly stem. Those scales are the rudimentary leaves, which do not need light. As a matter of fact, Indian pipe prefers deep shade. So these little flowers could dominate only slightly, in the sense of shading others out.

How might it rule, then? Indian pipe has long been considered a somewhat funguslike plant, which lives on decaying wood in the soil. Thus it could conceivably control other plants by taking away the minerals they require. But this would be very early robbery, the material still being in the form of wood. More recent research shows that perhaps the plant taps *living* tissue!

In 1960 a scientist named Erik Bjorkman injected radioactive carbon and phosphorus compounds into spruce tree trunks. Then he checked to see what effect, if any, this might have on Indian pipe plants growing below. He knew that the roots of this delicate plant usually are completely blanketed in mycorrhizal fungi, which also invade the roots of some trees. In this case, the radioactive materials passed from the spruce through the fungus and into the Indian pipe plants. So it may be that this easily crushed relative of mountain laurel, trailing arbutus, and bearberry —the hardy heaths—is sometimes a parasite on the trees it hides under. The question of dominance might as well be foregone for the moment. The idea is worth thinking about, though, and I have done so many times while walking in this woods.

While climbing the other side of the ravine in the summer I often pass through a zone of towhees. This is near the edge of the woods, and the birds have found an appealing opening in which to nest. In the distance their clattering "drink-your-tea" seems to reflect from the canopy. Up close, the song changes quickly to an oft-repeated *chewink*, a call that has come down as another of their names. Beneath one of their nests grows a furry flowering raspberry called "dewberry" whose fuzzy pink fruits I consider delicacies. So do towhees and other birds, and the race is to the swift, with the birds winning the greater share of the prize.

Along this route I have two favorite stopping places, one for spring and the other for fall. The blunt-leaved hepaticas becoming showy in March always draw my interest. Their lilac-purple petals form a backdrop, like the sky of late day, to the bright yellow stamens. It is usually a very glistening effect and reminds me of a particular movie actress who achieves the same effect with her eyes and, I suppose, highlights in her makeup.

In fall I stop beneath an angular black walnut up on the slope. Wrapped now in the forest throng but once possibly standing alone, where no companion crowded its outstretching limbs, the tree reminds me of Edwin Way Teale's "Lincoln Tree," named for its approximate birth date. Each terminal leaflet of the one or two dozen leaflets on each leaf has probably fallen by early July. In autumn the whole fluttery leaf usually breaks loose before those of any other tree, rendering the walnut massively black among lesser neighbors. A friend, who comes so often into these woods that she doubtless knows as well as anyone could when the leaves are going on their way, was only a few months ago telling a story about some white-footed mice that had a nest down in the bowels of one of the hollow trees up the path near the exit. When she banged on the base of the trunk they would scurry past an opening and into the upper stories—"Hickory, dickory, dock," she said.

Another large but easily accessible woods I am quite familiar with begins for me at the edge of a lazy brown creek and ends on a rocky ridge that is about a half mile away as the crow flies and 125 feet higher as I climb. Along the way, the woods can be divided into sections which together illustrate the combined effects of soil, water, and elevation.

Openings along the creek give us our first spring flower, which happens to be skunk cabbage. Whereas hepatica may arise demurely within its protective fur, skunk cabbage presses up boldly, like a rocket in metal hood rising slowly but certainly from its silo. Half a dozen brown long-winged flies flit among the cones. They like to pause on sunlit tips. Deep in the woods some skunk cabbages poked up like fine blue-green fingers last fall and were soon frostbitten. By January no remains showed above ground.

Violets here, as elsewhere, are regularly overlooked as "too common." Their blossoms of spring should be probed with a bit of wire to see how the clever pollinating mechanism works. The lines on the petals are admittedly attractive, but they are also distinctly functional. They act as nectar guides which point an insect in the right direction to the pollinating structures. Months later, ants and other insects will visit and carry away the sugar-coated seeds, usually dropping enough to spread the species further. Bonapartists chose the violet as a symbol of both the month of March and of Napoleon I. On the thirtieth of March Paris had capitulated to him. Later, as he lingered in exile at Elba, his return was predicted on masses of postcards bearing symbolic violets. Napoleon was called "Caporal Violet," meaning that he would reappear in spring.

Springtime today finds churches decked at Advent in the liturgical color of violet, referring to the royalty of the anticipated Christ. Our woodland violets come in many hues, of course, but the power of the name lingers on, even through such disclaimers as downy yellow violet and sweet white violet. Some of the names that have been derived from various shapes and other aspects read like a roll call of an Indian tribe: bird-foot, dog, arrow-leaved, lance-leaved, wood, and marsh violet.

Spicebushes down toward the creek bloom profusely yellow early in spring, even before their leaves expand. Their sweet odor pervades hollows and is quite as distinctive as the blossoms sprinkled along the slender branches. With hepatica, they may attract the first bees. In autumn the yellowing foliage adds a luster to this woods, a counterpart to the scarlet fruits, which are eaten by veerys and wood thrushes. Spicebush can be a friend to a camper. It hints that water is not too far away, while its wood is handy for kindling. It burns well even when alive. Spicebush leaves are famously aromatic when rumpled between the fingers, and the fruits have been made into a liniment and have served as a replacement for allspice.

Rather twiggy pin oaks tower over everything here. Some people attribute the name to the stubby but sharp crosshatched twigs that hold their leaves for a time and then die with winter's advent. In his *Fieldbook of Natural History*, the great Cornell University naturalist E. Lawrence Palmer says that the name is derived from the "practice of using the stiff pin-like spurs as pins to fasten timbers together, before nails were generally used." Pin oaks have a distinctive obelisklike appearance, with their bases often half-shrouded in a viny tangle of their own lower branches. These are among the largest limbs, for they become progressively shorter going up the trunk. Over-all, the whole frame resembles the far more graceful spires of pine trees. The pin oaks I see now may be the last of them, however, for few young ones are filling in below. Probably the ground is drying out because of the effectiveness of a channel that was cut through as suburban housing moved this way. Sapling sweet gums, red maples, and ashes are doing very well and hold more promise.

The easiest path to take into the woods today is a compressed track that parallels a creek. During summer, leaves of ironwood brush across your face and their branches make passers-by duck. In that moment of looking down while walking, a visitor may miss a hollow ash, with its smoothly rounded bunghole seven or eight feet up, just off the path. A small colony of honeybees has been living there for years. I occasionally call out a few by rapping on their wall with a heavy stick. Hardly any bodies or parts lie below, indicating that mice and other small animals are very active nearby and eat them wings and all.

A wider selection of oaks takes over as one begins to ascend the hill. The soil collects here yet drains well, and so a number of the largest trees are found to the right and left. Tall, straight tulip trees make up the lion's share of the canopy in places, and can be a nightmare to bird watchers during the summer. Anything flying up there is at about the limit of practical eyesight and must be spotted against a backdrop of gray-green leaves. It certainly is enough to convince anyone who has tried identifying birds in the woods that he will learn the *songs* or be in constant misery.

Records show that small spring-flowering plants take over more of this part of the forest floor than autumn ones do. I have never tried to find out if anyone has counted the people, but I suspect that their ratio is similar. Dark woods are famous for their spring show, even as meadow blossoms are linked to summer. It is worth keeping a phenology, or flowering-time list, just to see how rich certain places are when their moment for blossoming arrives. Fresh ideas come from such easy activities, too. For instance, I was just reading in one of Thoreau's *Journals* where he wonders:

> Are not the flowers which appear earliest in the spring the most primitive and simplest? . . . I observe that the first six [of the count Thoreau has made and presented to us] are decidedly water or water-loving plants . . . the 11th and 12th in cold, damp gardens, like the earth first made dry land; the 15th and 17th on dry . . . fields and hills, hardy. . . .
>
> This may, perhaps, be nearly the order of the world's creation.

Thus we have in the spring of the year the spring of the world plants.
— water-bottoms, bare rocks, and scantily clad lands, and land recently
bared of water.

Now the woodland gradient steepens to a point where jagged rocks
poke through regularly. They are jumbled enough to stir us out of the
reverie that so easily absorbs us on a smooth path where our feet glide
along almost like a hydrofoil. Again, as in the pin oak community, I must
look below the headliners—in this case, red and white oaks and tulip
trees—and note the news placed lower on the page. As any good journalist
knows, this is where one finds portents of the future, and here these
columns belong once more to ashes and red maples. It is a minority report now that will perhaps be the final majority word one day.

Maple-leaved viburnum rules the lower world of shoulder-high
tangles. It is a reasonable proof that this soil is draining well, for the
plant cannot survive in saturated ground. Among the roots of one viburnum cluster appears a mound of shale. A closer look reveals that it is the
debris pile where a woodchuck has dug a burrow—another proof of fairly
dry subsoil. I find a number of these signs about, marking burrows abandoned after the brood has gone and now hideouts for other beasts. Sometimes I am cautioned not to snoop too closely by a sharp order of skunk.
Woodchucks, or ground hogs, make two or more entrances, each leading
into a tunnel that may extend more than twenty-five feet into the hill; the
several chambers may be five feet below ground. The front door begins at
a mound, while the back exits have none and are more hidden. The best
time to find the owner is in the morning or evening when it will be out
feeding, usually well away from the burrow. Here they have too open a
view from the wooded escarpment to be caught unawares close by.

Suddenly the slope rises sharply and becomes a boulder fortress
that reminds me of a castle in ruins, tumbling down from its hilltop
eminence. The trees have been left alone longer, as though everyone had
fled for good or perhaps had been captured and dragged away. Great red
oaks rise like sentinels among the rocks. Large black oaks and ashes

occur less often, probably indicating that the soil was once quite damp and therefore right for young red oaks but not black; the ashes have simply been shaded out. Young black oaks in the understory show, as they do all down the slope, that even drier times are ahead. Possibly the day will come when one will refer to this place as Oak Town.

The stepwise nature of the escarpment creates successive stories. They receive more light than the woods below, especially in the hours before and after noon. As a result, sassafras, more commonly found in the open, has entered. Pines have not found their way in, although they too often choose just such rocky land as their fortresses in a competitive society. Similarly, both trees may colonize deposits of sandy dry soil. Sassafras is somewhat edible and definitely aromatic. Young bark from the roots gives flavor to root beer and other sweets; the oils go into perfumes, soaps, and various delicately scented products. In *North with the Spring*, Edwin Way Teale says that the Pilgrims sent the bark back to Europe in their first cargoes. Sassafras logs have been used to fence in the very fields the trees find so pleasant to occupy—they often fill in as thickets soon after the ground has been cleared—for the wood resists soil rot.

Finally, on the summit of the woods, white oak returns to the oak community. Like so many of our oak forests, this one promises to be a mixed-hardwood stand, which will number half a dozen species tossing together high overhead. Oaks can live well side by side because each provides for its own interior light. The branches that come off the trunk are arranged in a sort of spiral that allows no branch to lie directly above one immediately below. About five branches down will be found the first limb that is covered directly. Not all oaks show a stereotyped arrangement like this, bur oaks being outstanding for a crown which often seems merely a nest of branches. Also, red oaks and others will fork near the ground when the growing is difficult, and this makes for crisscrossing at the center.

Some oak bases here have produced several trunks. Growing conditions for these trees were certainly poor at one time, for such bases are stumps left after the woods was cut over. They made a comeback as sprouts, some having to engulf boulders to find room. About two hundred years ago, professors from a nearby university were not being very well paid and so were offered the right to chop their own timber in lieu of salary increases. Oak logs burn for a long time, and doubtless many a scholar read in the firelight provided through the night by an oak log lit at bedtime.

One last rendezvous with oak forests comes in nearly virgin stands which represent the major deciduous forests of North America where oak is more or less supreme. These are parts of the climax oak-hickory and oak-chestnut realms that are most famed as, respectively, northward and westward expansions of the deciduous forest from Texas to Canada and an eastern strip along largely mountainous terrain from northern Georgia into southern New England. The latter, the oak-chestnut, is a memory of things as they once were. Chestnut has been almost wholly wiped out, and pine has often replaced it, especially on drier sites. In addition, small oak associations in various other combinations occur here and there, as we have seen, oak-hickory being one of the many widespread clusters in this region. But before we change the name of the oak-chestnut association to something more appropriate for future generations we have to see how permanent will be its replacement. And that will take centuries.

I came to the climax oak-hickory forest by traveling dusty country roads with friends who would have to show me the way again should I ever wish to return. We followed the route of a wandering cow and, appropriately, found the forest at the end of a rutted drive. Like a green castle it rose from a landscape given over to farms, used and abandoned. How far back might it go? The understory gives some clue, for beneath an umbrella of white oaks and hickories the herbaceous layer was insignificant, while saplings of any sort were almost nonexistent. As a matter of fact, in the interior the majority of the youngest white oaks in full tree form were over fifty years old. Thus the canopy had been almost wholly closed for at least fifty years. Nothing had been culled out. Only a few hickory and black oak saplings had staked a claim on the near future.

Looking into further distances, though, were a number of weedy little white oaks and hickories. They were growing very slowly in the dark and were possibly twenty or more years old. I saw in them the efforts of the woods to recover after cows had been allowed to graze here because the farmland alongside became poorer.

Red-bellied woodpeckers past and present betrayed themselves by their long nesting holes and shy, elusive flights among the stiffening leaves of September. The presence of these predators indicated that the woods had aged enough to provide grubs in the dead wood up above. They also were helping themselves to acorns, which may not have had a much better future anyway, and to corn in an adjacent plot. Occasional cardinals, robins, and cowbirds reminded me that this was a fairly small woods and that a "thank you" is in order for the people who have preserved it in what appears to be its final, or at least most stable, state. Their many efforts on behalf of conservation are to me best summed up in this tract of land, a priceless and yet very heavily priced bit of property, guarded now by the Izaak Walton League of America. In this same county, fewer acres than these were sold as shopping centers for millions of dollars.

Tufted titmice here preferred the interior, but they could be called out with a high whistle in imitation of their rolling *peter-peter-peter-peter*. Like chickadees and other birds, the titmice had followed the woodpeckers in and now nested in their empty holes. Both titmice and their relatives the chickadees possess a mad curiosity, which brought them right away to the little commotion I made.

Every beam of sunlight that pierced the canopy glowed on a dozen or so insects passing through. Aphids drifted by on paddlelike wings. Small moths puttered from one hiding place under a leaf to another. Most prevalent seemed to be immature wingless leafhoppers and aphids, which collected in pale colonies on the lower epidermis of hickory leaves. Without fanfare, these sucking machines were drawing away gallons of sap drop by drop. Over-all, I cannot complain, however, if a few giant hickories or oaks drop out. Some of the hickories show interesting minute white semicircular fungi at the tips of their branches as they die, a living snow in the winter of their lives. Their death opens the way for new trees, probably young hickories or oaks for the most part. A more diverse forest would prevent the concentration of such masses of a few insect species. Thus in the end the death of a few trees can mean a longer life for a forest. The individual is sacrificed (though not deliberately) for the benefit of the population as a whole. But the dead one will eventually be back, after its tissues turn to chemicals that are absorbed by trees of later generations. Robert Frost said it of leaves in a stanza of his poem "In Hardwood Groves":

> Before the leaves can mount again
> To fill the trees with another shade,
> They must go down past things coming up.
> They must go down into the dark decayed.

All is not so easy for the insects, however. Have you ever noticed how really rare an insect outbreak is? How often has anyone seen a thousand caterpillars of more than a few species tearing trees down? What about the katydids that grind with their wings through the hours of dusk, twilight, and the first half of the night? Are they not munching as well as crunching? Well, probably not enough to cause trouble.

Why not? One good reason is that oak leaves go through a subtle change after their first few weeks of expanding in the spring. They become practically indigestible. Unless leaf eaters are able to withstand early spring frosts, they are forced to wait and dine later, on foliage of lesser quality. One way that insects have of getting around this is to develop enzymes in their guts that reduce the plant poisons. And, as you might have guessed, the same physiological mechanisms which enable insects to produce antitoxins to overcome *plant* defenses may also operate to save them from *our* insecticides! So the balance may swing back and forth between insects and plants, with ourselves usually thrown in on the plant side. An insect outbreak may therefore signify either an "improvement" in the insect or that a set of leaves has not yet acquired resistance.

Insects that feed on a single species, or even family, of plants may evolve countermeasures for only the one or two worst natural poisons they encounter and may then be able to transform the poisons into chemicals that act against their own predators! Is this "good" or "bad"? Remember that predators are often necessary to keep the prey from becoming so numerous that it consumes all its food supply, thus committing suicide. Some plant defenses, which may come into play after chemical repellents have stopped almost but not all insects, seem to be aimed at only certain insect enemies. Probably the best-known example is the mattress of minute hairs, or trichomes, which in some cases are known to hook caterpillars to the very leaves they would otherwise devour. There the larvae die, of either starvation or bleeding punctures. Such defenses, Dr. Lawrence Gilbert, of Stanford University, says, may be useful for the moment against only a single species. One plant, *Passiflora adenopoda*, which uses the trichome defense as an effective shield against a heliconine butterfly caterpillar, also has a way of stopping other enemies. Nectaries located outside the blossoms attract predaceous ants, which function as guards.

Oak-chestnut forests, the final type we will consider in this chapter, probably undergo less wholesale destruction by insects because in the absence of chestnut trees they have acquired a greater mixture of associates less likely to acquire huge concentrations of pests. In a younger forest I visited, the trees were uniformly small. It had once been a field. Now red and scarlet oak were gradually taking over from red maple and black birch. Few weeds had been able to last, although as the oaks come in, a narrow-leaved fescue grass seems to be following. At present, erosion is a major threat to the good life, since there really is nothing to form a sod.

A much older oak-chestnut forest lay next door. Here red, scarlet, and chestnut oaks dominated, in overwhelming fashion, a mixed-hardwood combination that included a fair sprinkling of red maples and a thin supply of black oaks (whose leaves can usually be distinguished from those of red by being shinier and having lobes that may expand toward the outer portion), black gum, and black, or sweet, birch. The future, as recorded in the understory, seemed to belong to red maple and black birch, though the shrub and small tree layer offered relatively abundant chestnut oaks, as well as black oaks, hickories, and red maples. I wondered how long the red maples would hold out in the gravelly soil here. Lucy Braun notes that black birch actually dominates the upper reaches of a number of rocky slopes in Pennsylvania, and therefore I expect *it* to last in this forest.

Perhaps a dozen birds rambled through the canopy when I was last there, in the fall, but more evident were the mammals. Even louder and more frequent than bird calls were those of chipmunks, which chittered from the canopy like grasshoppers from the tops of weeds. Deer scat, which I understand is dropped at about the rate of thirteen piles per deer per day, proclaimed that this major herbivore of the region was an occasional visitor. White-footed mice had made quite a few digs around stumps; I have seen some woods where the best evidence of their activity was gnawed bones and antlers, from which they obtained calcium. Where the shed antlers are conspicuously small, the local soil is probably deficient in calcium, which the deer get by browsing.

Of the smaller animals, the salamanders probably gave the answer to my red maple question. So abundant were they that every human footstep on the leaves must have pressed one and shaken two more. Also gray springtails, which love the damp rotting leaves, leapt everywhere like bits of shot. Before I left I dug up the black tough larva, or "leather jacket," of a crane fly. Since it usually prefers moist or even soggy places, I presumed that it was the final arbiter and that the red maple would probably do well.

Insects were so prevalent, now, that autumn in this woods belonged to them. Masses of aphids had settled on the leaves of chestnut oaks. They were under assault by their own kind, however, as syrphid fly maggots wriggled through and plucked them up like so many breakfast buns. My own battle came with sticky silken threads that dangled from the canopy into every opening. At the terminus of each guy line swung a pale green caterpillar, the larva of a leaf skeletonizer. For the first part of their lives the caterpillars had reclined inconspicuously inside the leaf, which they hollowed out. Then they broke free and turned on their former prison, gobbling everything except the veins—which remained aloft as a screen of skeletons.

On this trip, as on others to many oak woods, I saw dozens of different-shaped oak galls, primarily on leaves. Some were quarter-inch corky spheres. Others were a tenth as large but as hard as BB shot—in an air gun they might be murder. Serpentine rows of galls along leaf veins often suggested puffballs, while hairy ones resembled fruiting slime molds.

Usually these are the homes, and larders, of larval gall gnats or gall wasps, though most orders of insects have one or more species that make galls. The insect injects the plant with a chemical allied to the auxins, or plant-growth hormones—into a leaf or other part that is actually growing at the time—and a gall soon appears. Mature plant parts usually cannot be stimulated into further action. Therefore most insect galls rise in the spring.

Ross E. Hutchins, in his book *Galls and Gall Insects*, notes that gall makers tend to attack the more recently evolved plants. Algae also have galls, however—though they are the work of nematode worms—and at least seven species of flies induce galls on mushrooms. A mite or so has attacked the lichens. But the vast majority of galls occur on flowering plants. Members of the oak family take the prize in North America; at least 805 species of insects and mites make galls on them, with another 563 species scattered among ten other plant families.

Oak tree fossils show no evidence of gall invasions, although galls are known from leaves of the Tertiary period, 50 million years ago, and even, Hutchins says, from Cretaceous leaves, more than 100 million years old! Thus, he observes, the preference for oaks is quite recent in the scale of things. Perhaps it shows that oaks have not yet developed a chemical defense. Or it may point up a nice lesson about getting along together.

A parasite that destroys its host may be well along the road toward eliminating itself.

I would like to see a chart that traces the evolution of gall makers. Dr. Asa C. Chandler was speaking of other parasites when he wrote these lines in his *Introduction to Parasitology*, but they might conceivably apply to gall makers: "Since the parasites have a less changeable environment than their hosts, they tend to undergo evolutionary changes more slowly, so that while a host is differentiating into new species, genera, families, or even orders, the parasites may change relatively little." An insect that makes galls on more than one species of plant produces galls that look alike. Through this characteristic it might be possible to trace the evolutionary pursuit of gall makers after their hosts. Plants of similar environments might have been more important than "blood relatives." Thus unrelated trees that were characteristic of lowland or upland sites might have been as likely to share parasites as were new species or subspecies of the same tree. The gall might be enough a part of its own particular environment to make this true, even as Chandler says it is of other parasites: "In some cases, however, inherent host characteristics are of less importance than similar environmental conditions resulting from similarity of habits or diet and a parasite may adapt to phylogenetically unrelated hosts." If this should prove true, imagine what the evolutionary radiation of gall insects from oaks could be! I like to think that we have plenty of evidence to work on in our own local oak woods.

12 | *Cold Places and Their Tall Maples: The Lovely Deep Dark Woods*

If it were possible to enter the tints and shavings of a mellow painting, it would be possible to touch the colors and oils that one normally views from far off. If it were possible to step inside and find the deeper layers that burn their way out to add subtle depths of color, influential but never wholly tangible until the moment, then it would be possible to understand far better what the painter had in mind as he labored week by week over his creation. If it *were* possible, then we would have the tints and flakes, the depths and changing motifs we *do* find, in real life, every autumn when entering a maple woods.

Our maple forests, primarily a northern expression of evolution's deciduous adventure, have for centuries drawn people to this continent simply to see these colors—to enter the painting in person, as it were. New England was the primary spokesman for this display, which began at the summit of the mountain ranges and spread downward like a slow flood. Lingering warm periods, with the chance they gave for drawing out the deeper red tones before the leaves fell, acquired a special name, Indian summer.

Autumn, however, does not rule the seasons, and many visitors who arrived between May and September were depressed to find other, more somber tones, especially deep inside the older forests. Through these months darkness ruled beneath the huge closed canopy. Shrubs and weeds were sparse. Tree trunks stood so far apart that two wagon teams could drive between them side by side.

This gloomy atmosphere soon found a ready companion in the Puritan doctrine of original sin. Demons roamed the forests in spirit. We see their ghosts in literature relating to the period. Nathaniel Hawthorne puts us there especially in his allegorical drama "Young Goodman Brown." This pious fellow reaches what are supposed to be the innermost truths of men, the sins of Adam and Eve, through his adventures in a great forest. Goodman finds that he is accompanied by the Devil, who "plucked a branch of maple to serve for a walking stick, and began to strip it of the twigs and little boughs, which were wet with evening dew. The moment his fingers touched them they became strangely withered and dried up as with a week's sunshine." Whether this was dream or nightmare Hawthorne never said, but the attitude toward the shrouded forest lingered on, and appears even today. It is perhaps strongest in the poetry of Robert Frost, where "The woods are lovely, dark, and deep," and where one can "come in / To the dark and lament."

Contemporary anthropological thought says that we human beings as a species do not really enjoy great forests because a long period of our evolution occurred on savannahs, where open scenes were broken by mere groves of trees. Be that as it may, and for all the mood above, I myself shed any doubts by getting as close to the inner workings of the woods as I can. It becomes one of the richest experiences I know. In climax maple forests—which means sugar maple—the most prominent partners are beeches to the northeast and basswoods to the northwest, with oak and hickory on poorer land and along the prairie margin. Their companions are likely to include American and slippery elm, red maple, black cherry, and ironwood. None are foreboding in themselves. A closer look at a few dispels the earlier rumors about demons and invokes the *higher* spirit of the woods speaking in its own behalf.

Black cherry is a native American that travels around through dry woods in the eastern states, its edible dark purple fruit distributed by various animals. While yet a young tree it is easy to recognize by the leaves, shiny green above and paler below. I can often identify the trees during leafless months by new egg masses of tent caterpillars, which form glossy black muffs about the twigs. Older masses, from which the insects have emerged, show the white insides of the eggs and so are light in color. Driving down a road during May I can often recognize black cherries by the silken tent caterpillar nests gleaming whitely from half a dozen branch crotches. The elongate elliptical shape of the tree coupled with these tents is a dead giveaway. I have seen a tree that was completely stripped of leaves in mid-May make a complete recovery by June 7. The drain on soil nutrients must have been terrific. A tree that has been able to develop in a sunlit spot will be more likely to reach its maximum height of about one hundred feet, and then no one can see leaves, tent caterpillar egg masses, or nests very well. The bark, however, is a sure give away, being obviously flaky. Some people call it "burnt potato chips."

It was the fruit of the black cherry that became famous as "Rum Cherry," says Euell Gibbons in *Stalking the Wild Asparagus.* New England colonists added the berry juice to West Indies rum, sweetening it and giving it the richer color of a cherry liqueur. Cultivated cherries, on the other hand, are imports—not only to America but also to Europe, having come with the Aryans from Asia. Around 70 B.C. the Roman general Lucullus brought some cherry pits home from the East. Then, when Caesar's legions went ashore in Britain, they took the fruit with them, and so cherry culture took another long jump.

Where tall sugar maples and elms are associated, I am often impressed by what must have been the scene as recently as perhaps forty years ago. You have to stand beneath these trees, with a few branches separating you from a blazing sun, to appreciate the kind of green light that comes through. The leaves of both trees are thick, those of American and slippery elm especially so, and sunlight arrives as though the leaves were incandescent. I have mentioned the autumn colors, as everyone does, but you have not lived until you have seen this other sort of light, especially in early spring, when it is very yellow in the morning—about six-thirty a.m.

A few of the small engraver beetles, insects that make those fan-like tunnels on the surface of the wood just beneath the bark, have done about as thorough a job as could be conceived in wiping out the American elm. Two species of beetle, the native elm bark beetle *Hylurgopinus rufipes* and the smaller European elm bark beetle *Scolytus multistriatus*, carry a fungus which causes the leaves to wilt or yellow and then fall off. Almost inevitably the attack is fatal to the tree. Spores of the fungus flow through the tree's vessels with the sap, producing poisons and eventually plugging the tubes. As the tree dies the fungus switches to a new role and feeds on the dead material, thus converting from parasitic to saprophytic behavior!

Sometimes the disease continues its parasitic life by invading a neighboring American elm through roots that have become grafted together and formed a living bridge. Our city planners who have planted elms in rows along streets have in some cases made this a chain reaction in which trees die one after the other, like falling dominoes. Usually, though, the disease is carried by the two beetles, which seem to have been relatively innocuous until a few decades ago.

The American beetle has probably been here for ages, then as now chewing out galleries under the bark in which to lay its eggs. The larvae burrow off on their own and create characteristic radiating tunnels. A string of eggs pocketed in niches along the beetle's path has a fan shape that suggests a house centipede. Around Boston, people were familiar with the smaller European elm bark beetle at least by 1904, but it, too, had a record of only minor infractions then. The fungus was first noticed in the Netherlands around 1919, and so it had already acquired the name Dutch elm disease before coming abroad. Within eleven years it was shipped to America, in elm burls that were to be used for wood veneer. From there on the beetles took over, the major carrier being the European species.

The relationship of tree, fungus, and beetle is an example of "the eternal triangle" in which one is the loser. The adult European beetles prefer to breed in damaged or dying elms, such as are found where heavy blizzards weigh down the branches and split the Y-shaped trunks. In addition, every time the beetles feed on twigs and transmit spores of Dutch elm disease they are setting up more new breeding grounds for themselves. The elm is, of course, the odd man out. Not all elms suffer from this disease, though, and so the genus (*Ulmus*) seems likely to survive. While American and European elms are highly susceptible to infection, Asian types, such as the Chinese and Siberian elms, are not. This suggests that the disease originated in the East and not in Holland. Probably the first host survived, or the fungus would have died where it was born.

There is a traditional picture of the American small town where streets pass under a bower of stately elms. And so it is that these natural riverbank trees, which can withstand flooding, drought, and other streamside conditions, have found a home in towns and cities. Their spreading roots, which once kept them from falling into the river, now reach out through huge areas of a local park. The shallowness of the roots, which kept them close to oxygen even during floods, now helps them take in oxygen through trampled soil. They lie huge and black as burned bones where constant walking has killed the grass and scuffed away the soil, and I am quite sure that the amount of root equals that of canopy. When a new street goes in, elms are among the first trees to be planted. They take transplanting well and grow quickly, valuable characteristics which have enabled them to live for millions of years along floodplains.

Unfortunately, towns have developed into cities, especially factory-filled cities, and the steps up from the forest of the riverbank to an urban setting may be a march to death. The elm's rough leaves easily pick up dust, soot, tailpipe emissions, and all the other airborne particles so common to cities. The tree may suffocate or even poison itself. It is no wonder that native elms, caught between these conditions and attacks by Dutch elm disease, are fading from our landscapes. Ironically, their dying often has a touch of the same paintbrush that for so many autumns branded them as being in healthy metamorphosis. The first symptom in sick trees commonly is a yellow spray of branches. I have seen rows of the trees that had struggled through at least a century of cultured existence finally give in to the disease—fountains of green and yellow, "slain upon . . . high places," going down along the street.

Whereas elm has long meant elegance to everyday America, basswood has not. No slur is intended, but basswood simply has never attained the fame of most of the tall members of the maple gang. I imagine that part of the obscurity comes of its being more prevalent in the upper midwest, and so it has suffered from the same disregard as many other trees of this region. The maple-basswood forests of Minnesota may, in fact, have drawn more attention for their birds than anything else. According to one study, these woods are preferred residences for pine, mourning, and myrtle warblers, broad-winged hawks, white-breasted nuthatches, and ruby-throated hummingbirds. I myself first really noticed basswood as a member of *northeastern* woods when I began picking up its seeds in areas of the richest soil. The pea-sized woody fruit terminate a slender stalk that is attached to the center of a straplike leaf; together with this single wing the seeds go spinning off somewhat crazily through the trees on gusty autumn days.

The name basswood is a corruption of the original bastwood, which referred to the fibrous cortex of the bark. Iroquois Indians and early farmers made rope from the bark. My interest in it has included a chilly hour or so of catching male linden looper moths, whose wingless mates are likely to be laying their eggs in bark crevices nearby. Flattering the warmth of a front-door light on a wintry Thanksgiving evening, these white moths, about the same size as a cabbage butterfly, draw attention immediately. A few of us once had a mothing party on a weekend that also brought snow past the same lamp.

Our hosts were Bill and Virginia Welch, of Danbury, Connecticut, who at the same time introduced my wife and me to their flying squirrels. Several pairs occupied nests in trees by the front door of their woodland home, called "Stonybroke" after the rocky and boulder-strewn hillside. When I noticed that the lettering on their new station wagon spelled the name "Stoneybroke," I questioned them about it. Ginny, never one to hide the facts, said, "For a while there, we couldn't afford the extra *e*."

Basswood, a close relative of the European linden, has sometimes been brought into the city. The two trees may even flourish side by side in America, for settlers brought the linden over early, perhaps because of a long romantic association with it that shows up in English poetry. The father of Carolus Linnaeus, whose name is more correctly stated as Carl von Linné, adopted the Linné from a favorite old linden in his own garden. Actually, either of the trees might also be called lime. George Washington planted such lime trees at Mount Vernon. Lime is another of those almost untraceable names, which, I understand, in this case comes from "line." This is said to be a variation of "lind," itself a reduction from "linden." Since line can also be cord or rope, I wonder if possibly the name actually began as a reference to material made from the bark, the over-all derivation going from "line"—in the sense of cord—to "linden."

When I was a boy my mother and dad brought a basswood home from the Adirondacks and planted it by our driveway. There its great leaves flapped in the company of another guest, an apple which produced each fall the hardest apples in our neighborhood. Between the two of them, from May to July we had a copious nectar flow for bees. Possibly that sweet-tasting apple also came from the deep woods, from a logging camp where some lumberman had tossed his core.

Twenty yards from these bee trees stood a huge sugar maple, one of the remnants in our neighborhood that spoke of the maple forest once there. Some years, as winter declined, my dad would drill a half-inch hole in the trunk of our tree and insert a pipe to tap for sap, which became syrup only after hours of boiling on the stove. Red and silver maples (which we did not have in large size) offer good sap, also, but it contains about half the sugar per volume. This can be significant when one realizes that it takes around thirty gallons of sugar maple sap, or about ninety-six hours of steady dripping from a series of trees one foot in diameter, to yield a single gallon of syrup. Fortunately, maple sap occurs in such abundance that there is little danger of excessive bloodletting, though on the average twelve or so gallons is about the limit any one tree will deliver. Only once have I heard of sap being really thin, and that was in a historical account. In New England, in the year 1816, not only was there a drought, but every month had a frost, with July and August suffering through snow; that year became known as "Eighteen Hundred and Froze to Death." At college we used to have "sugaring-off" parties where we boiled both syrup and sugar into existence. These events took place in the mountains in early spring, before the buds had begun to swell, when the days were melting and sunny (some years not so, but the parties went on in full force anyway) and the nights nipped by frost. During spring, insects by the hundreds often have their own sap licks, at and below the opening where a maple has ruptured and the juice is flowing out. Down the trunk will stretch a gleaming stream flanked by banks of paper wasps, yellowjackets, various bees, and tributaries of ants traveling back and forth between their nests and the sweet liquid.

Wisconsin, New York, Vermont, and West Virginia—all northern, mountainous, or both—have chosen the sugar maple as their state tree. That emphasizes the unity of these forests, whatever their individual differences. I think of the sugar maple as a forest's forest tree, showing characteristics which reveal a true interweaving with the life of its place. Sugar maple seeds, like those of such other climax forest trees as basswoods, elms, and the other maples, are fair-sized and in spring can pierce ground litter with their shoots. Thus the heavy foliage cast down in autumn does not impede the resurrection in spring. Then, too, the saplings are patient. They can endure deep forest shade, growing maybe only an inch each year until light comes. Many of those little trees of the understory may actually be older than you are! When an opening finally does release them they may spring up at the rate of about two feet a growing season. The consequence of this watchful waiting followed by powerful growth is that maples can suddenly take over another kind of forest, killing it off with their own dense shade. Finally, this shading will help enforce other aspects of the forest regime. Sugar maple leaves open early in spring and rule throughout summer, influencing the flowering and leafing-out times of many plants below. So, while responding to the annual rhythms of temperature and length of day, maples instill their own particular cadence into forests.

Curiously, the land community best equipped to defend itself against maples and their compatriots is grassland. To that can be added less formally organized sites like burned acres, heavily trodden places, and farmed fields. These are often too dry for the moisture-loving seeds and shallow roots to invade. Maples, however, being long-lived, generally capture the rewards that so often come to dumb persistence. Let a marsh fill in, a swamp arise, and the drying earth receive its tall oaks—the embryo maple forest waits, uses the last as its womb, and is finally the king. It can take over almost any kind of forest.

Shrubs and weeds that are characteristic of the maple understory have this same deliberate approach. Among the shrubs, maple-leaved viburnum and the viburnum called witch hobble, or highbush cranberry, stand out in my mind. Both have three-lobed, opposite leaves suggestive of red maple or, more true of witch hobble, mountain maple. Maple-leaved viburnum makes a nice specimen for sight-identification tests for students of natural history. Both these trees tend to be pioneering sorts, the maple-leaved viburnum preferring drier places and witch hobble wetter ones. Like so many shrubs of deciduous forests, these members of the honeysuckle family are spread by the birds and mammals that eat their berries. This does the animals a favor later, for they use the shrubby part of the woods for cover. One of the best-hidden exits from a wood-chuck den I know of emerges beneath the dark green leaves of some short maple-leaved viburnums.

Herbaceous plants of the deep woods can be divided pretty much into two categories, based on reaction to shade. The largest number of species comes under the heading of "shade endurers," which generally appear early in spring, blossom in the few weeks of warmth and sunlight, and then endure the summer shade. Most of these species are perennials that collect and store food over their first autumn and the following spring, or even through another whole year, and then expend the lion's share of their reserves in the final summer stalk and its seeds. To me the most striking of the biennials is cardinal flower, whose scarlet birdlike blooms peer across woodland streams or even from the middle of slow riffles. On the other hand, the annuals in this category seem to have the least problem, since they live but a year. One of the best known of these is jewelweed, which may be encountered in marshy openings. Its plants borrow a page from the book of oaks, hickories, and walnuts by making a strong start in life with their large nutritious seeds. Jewelweed stems are fairly translucent, and when the lower end is placed in colored water the movement of fluid in the vessels can be followed rather well. The stem is full of liquid, and some people use it as a salve on the skin for poison ivy.

In the second category of forest herbs are the "shade-escaping" woodland flowers, which bloom before the trees have put out leaves to shade them; they are known as spring ephemerals. These herbs give maple forests a remarkable carpet that has an almost fairy-tale rise and fall during a part of only one season: spring. Their ephemeral life on the stage is Cinderella-like in its brief beauty. Compare that life to the songs of spring peepers down in the woodland marsh or to the Ephemeroptera, the mayflies, which emerge from a shaded brook to live as adults but a single day. For each the time to depart occurs suddenly. As Isaiah said, "And before morning he is not."

Spring ephemerals demonstrate one of those signal approaches to life which single out sugar maple forests. Other woods have the ephemerals, but the most magnificent displays occur in the rich soils of moist climax maple stands. During that flash of light and warmth between the end of winter and the first expanding of tree leaves, the forest floor blazes with blossoms. For a moment there is a glow in even the bleakest interior, the place where summer gloom has a creeping chill. During this fraction of a season the flowers are pollinated and the leaves build most of their reserves for producing this year's seeds and preparing for next year's resurgence. Most energy goes into making seeds. So little is left for stem production that the cellulose skeleton is very weak, with much of its sup-

white baneberry   may apple   hepatica   sugar maple   jack-in-the-pulpit   maidenhair fern

wild ginger   spring beauty   white trillium   trout lily   Christmas fern

port coming from *water pressure* inside. Pick a flower and watch it wilt before getting it home. Step on one and you have squashed it out of the dance. But unless the root or bulb has been injured all may still be well. This is where the food is stored. And so thorough a collecting job does the plant do that "spring ephemerals" often bloom year after year after year —outliving many of the woody giants about them.

Remember back to your first acquaintance with some of them and try to recall how brief the experience was. I have, for instance, relatively few photographs of trout lilies, spring beauties, Dutchman's-breeches, and toothwort. Yet most of the field, marsh, and other plants are so well represented that they occur in my files under a diversity of titles. Spring beauties do appear twice, for another aspect they illustrate remarkably well is pollination. Their white petals have pink stripes that guide bees and other insects in to the pollen and nectar. The bees are almost surely fertilized females which have overwintered and now depend on the success of early bloomers. Dutchman's-breeches turns up among garden flowers as well as among the ephemerals, since it is first cousin to bleeding heart.

If I had the pictures, trout lily could travel about as widely in my collection as any plant I know. Because it is a member of a family that first evolved, along with most of the trees of temperate-zone forests, during the Cretaceous period, it could go into the historical geology section. It also may be a remembrance of the ice age, when rapid life cycles were necessary for some plants to keep alive between snowfalls. The greatest claim on my attention, however, comes from the trout lily's elegance and from some mathematics. Those plants with single leaves do not have enough food supply to blossom and produce seeds, while those with two leaves do. It may take the plant five to seven years to arrive at the two-leaved state and bring out the initial blossom. From then on, it will flower every other year on the average, building up stores in between. Like those of other early plants, trout lily leaves get some protection on bitter days and nights from the sugar in their sap, which acts as an antifreeze. The blossom also gets protection by closing up at night and on dark, stormy days.

Trout lilies often occur in patches, where the mottled leaves give a wavy camouflage of broken lines and indistinct images. Here a careless step can crush the hidden nest of a hermit thrush or the closely related veery. Woodlands that have spring ephemerals are dark through much of spring and summer and in those times are often difficult places to spot birds, whether on the ground or in the trees, but fortunately these two species have very distinctive songs. I particularly enjoy the ringing notes of the thrush. Male birds in general have songs that distinguish them clearly from their nearest relatives, which is important in the mating game. But more interesting is how similar the various alarm calls of the forest may be. They provide easy group communication within a dark environment about a problem all the birds are likely to have in common.

Spring ephemerals choose one of the most difficult times of the growing season to try to break through the forest litter. They arrive, first thing, while the litter is still about as thick as it was in autumn. Later on, earthworms, bacteria, and fungi will at least partially clear the way, far more so in maple than in other woods because the fallen leaves of maples, basswoods, and various associates are regularly still high in nutrients. It is worth looking at some aspects of the story of photosynthesis to see what a remarkable event it is, so influential a part of woodland ecology. The color sequences in maples make them a particularly happy jumping-off place for the story.

From spring through summer, maple leaves have the shining green color that makes these forests attractive even as a roadside display. As the autumn colors begin to range toward yellow and red, foliage more hidden from sunlight remains green. Some of these leaves may even drop off before their chlorophyll has had a chance to disintegrate, as is usual at season's end, and they are therefore still carrying on photosynthesis at their death.

A direct product of photosynthesis is the chemical phosphoglyceraldehyde. It is very reactive and is often rather quickly changed to the more familiar sugars, starches, or even oils. Otherwise the aldehyde may go into the many active chemicals needed for respiration, the creation of more aldehyde, and the capture of carbon dioxide. Sugars initially travel pretty much throughout the plant. In such plants as sugar beets and sugar cane they are stored fairly soon and give the sweet taste. In plants like maples, which live past the killing frosts, roots and trunks collect the sugars and convert them to starch for storage over the winter. Later, most notably during spring, the starch is changed back to sugar and flows in the sap to help build new plant parts—we interrupt some of this flow when tapping maples to make syrup and sugar. The best-known plant oils are probably those of olive oil and peanuts. Less commonly recognized are oils that float on stream surfaces, giving a slick appearance which is often attributed in error to automobiles. Where a slow brook in the maple woods forms pools that carry this sheen, and the banks have a rim of ferns and ground pines, the scene can suggest the Carboniferous period of several hundred million years ago. In those times such plants darkened the swamps, and their decomposed matter was eventually added to the morass that became coal and oil. Some early forms grew more than a hundred feet tall. In the Coal Measures of Nova Scotia and New Bruns-wick, a twenty-foot-long fossil trunk stands where it was buried by a meandering stream that frequently leaped out of its channel.

The yellow leaves of maple trees have ceased their production of phosphoglyceraldehyde because their chlorophyll has broken down. On their undersides are revealed yellow carotenes, which had been present all along but were masked by the dominant green of chlorophyll. Caro-tene—from the word carrot—gives us vitamin A as well as the mellow color of carrots, oranges, tomatoes, butter, egg yolk, and maple leaves. Green spinach, surprisingly, has even more carotene than an equal weight of the yellowest egg yolk! It seems likely that carotenes in the leaf help to produce chlorophyll.

For the leaves that go into a violently red tone there is a richer autumn story, one of sunlit days and cool nights. While summer weather lies over the land photosynthesis continues; sugars flow abundantly from the leaves and downward to be stored. But then, as a chill creeps into the season—especially on clear nights when temperatures can drop precipitously—the departure of the sugars is slowed. Delay takes over. And finally the sugars left behind in the leaves change to anthocyanins, which give the red and purple hues of autumn after the death of chlorophyll. Single leaves often show the sequence, with darker hues to the outside, yellow tones nearer the ribs, and the remaining chlorophyll turning the indentations of ribs into green valleys. A leaf that has been overshadowed by another has photosynthesized less and so will hold less anthocyanin, the result being a lingering imprint in green or yellow. Long, slow autumns bring the colors imperceptibly. Icy blasts put a whip into the air and send sudden blazes of red across the hills, especially over acid soil.

Maples are not alone in such a response to autumn, but they are outstandingly varied within each individual tree as well as in their great quilted stands. Hour after hour you can drive through a countryside overflowing with autumn's abundance. As a matter of fact, the yellow clouds of tall tulip trees and the piercing flames of red issued by narrow black gums bring a relief, a punctuation in the passing scene. Basswoods, beeches, and occasional elms soften the view where this sort of forest dominates. In the fields and along the forest edge the scene is the same, with those trees that can produce quantities of anthocyanin often bringing on a fiery look, while others infuse the tawny yellows more widely associated with the season. A field turning to a woods, especially a maple woods whose flanks are spiked with green cedars, can have an autumn glory that seems the heart of our north country.

Nutritionally well-stocked red and purple leaves are at least one reason for the great success of the humble earthworm, whose unremitting (if unwitting) labors in our behalf remind me of the tireless efforts of the Badger in *The Wind in the Willows* to keep his friend Mr. Toad solvent socially as well as economically. But I do not measure the worm's success only in contemporary terms of aerating the soil, promoting water passage and drainage, lifting up minerals from the subsoil to the top, converting leaves to fertilizer, and the like. I am more astounded by the way the European earthworms, or night crawlers, have wriggled their way into prominence since their introduction to North America only a few hundred years ago. Very possibly our northern earthworms were largely wiped out by the glaciers and these have replaced them, much to the benefit of farmers and robins.

Curiously, if approached right, earthworm ecology has a romantic flavor. On one of the first truly warm nights of spring, standing quietly in a maple woods one can hear earthworms moving leaves as they forage among the litter for the choicest pieces. The sounds, jerky and scratching, may come from all sides if the frost has been gone for a while, but they will fade as the stars ride high to announce a cold snap, which your steamy breath says is here right now. The next day the ground is likely to be peopled all about with turrets of mud erected of pellets piled an inch or so high. If the soil was at all wet, the travels of the worms will still show as streamers leading from the bases of these mounds.

One day I discovered a night crawler extended along one of these paths and touched its head. The beast hunched backward as though passing rings of fat down its length under the skin. It backed out of sight through a hole in a rut. I dug in after it with a twig but soon realized I was obviously losing the race. A few inches away stood one of the mounds, so I skipped the poking method and just pushed the castle from its moorings. There lay the worm, flat and reposed. That was enough. During the night the worm had been piling up bits of leaves, bark, and even white pine needles and then covering them with excreted mud balls. Eventually bacteria in this midden would reduce the raw food to something more edible. In the meantime, the worm could be out collecting and building again. That was where I had found it on one of those rare occasions when it was abroad in daylight. Many dangers await such wandering worms, not the least of which seems to be the lethal effect of ultraviolet light on the thin skin.

By turning leaves into mulch or a finer component of soil earthworms help change a rough litter to a soft one. This is especially true in maple woods, where the leaves are very much to their liking. And so these deep woods become quieter places to walk. Sounds of disturbance are muffled, allowing those of the woods alone to filter through the leaves, both high and low.

13 | *Mixed Forests in a Changing World: Passing Scenes*

Throughout that golden morning in the height of autumn we had been traveling northward in one of the oldest forests of the eastern deciduous forest formation. It was a candyland of colors, but all shifted toward the red end of the spectrum. Maples and oaks, hickories and beeches, gums, poplars, and birches—they seemed to have been hurled together in a vast mixing bowl of species, a forest conglomerate given this one chance to mingle and offer an autumn that might have been unparalleled anywhere. Or was it the reverse, that this forest was a brilliant fragment of an original togetherness that ten thousand or more years ago broke away into natural divisions as trees, shrubs, and small flowers probed the north country in the wake of the last retreating glacier? Whatever the sequence, the unity of a diverse nation of trees had given this part of the great eastern deciduous forest its name of mixed mesophytic.

The term mesophytic was coined in 1916 by the botanist Lucy Braun to refer to moist soils with good drainage. The soil chemistry in a mesophytic forest occupies a middle ground. Neither the acids nor the alkalines of the humus have a chance to accumulate separately over large areas, such as we find in other forests. Characteristically the soil is dark, with a porous humus that is rich in such chemicals as calcium and potassium and is well stocked with bacteria and earthworms. The mixed groups of trees come to this varied environment as to a gathering of the kings, with each able to find a place. Trees that elsewhere stand above all others are coequals here on the Appalachian plateau where the glaciers did not touch. Throughout that day we were on the Mount Olympus of American forests, where the gods of the realm had gathered as early as Tertiary times.

As in all groupings of long standing, however, pairs and triplets and others had gotten together here and there, like the small social knots at any large party. Just past noon we turned down a valley and headed straight for one of these associations. Even from several hundred yards away, it stood out beyond the massive trunks of red maples and red and black oaks with a luminescent brown—a stand predominantly of beeches on an island that divided the forest stream.

During these last days of October Beech Island was a world of paper. Leaves that had changed early hung in twisted and coiled bits of crinkly translucent tissue. They seemed less leaves of trees than straw-colored ornaments brightening up a forest that itself stood out like a jewel among the heavy melanized browns of oaks. The younger beech leaves had yet to curl. Their straight veins that parallel each other quite uniformly gave them the neat appearance one associates with ruled note-paper. I could see small red splotches here and there on perhaps any four or five out of a dozen such leaves chosen at random. Anthocyanins had collected where sap passing in the veins had been jammed up by mite galls. The underside of the leaves revealed the lumps so typical of galls. Th upper surface was depressed into dimples, very much as though drops of red ink had landed and created the kind of lump made on paper where it has been sprinkled with water.

Although tulip poplars, black and sweet gums, white and red oaks, and a few American elms gave some relief, the island was totally under the rule of American beech. Furthermore, this was likely to be a self-perpetuating condition, since the understory repeated almost the same tale. A notable visitor from a tropical family stood out for its drooping long leaves that gradually widen toward the tip, terminating in a quick flourish—the visitor, pawpaw, belongs to the family Anonaceae, which is extensive around the equator but sends only this one representative to investigate the high north. Diminishing in height and over-all size as it goes, pawpaw follows streams like this even into Canada. In many places it will grow as a shrub rather than a tree, and both types have become popular as attractive ornamentals. On Beech Island the two forms appeared, the shrubs making up a high proportion of the shrub layer. None of the famous fruit had lasted this late in the year. Its soft leathery skin can easily be removed to get at the nutritious pulp inside, which is supposed to be sweet, edible, and not necessarily to everyone's liking. Opossums and raccoons go a long way, though, for such fleshy fruit—even to the urban garbage can and probably to Beech Island.

Herbs of the ground layer were too scattered to be really impressive. This was in strong contrast to some oak forests we had just passed through, where a broad, roughed-up plot might be filled with enchanter's nightshade. Bottom-land forests elsewhere sported dozens of flop-eared hepaticas laid out in a loose garden for several dozen yards along the stream bank. Even among the few herbs here we could see no distinct society. Sedges were more prominent than grasses, which made sense down in a draw. Evergreen partridgeberry wound along like a furtive thought, sparkling here and there in red "two-eyed" berries which might survive into next year's blossoming if not eaten first. Bedstraw, a closely related annual, was, if anything, even more self-effacing. Not only do its stems lack the woodiness of partridgeberry, but also they are almost excessively weak. The creeping strands support themselves on almost anything ahead or below, holding on by bristly little backward-pointing hairs on their square stems and their long, narrow starlike leaves. Bedstraw placed over an arm will hook on, and feels like a sluggish caterpillar. Perennial yellow bedstraw from Europe is a bit more self-sufficient, as is shown in its more erect posture. By old superstition it was reputed to induce fertility when draped across a bed.

No doubt our heavy-footed raking of oak leaves along the way had alerted every large animal for half a mile, so we saw only the smaller, less speedy ones of Beech Island. From their diggings and twisted scat we estimated that one family of red fox were residents. Raccoons, passers-by, had left scat along the stream bank. A few skunks had burrowed here; one opening carried a fresh odor. Deer tracks appeared here and there. These animals prefer the maples and birches of such mixed forests but leave the beeches strictly alone. By their selective browsing they can actually change and control the character of a woods. Red maple, a dominant in the surrounding forests, had few saplings out there and none on Beech Island. Possibly the deer were devouring them almost as fast as they grew to munchable size.

We kept on scuffing through the leaves to see what the beech litter had to offer. Curiously, no salamanders appeared, though the Appalachian plateau forest as a whole is for them perhaps the richest known place in the world, exceptional in its numbers of both species and individuals. Dozens of spring peepers leaped away, quiet now in a forest that in spring must have resounded like an aviary with their whistles. These frogs truly belong to the woods, where their dark skin with black stripes—most notably the cross on the back—blends in with twigs and leaves on an irregularly lit forest floor. They have a curious migration. Beginning in pools in the spring, they move high into the trees during summer and eventually return to the ground with autumn days. On almost any warm day of the year their voices may start up, much to the surprise of someone walking where snow is plummeting down from the trees.

Leaves were filling the forest floor so deep that the creek around Beech Island passed almost unnoticed—a buried thought—that is, until a pair of wood ducks took off with a blast of quacking that rattled loudly down the creek as they sped away at shoulder height. None of our other ducks can match this boldly patterned drake, and none that I know of better breaks the somber tones of most woods. I was sorry we had sent the pair pelting away among low branches. Fortunately, wood ducks are admirably equipped to fly such obstacle courses, and are adapted, perhaps, to dodge the raccoons that so easily climb the hollow trees where the ducks nest. Wildlife managers sometimes construct houses for them on stakes, with inverted tin cones just below the nesting boxes to repulse raccoons and other enemies. Agile young wood ducks nested in trees can actually escape from some raiders by hooking their way upward with bill and claws, "like flies walking on a wall," Edward H. Forbush says in *A Natural History of American Birds.* And a good many of these young birds may be on the move at one time. So tight is the supply of tree holes in the woods that one has been recorded as holding thirty wood ducks and five merganser eggs at the same time!

Mixed mesophytic forests would seem to have so many components that none could act in conjunction with others. They do, of course, and spring changes reflect this extraordinarily well. The dynamics of the opening moments of the growing season are so interrelated that a change in one factor may reflect a significant change in another. A few springs ago I made a study of bud and leaf growth on two woodland beech trees in a forest of this sort, using twenty twigs and more leaves and leaf surface than I care to remember. While friends were measuring a number of other aspects of spring phenology, or the "shape" of spring, I graphed foliage growth of the trees that were king in this particular woods.

On April 8 the beech terminal buds averaged 15 centimeters in length. Measurements on April 29 showed them to have nearly doubled, to 28 centimeters. During the succeeding week the buds unrolled into loose twists of leaves, which averaged 34 square centimeters of surface area on one side for all the leaves from any one bud. By May 13 the surface area had leaped to an astounding 120 square centimeters, nearly quadrupling during a single week. In other words, between April 29 and May 6 the foliage changed phases, while the next week saw a shift with a great thrust of growth that could only drain the resources of the forest floor in one fast gulp.

All across the spectrum the effects of spring were sweeping the forest. The trunk circumferences of two red oaks, a red maple, and a black cherry increased an average of about six inches at chest height! The dry weight of the spring beauties had been rising steadily and rapidly between

April 8 and 29. Then, just before the canopy of beech leaves opened, they blossomed. But the coming-out party was doomed. By May 6 the population had suffered a considerable decline, and on May 20 most of these gentle plants were staining the forest floor. All over the woods the spring ephemerals had fallen.

Those in our group who were measuring water movement in the ground had erected a level wooden platform some sixteen inches above the soil surface. From there they could measure the distance to the surface of ground water below. As the water table sank they dug pits and followed it down until further pursuit seemed unnecessary to give the picture. On April 15, the high-water mark of that spring, three woodland ponds were measured. Two had risen to within a foot of their planks, making the pools about four inches deep. The third lay in a pit, and its surface came to about an inch below the average soil level there.

Then, between April 15 and 29, when beech buds were doubling their length, the water level dropped two inches. And during the week of leaf emergence and wild flower collapse it plunged another ten inches. The two higher ponds dropped so far that their water table was now seven inches below the forest floor. A week later it was better than two feet down. The third, shallower pond had disappeared before we arrived on May 6.

If you were to spade up spring ephemerals like spring beauty, Dutchman's-breeches, and trout lily, you could hardly have a worse effect than what happens to them naturally.

Other mesophytic woodland flowers remain past the blossoming season as examples of a more enduring life style. For instance, the heart-shaped parasols of wild ginger hang on in the gathering darkness long after the brown blossom has closed. It blooms so close to the forest floor that I would expect the fused petals to be rubbed raw during spring storms. The stubby stem points outward unwaveringly, however. Like a hidden treacle trough known only to the initiate, the yellow center with its pollen and nectar is host to little insects such as flesh flies and fungus gnats. They jiggle before your face as you lie prone.

Suddenly the flies are gone, like all the crowd of pollinators streaming by at ankle height. Ginger, radiant brown where caught by the sun, fades in death and joins the leaf mold at its lower lip. To every side crusty leaves clutch some bit of the forest floor. They conform to the variant shapes of twigs and exposed roots, chips of bark, even the coils of empty snail shells.

Life in the forest seems to move higher, like the twinings of moon-seed vine, when summer enters. The birds move from the shadowed rafters to the green roof outside. Here and there the excited ways of spring remain, such as in a shaft of light breaking through and filled with tiny insects riding it like motes of pollen.

Finally the growing season ends, and one plant especially seems to stand out in the change. The wandlike stems of Solomon's Seal often nod even into the gusts of winter, until they are buried in snow. A few dark blue berries jouncing from long strings at the bases of the leaves may ornament the stalk. The root survives longest of all. Each year, as it stretches farther and puts up a new frond, it leaves behind the old seal-like scar where last year's foliage grew. So the actual age of a plant can be traced by uncovering the rootstock and counting the marks.

This, then, is seasonal change in the mixed forest, but there is also a longer course of events, the scene that is played out over decades and centuries. Some years ago one upland mixed forest, dominated primarily by sugar maples, brought this most strongly to my mind. I could see within the space of a few hundred yards a story that might have begun with our country's westward expansion. The story is set in the midwest, where so much of our nation's early history took root, in a low-key fashion that is rarely sculptured on village statues.

Rising on one of the rolling slopes above a meandering river there is a mixed-hardwood forest that survives today only because the gradient of its floor has been too steep to keep in cropland. The soil itself is flowing slowly toward the river, as it has done for millennia. Curved maple and cherry, oak and ash trunks lean back into the force that urges them downhill. Many of the maples rise now in seventy-foot arcs, like poised bows held taut.

When I came to this woodland one morning in May, I arrived just in time to see the last of a nearby green alfalfa field falling to a tractor and harrow. Back and forth the machines clanked, devouring dark vales and shining green knolls. I walked into the passing domain of chipping sparrows and white cabbage butterflies, breaking a narrow defile through the legumes the farmer was counting on to fertilize his field with their nitrates.

I flipped over a cluster of the oval leaves, an old habit of mine. On one stem an insect thorn, a green buffalo treehopper, rapidly sidled around, mirroring my moves. Its burnished disguise vanished. From my angle, the pointed costume was undoubtedly a three-cornered hat worn by an incredibly shy gnome. Then, as in the fields I had regularly gone to at home some twenty years before, the insect caricaturist threw away its comical pose and catapulted backward into the shingled gloom, where I lost it. By high noon it would have to wing toward the woods, however, or be churned into the advancing furrows.

I never saw the end. Perhaps they are there again this spring, the treehopper and the tractor with its helper, vying for a few acres or square feet of upland meadow. But I did see, or thought I saw, a question in the farmer's mind. Between the woods and the ground he would soon put under seed he had left a wide strip—fifty feet or more—paralleling the tractor run. In it there were no alfalfas linked in a single-species stand for acre after acre, no stubs of wheat from an earlier year. It had, instead, a thick mat of grass and clover that seemed to have been planned as a stay against runoff, a gesture to protect the river from the bared land.

On top of this pleasant deep lawn the farmer also had kept some thistle and burdock. In their way they were playing the same role as the remnant apple trees some suburban dwellers keep on their lawns. The apples go blotched with disease, the limbs crack and fall, and all is on the picturesque side. So the thistles had a charm, interlocked as they were and blown this way and that. Bush-size burdocks make unkempt shrubs with ponderous fronds—the sort of ungainly appearance I suspect people of admiring in the elephant-ear trees they raise indoors.

There might be a bit of more distant family history to be read in that lot if one began with the woods and worked back from there. By looking at today's evidence and using some knowledge of plant succession, the way one plant species comes in as another fades, I thought I could reconstruct some of the story.

For instance, the largest and most numerous trees were sugar maples. Over half of the understory was composed of maple saplings that were running six inches to three feet tall. Clearly the forest was too dark, for one thing, for other tree species to compete, and the land was soon (well, within a century) to fall completely to the maples. In this part of the country, a good untouched stand of trees tends to end up that way, along with beeches mixed in, so the process here was well on its journey to the end, or climax, forest.

Such matters take time. As a matter of fact, the earlier transition from smaller growth, like dogwood and ash, to the domineering long-lived types can take seventy years or longer. Since the oldest maples here appeared to be no more than a hundred years old and probably had been preceded by a series of "trash" trees like ash and dogwood, the forest's place in the farmer's family history might go back over one hundred years, to days when it was an overgrown riverside.

To look at things as a dramatist might, there was once a grassy dip by a meandering stream where boy and girl used to recite poetry to each other under a tall, spreading maple, itself a remnant from another maple forest of many years before. Perhaps someone had loved its kingly stature —or maybe it had been easier simply to let it stand. At any rate, we can try to reconstruct a guesswork sequence of events beginning just before the Europeans came to settle in this neighborhood.

1750:   Indians canoe down gentle clear waters of the river and shoot deer that gnaw red maple twigs along the bank,

	leaving behind as a food reserve those deer hiding up higher, among sugar maples.
1800:	Sinewy pioneer chops down the last maples on his piece of land, skipping a few of those on the riverside, and he and his descendants continue successful farming.
1860:	Grassy sitting spot, where young people sing in afternoon and evening "down by the riverside," under shade of a two-hundred-year-old "wolf tree," a sugar maple left by grandfather.
1890:	A few fair-sized sugar maples in a young woods of ash and companions. The old wolf tree died and was blown over ten years ago, but not before it cast some successful seeds.
Today:	Maples dominate canopy and understory. Hump on forest floor is remains of moldering ancient wolf maple.

After the oldest son was killed in the Civil War the farm by the bluff retreated from song and love. Life went on, but more sparely. Around the "wolf tree," a giant that in the forest before 1860 had dominated a very wide patch of ground, the lovely open shade became crowded. Shrubs and small trees of other kinds came in on the grassy sward. The shade deepened. Most of these new weed trees could not reproduce themselves, though, since the shade of the parents killed off the seedlings.

Succeeding farmers in the family continued to cultivate the uplands but let the forest grow rampant around the old maple. Perhaps there was a story in the family about the tree and the boy's will to return before it blossomed twice more. After it died the story may have been shifted slightly to include a mother who waited for her son, the tree being the lamp she kept lit by the side of the river that he would perhaps come home on. Nearly one hundred years later, the offspring of that tree, being tolerant of shade, were ruling the new forest. In a few more decades it might be wholly sugar maple. A mist of shrubs, dogwood, ash, and companions would stream along its flanks as they had on the riverside feeding grounds of the deer more than two centuries before.

The present tenants of the farm, seeing beyond the woods now, were growing grass on that upland strip to protect the river from topsoil that was exposed every spring. Maybe one or another of their children, home for vacation fresh from a college course in geology, had pointed out the gradual slumping of the soil that was causing tree trunks to bow and had suggested it could be prevented by cutting down most of the trees and putting in grass. But the farmer had doubtless said that this was a "natural" flow of no great consequence and had held out for the woods. A brother was writing a family history and he, too, though a literary sort, asked that the trees be allowed to live.

14 | *Forests of the Smokies: Northern Summits in the Deep South*

The forests of the far north begin where the first scattered trees break the low flat wilderness of tundra. From there a thin lichen-woodland of small trees and lichen-covered ground spreads southward and gradually rises into a towering escarpment, sweeping toward the sky on dark green boughs. Trees of the few species of this boreal forest, this American taiga, may become so densely interwoven to the east that forest animals are born and buried in a perpetually gloomy winter.

If the *aspect* of the coniferous forest is peculiar to itself, however, some of the species are not. And a number of them survive as remnants of the ice age in forests that extend far south to the Great Smoky Mountains of Tennessee and North Carolina.

Occupying a great range, these trees also enrich the hemlock-hardwood tier lying north of the Great Lakes. This "Lake Forest," with its closed green summers, fiery autumns, and stark snow-locked winters, was once the most written-about plant formation in the United States, before the lumber industry discovered the commercial value of white pine. The overtopping spires, the distinctive layers characteristic of white pine branching—these were overtaken by the rolling aspect of a climax community that includes many of our favorite softwoods and hardwoods, such as hemlock, maple, and beech.

The hemlock-hardwood forest merges in turn into the deciduous forests of the Appalachians, forming a transition zone between the northern coniferous realm and the deciduous communities of lower latitudes. For the first time basswood and yellow birch appear beside striped maple and sweet birch. Along mountain streams, however, small locally pure stands of hemlock are often found. Beneath their dark branches the air is noticeably cooler. Almost the whole eastern United States is cloaked by this "summer-green" deciduous forest formation. Rain is plentiful, the summers and growing season long, the soils and topography diverse. These trees give America its magnificent autumn colors. While such deciduous tracts are still extensive in Asia, their representatives in Europe were either cut down by man or destroyed in an icy trap formed by the advancing hammer of glaciers and the anvil of high, east/west-extending southern mountain ranges. A few North American relicts, long separated from the main body, may be found in Mexico and in deep ravines and canyons of the southwestern United States.

But nowhere is there a more complex forest community than in the southern Appalachians. These oldest exposed mountains, untouched by seas since before the Tertiary period, have about all species and the greatest size of tree found in the entire eastern forest complex. Yet, in spite of the antiquity of the Appalachians, environmental conditions have been so stable that contemporary mixed-mesophytic forests there are closely allied genetically to the mixed forests of the Tertiary period. Fir and hemlock flourish in nearly pure stands.

Along the mountain crests that wind almost a mile above sea level, remnants of the northern boreal forests maintain a last stronghold. A dark horizon seems penciled in by the deep greens of spruce and fir trees. Here a peculiar species substitution has taken place. The white spruce and balsam fir of the boreal forest have been replaced toward the south by red spruce and Fraser fir, species not easily distinguished from their northern ecological equivalents. This illustrates the point made earlier about mountain ranges carrying many plant and animal species that are far out of their normal latitudinal limits. Thus, in western parts of the United States one speaks accurately of "arctic" tundra of the north and of "alpine" tundra high in the mountains. Eventually mountaintop species may occur in stands hundreds of miles apart and may mark the terminal point of glaciation.

Mountain terrain affects the flow of the seasons as though they were strung on strings. Autumn and winter come earlier, spring and summer later, to the higher altitudes. Yet when the hour has arrived in the Smokies, spring rushes through the highest forests and grassy balds like a crackling fire. May is old when wood anemone petals flatten out in the dark. Fiddlehead ferns unroll long after those on ravine walls in Connecticut have done so. But, unlike the slow-savored spring of the north, spring in the southern mountains scatters rapidly across the summits like flashing dice.

Lower ridges appear almost piebald by comparison. On dry north-facing slopes tiers of pine predominate. Table-mountain pine is most common on ridges below the boreal forest species. Farther down, table-mountain pine is replaced by pitch pine, noted for the short-stemmed cones that may occur almost anywhere on the trees above ground. Nearest the valley floor, scrub pine dominates.

Nearly uniform swaths of oak may be seen across the mountain coves from these pine steps. The concept of "limiting factors" could hardly be expressed better than in these two communities, oak and pine, confronting each other in clearly differing habitats across a cool ravine.

On the waistline of ridge after ridge, a pink blur appears and gradually spreads across the mountain range in spring. Late one May I stood with a half-dozen friends enshrouded in a few hundred of the millions of soft blossoms that compose this hazy sash. The knees of my pants were slimy with mud, and my cheeks felt inflamed from tiny cuts. Then I bulldozed my way upward once more, emerging finally fifty yards higher up the mountain. Standing to my full height for the first time in perhaps twenty minutes, I looked down over the tangle I had escaped. For nearly

150 yards down the mountain ridge pink rhododendron flowers slid gently among each other. Mountain laurel, clinging close to the base of the rugged jutting rock, which was peeled bald for a few yards, shed white petals in the after bloom. This was one of the famous "heath slicks," or "heath balds," of these southern mountains. I do them no injury by remembering that they were slick underfoot, that spongy and quaking humus slithered away at every other step. The low pH (high acidity) of this soil probably plays a large role in maintaining the purity of the rhododendron stands.

To me no flower matches the ultraglassiness of rhododendron blossoms. The pink cups allow a softer light to pass into the shadowed tangle beneath the canopy. Along the rock ribs the mountain laurel here seemed papery and weedlike, the unopened blossoms suggesting aster-shaped children's candy.

As we scrambled down the ridge flank, aiming free-hand style toward the road along the next ridge, a friend and I followed a corner of the slick. The ground fell away before us until suddenly the bushes ended at a ten-foot overhang. We dangled like parachutists over the bounding waters of a twisting mountain stream. Wading across it a few minutes later, we could see up and down stream only a few hundred feet. But we knew that upstream, several miles beyond the first crisp turn, lay the beech-filled cove of a vastly different environment. We were following one of the routes of the southern junco, which trace their migration routes up and down the mountainsides. For every four hundred feet of altitude they fly, they accomplish an equivalent of about four days' travel northward or southward.

Near the top of the Carolina junco's range, beech becomes the dominant tree. "Beech gaps" wedge into the upper reaches of many coves, the anvil-shaped community often being jammed against the canopy of a spruce-fir forest. I once sat astride a fallen trunk of beech which stretched up a slope like a giant rope, and immediately to my left and right were those two kinds of forests, separated by unseen factors. The gray beeches here grew only a few yards apart—the tree usually arises vegetatively from root suckers—and their gnarled and twisted trunks rarely attained the diameter of those in open stands. I was in a matchstick forest.

Small trees and shrubs grew like persistent weeds around the beech bases. The leaf and small-branch fall of such a forest has been estimated, in terms of decay, at about two tons per acre per year. Above the slowly flowing woodland floor drooped the leaves of mountain maple, suggesting yellow cutouts. Ropy, shining club moss wound past nettle stems.

In one lilliputian clearing the yellow bloom of boreal clintonia bobbed in the May breezes. With the sun's rays falling directly below it, the plant might have been a lantern illuminating a leafy park. Among the plumes of shield fern we found a genetic oddity, the octoploid "skunk" goldenrod (*Solidago glomerata*).

It is the coves that give these ancient mountains their graceful slanting contours. To the observer five or more miles away, their flanks seem to flow across to each other. To someone gazing down a colonnaded slope through a break in the trees, the sound of an icy stream stirs thoughts of a precipitous downhill flight. Farther down, a tough undergrowth of bushy mountain holly and serviceberry can easily rip pants and shirt and, like knives, cut wrists and neck. Tree trunks—those along the Appalachian Trail are occasionally scarred by the clawing of bears—are anywhere from two to four yards apart. The bluish-hued bark of silver bell stands out. The sculptured bark of yellow buckeye disclaims its family ties. And one may predict that within a few yards will be found a tree peculiar to these coves, the basswood *Tilia heterophylla*. All these species that give the coves their distinctive vegetation are probably their own best friends, contributing toward the cooler temperatures and higher relative humidity which help maintain the hardwoods.

Boulders have gathered in the creases of many coves. According to Dr. Hal De Selm, of the University of Tennessee, "some are of tremendous size, and, piled in wild assortment, they no longer fall from the cliffs above and slide downslope. Their immobility today suggests a cool, moist Pleistocene climate for their origin and movement to the present position."

Man's influence began to be felt in the early lumbering periods, when, as lumber camps were dying out, tulip poplar moved into the slash areas. Now the poplar is commonly seen at low elevations in the coves. With travel through the giant forests easily accomplished by auto, man's progress is too often traced by flames. And the window burned into the forest canopy may open in spring on the pink blossoms of fire cherry.

15 | *From Lake to the Conifer Summit of a Mountain in Glaciated Country: Up, Up, Up the Storied Mountain*

In the northern, glacially eroded part of our country, the ascent of a mountain often begins at the edge of a lake and ends on a summit of conifers. The first steps are taken in darkness, for the rocky mass rises abruptly and throws its shadow far out over the water. Mornings are short. Dusk comes early.

Along the western shore of Lake George, in northeastern New York State, summer mornings usually open with a harsh sunlight that flickers across gray waves and brings the brightest part of the day to the lowest rooms of the forest. Like the wind and water, its full force blazes unchecked into the bases of beech, maple, white birch, and white pine trees that mantle uneasy rocks. Within an hour, however, the green Adirondack umbrella reasserts itself. Tall dead tree stubs where belted kingfishers frequently pause to stare down into the shallows no longer suggest black candles but retire into their more familiar secretive role. Old protruding branches once again suggest the rifle barrels that early American patriots learned to brown, as camouflaging, when fighting the French and Indians. By nine in the morning, standing among the last beatings of little white-caps, I have had to use a flash unit to photograph a fresh-water mussel that every now and then parted the water and broke the ripples into silver shingles.

Morning lasts longest and the day closes most suddenly on the lake's western cliffs, such as the steep slabs of Rogers' Rock, a seven-hundred-foot slide named after Robert Rogers, leader of the Rangers who fought in the French and Indian Wars of the middle 1700's. So desperate is footing there that cedars and pines hang from fissures like giant ragged mosses, leaving a dominantly broad-leaved forest to cloak the sidelines. From out on the lake a great rent appears to have been torn in garment and flesh, revealing much-abused bone. When winds blow out of the north, clear skies make this shining cut one of the boldest landmarks for the whole thirty-two-mile length of the lake. While south winds bring warmth, they often threaten with haze and, finally, thundershowers.

The events of one August morning gave me a peculiar glimpse into what winter might look like here at the base of the slide. At six-thirty, sunlight was flashing off the lake and illuminating the rooms of our lakeside cabin with what people elsewhere would consider a ten-o'clock brilliance. A difference was that speckles jiggled about, not on the floor but on the ceiling. By a quarter to seven everyone was out on the lawn, on the dock, or in the cold water. Then it floated in, a shimmering white curtain being drawn across the face of the far shore and mountain range. A heavy fog, wavy internally with countercurrents that shifted its streamers and puffs but definite as to its main force as it moved slowly from left to right down the lake, slowly cut off our distant audience of early risers and tall trees. Then, as though one of those clear northern breezes had sat on it—not parted or shredded it—the hanging cloud sank down onto the lake. There it lay for minutes in a flat mist only a few feet thick. My older daughter saw the picture best, seeing winter at Rogers' Rock when she called out, "It looks like ice!" That evening, reading, I recalled the scene while imagining other times here. I have never been at Lake George during December, January, or February, but I saw in that morning whiteness how on a number of occasions Captain Rogers and his independent Rangers could have sped after their quarry on ice skates—a quarry that returned the favor with similar dash.

Certainly there is no easy route around this edge of the lake where the bank plummets, straight down through hemlocks and over mossy bedrock, into charging water. Rogers' men could have hidden practically in the open there, wrapping themselves in green blankets and merging with the undulating turf. The only gradually descending shoreline near the Rock occurs in sinuous embayments, which may even be backed by cattail and jewelweed marshes. Within such bays quillwort and horsetails can find enough quiet here and there to give places a grassy appearance. Sunfish hover, especially among the ribbony leaves of eel grass, where only the slices of their shadows indicate that the brown you see is flesh and not dun-colored muck. As a matter of fact, if the fish depend on these tall streamers for cover they have chosen well, for eel grass seems to be the dominant weed of many inlets here and in other lakes.

Eel grass, or wild celery—whose distant salt-water relative, eel grass, or grass wrack, is better known as windrows along beaches on both the east and west coasts—has curious coiled underwater stems that immediately attract attention. They may also be deceiving, for the twists enable female flowers to rise and rest on the surface—attached to plants that might be rooted half a dozen or so feet down! While rowing over a patch in our cove, I noted that the bottom of the lake would disappear several strokes before the eel grass did. All down the bay I could see dimples where stems had relaxed and their tips had surfaced. The yellow-green flowers at the ends of the stalks made me think of funnels at the top of spiral drains, holding the lake at a certain level. Actually, the process is somewhat the reverse, for each corkscrewed stem has enough spring to keep its single flower bounding the top as waves rise and fall. Into the depression the female flowers have created float male blossoms, which break free of short stalks below after their pollen has ripened. They come bobbing along like toy cargo vessels. After the female flower has been fertilized and the seed begins maturing, the impressionable stem contracts and draws the blossom under water. The Greeks of classical times would have enjoyed this event for its suggestion of a god retrieving his daughter, who would give birth to another water nymph after her interlude in the human world. Eel grass seed simply drops off into the mud and becomes another wraith in the underwater world of Lake George. Into such aquatic jungles Rogers and his Rangers must have many times dipped their oars, wrapped in lengths of blanket to deaden their sound.

I have many times climbed the mountain which broods over this lake, traversing a physical and historical giant that has been worn over millions of years into gently rolling ridges. For thousands of years other human feet have found these slopes amenable to walking or even running. One day last summer I began where Indians must have passed many hours, among the paper birches that gave them canoes, and set out to hike to the summit of Rogers' Rock.

It was often an intensely human trail that initiated many thoughts of ancient and modern events. For instance, close into the lee of one projecting peninsula of white pines and birches several dozen stalks of pipewort poked out of the water like miniature posts. In my mind I saw them as actual stakes that might long, long ago have supported fishing nets or possibly the dwellings of lake people. Again, on one of my days here, I had seen a family of four farther out in the lake, half-swimming, half-floating, as they paddled in toward shore, gabbling as they went. On the floating dock they were aiming for sat five or six women, a changing population, talking about this and that as they guarded their own children and those of absent neighbors. Occasionally an especially agile child would flip out of the water onto the weathered planks, arch over the crowd below, and spring away in a curving plunge. Mothers admonished, mothers encouraged. I think that somewhat the same scene must have happened year after year for perhaps five, ten, or more thousands of years. Surely after the glacier left ten thousand years ago, Indians had camped around Lake George, perhaps in this very embayment. Like us they probably could have been found on warm summer days swimming and talking, sitting and visiting, watching their children. Doubtless some of the brood were obviously better athletes than the others and drew attention by their lithe movements. I have no doubt that "good form" was recognized then, and that it was about the same as it is today.

So, as I left the yellow morning light that caught the arc and swing of lakeside birches, almost as much of me was living in the past, both storied and unwritten, as in the present. Even white oaks along this path meant more than their unimpressive stands would seem to indicate. I saw them as creating the environment essential for the sugar maples that have made our north country legendary. For far longer than any human memory, to Adirondack red squirrels the oaks had doubtless meant caches of acorns and hefty clusters of leaves, the latter to be stuffed into the walls of winter nests high overhead. The scratching noises a squirrel makes dragging a packet of leaves up the trunk of a tree are worth listening for. One will rush and stop again and again, like a dog digging through litter after a mole. If the observer is standing on a slope well uphill from the base of the tree, he may think at first that he hears some large animal stalking nearby, approaching in short dashes. To anyone desperate for food, as Rogers' men sometimes were, the scratching is a clue that meat can be had—though only a fistful.

Clambering along the rocky fringe of the lake edge, I parted with a number of odd companions, such as alders and shagbark hickory saplings. The hickories really had little future down there where the water lapped—I can still hear the slapping when I close my eyes, and can remember one steep bank that ended in a bed of boulders. It was not, however, the threat from the lake that promised most trouble but, rather, the insects that were following the shoreline. Above me, crevices under a few shingles of bark looked as if they had been stuffed with wads of russet rug matting. These turned out to be old caterpillar skins and the pupal cases of gypsy moths. The infestation was apparently only beginning here. As a matter of fact, this was the last place I saw signs of them in any force until I reached the summit. Possibly the mildness of the invasion by the lake was due to the relatively low percentage of oaks. Again, maybe the gypsy moth population there was simply at a dip in its fluctuation, in what has been termed the innocuous phase. If so, then the top woods were thoroughly within the epidemic phase. It had been going on up there for at least two years that I knew of, and the end might be nowhere in sight. Back toward the beginning of the 1900's, an "outbreak" centering in eastern Massachusetts lasted a decade or so.

Fortunately, female gypsy moths are practically flightless. They have heavy abdomens, so stuffed with eggs that they apparently are the equivalent of burlap sacks of potatoes—quite a drag on the wings. The females therefore lay their eggs within whispering distance of the place where they were fertilized. The males, comparative dwarfs, pick up the strong sexual odor of the females from as far as a quarter of a mile away. By the middle of July males can be seen zigzagging along a few feet above ground, not searching for food, since neither sex partakes of any, but in the throes of the major drive of a brief life span. The true spread of the species, however, occurs on hot May days, when powerful updrafts emanating from the woods pitch the newly hatched larvae aloft like soot off a fire. Gliding along on their fine hairs, gypsy moth caterpillars travel at heights of two hundred feet or more and can be carried by prevailing winds for as much as twenty or so miles. They may be less than one-eighth of an inch long, but no doubt they can be very annoying to boaters caught in a downdraft over the lake. Dr. John J. Kirk, a leader in conservation education, has told me of the end of those that invade cabins via the chimney route. They go *ping* as they land on the metal flashing of the fireplace, before they wander out onto the cabin rug. On cold days, they go *sizz* when toppling into a fire.

This day, only the tall trees by Lake George showed signs of infestation. The witch hazel, alder, and flowering dogwood trees nearby appeared to be unscathed, though it was just possible that any injured ones had already put out new leaves. The young caterpillars are born late in April or early in May, from a tan patch of eggs that has been plastered onto bark or some other surface the previous autumn. Toward the end of June the full-grown caterpillars, now about two inches long, are transformed into bullet-shaped pupae that have a shellacked sheen. These hang loosely from some few silken strands and are thinly caged behind several more threads. The July survival rate seems to indicate that their natural enemies have quite a bit further to go before actually controlling gypsy moth spread. Everything from birds and mice to beetles and wasps has been looked to with hope. A parasitic ichneumon wasp has shown promise, in that it stings about a thousand times more larvae than it lays eggs in. Bacterial diseases are being tried, as is a synthetic sex lure which attracts males even more surely than does the real thing. In some places, birds have been known to reduce gypsy moth populations to about one quarter of their presumed original strength.

Right now the best defense appears to be the ability of defoliated plants to put out new leaves. I imagine this could be disastrous, however, along a fast-eroding shoreline or other area where few minerals collect in the soil. The evident success of alders around Lake George was doubtless due in good measure to their hardiness in the face of the worms and to their lack of competition here. Alders can be their own worst enemies, incidentally, because their roots customarily grow nodules that are infected with bacteria, which fix nitrogen gas and oxygen into the chemical compounds that all plants need. By making the soil more nutritious the alders invite competitors. In tight thicket growth, where it is difficult to identify individual plants, a lopped-off twig will show by its triangular pith whether the shrub is actually an alder. By one means or another Robert Rogers knew them, for they became ropes whereby the logs of his rafts were lashed together.

When I turned from the woods at the edge of the lake and entered the denser forest of the mountain slope, I entered a world that made the first seem a display case by comparison. To find a counterpart of the ant lions I had seen boldly digging their funnel-shaped traps in sunny bare spots, I had to dig under a great comforter of leaves to chase down furtive predaceous ground beetles and snaking centipedes. Instead of the Baltimore orioles' nests I had seen sagging, white and obvious, out over the lake—a habit they retain over city streets—I had to follow high branches out one fork and then another, trying to pinpoint nests that often seemed like thicker patches of lichen. If minute and perched on a limb, these might be the work of a female ruby-throated hummingbird, or perhaps they were the art of both red-eyed vireo parents if they were no more than small and wedged into the crotch of two limbs. The voices of birds became louder as the individuals became less visible. I could see how Robert Rogers and his men might slip their signaling imitations in among the real calls.

My path was determined initially by the V-shaped cut of a slender mountain stream. I could have followed the furrow by sound alone, for two days of a cold storm had raised the stepwise fall of the spring water to a brawling downpour. This twenty-eight-hour rainfall was the offshoot of a hurricane that had drifted slowly up the North Carolina coast, ripping up the land there and causing record floods as far north as New York City. Long and unusually cold rains can ravage birds, whose feathers begin to lose their insulating property as they become soaked. This rain, fortunately, had been relatively short—though effective here. The sound of the mountain torrent echoed a hundred yards out from its rock-walled elongate megaphone. Weak herbs flopped on both banks. A musty odor of rotting leaves filled the air where whole branches lay soaking. One fifteen-foot section of sugar maple had dropped lengthwise down into the cascades and landings of the stream, forcing the current to slow and form temporary pools. Evidently leaves had steeped for some time there, for their heavy tea-like odor filled this part of the ravine.

Behind me I left a trail of another odor, from all the rank growth I could not help but step on. Parades of wild ginger indicated the richness of the woodland soil—I was three months too late to catch the opening of the brown cups, which now lay in the company of last year's leaves. Indian pipes rose whitely, a hint of their relatives the blueberries, which were already fruiting higher up. The bright button eyes of baneberry were out; their ability to make people sick may have accounted for my spotting so many of the tallish spikes simply by the gleam of the berries, which few people stop to pick—the name of the plant indicates its history as a known poison.

The most constant color of the living woodland floor was provided not by flowering plants, however, but by the ferns, especially Christmas fern. So an even better season to be in these woods might be around Christmas time. The evergreen fronds persist through the snow—deep here on the lake side of the mountain, and of little aid to the French and Indians, who were often shocked by Ranger attacks in the worst weather. One famous fight under such conditions has been called the "Battle of Snowshoes." We had had a very wet spring and summer this year, and the fern's feathery leaves, with their Christmas-stocking leaflets, or pinnae, strung up the axis, may have been a second crop. Sunlight is so spotty where Christmas fern grows that it is difficult to get a photograph through naturally back-lit fronds. But the dark orange of the spore spots, or sori, on the upper pinnae comes through rather well when the light is right, and I have noted the time of the best lighting on one day in order to set an appointment there for the next day's show.

Another kind of appointment had been signed up for by a fern it-self, the northern maidenhair fern that does so well in the rich soil of shady beech-maple woods—a soil whose value was well appreciated by Rogers, according to his letters. A meeting of the fern with American beeches and sugar maples was due to occur here soon, and in many places farther away it had already taken place. Some people living nearby have let the fern's ebony curliques run free on shade lawns, where they have escaped from the woods out into the noon sun. Maidenhair ferns make a border planting that shifts over the summer from forest green to the reddish tones of early autumn.

Heavy undergrowth like these ferns and the low flowering plants creates a loose, damp microclimate close to the ground. Three- to four-inch-long millipedes give a junglelike aspect of giganticism. When laid into deep fissures of bark they can be about as startling as snakes. Red efts, which are salamanders with wanderlust, are somewhat more pleas-ant. They begin life during the spring as eggs in one of the clots of the mountain brook, emerge as gilled young, and then, perhaps by mid-August, resorb their gills and step out onto land. This last move is an extraordinary change, and their evolution has so focused on it that the departure from water occurs primarily at night when the air and land are damp with dew.

On land, efts often take on a vermilion color that contrasts sharply with the mosses and dank leaves they live among. In their new home, which is often as moist as a shower room, only some of the fungi outrank them in brilliance. Like most reptiles, their legs now lift the body so that they can run agilely—reptile legs are placed more directly under the torso, while these amphibians accomplish the same thing having longer limbs. Efts are so nimble on land that they have survived what would seem to be one of their less protective daytime mannerisms, the habit of dashing out in public, especially after a rainstorm. Once, when we were leaving Rogers' Rock at the close of a thundershower, our departure was delayed, happily, by one of these salamanders in the driveway. Their bold coloring, though, like that of Monarch butterflies and their caterpillars, acts as a warning that here is a meal definitely not worth the eating. When this hint fails, their repulsive taste usually convinces and teaches the unlearned predators. Any consumer left over and still willing to try after that may soon die, punished by poisons produced in the eft's skin glands.

This protective mechanism persists into the next stage, one to three years later, when the salamanders return to the water. Their wanderings in the interim may have carried them several miles from their birthplace. With luck, though, one or more of each sex finds the same spot, and here they mature rapidly into reproductive adults. The red, rough eft skin becomes as green as waterweed and as soft as in its aquatic larval stage. Once again this skin can take in oxygen. The tail broadens out once more into a flipper. Undulating movements the male makes with his tail may even excite the female into mating with him. Then, like most amphibians, the female deposits her eggs in a watery environment.

Red-backed salamanders have gotten further from the aquatic limitation by nestling their eggs in simply wet places. Their larvae stay right inside the jelly egg coats, and the free young ones keep their gills only briefly.

As I knelt among tall ferns to dig out one of the elusive wood frogs found here—they can leap farther at a single bound than most other kinds of frogs—or braced myself from side to side on boulders and birches to drop into a bowl full of horsetails, I could visualize the perspective the Rangers and Indians must have had here. Hidden from anyone walking below, I could imagine what it was like for the small companies of Rangers looking down on hordes of Indians on the warpath. One of the Rangers has told of hiding in the woods and watching an Indian party strip and mutilate a companion who was caught when the warriors broke into the soldiers' camp. The prisoner screamed for a tomahawk with which to destroy himself, but the man in cover was afraid for his own sanity if he gave him one. Torture was not an Indian invention, of course, and the practice of scalping may have been introduced into the New World by Old World civilizations.

Farther up the mountain an opening along a ledge gives another view. Surely many an Indian, many a settler, must have stared out from here down the length of the lake. This was the way the morning fog had been heading. It was the direction swatches of water, "cat's-paws," would appear to be traveling about half the time. Toward this end would blow the northerlies that keep the sky clear, while from the other end of the lake would come the mare's-tails that often accompany south winds. One has to step back from the ledge and go around to the other side of the trees in order to see most of the woodpecker holes, for the birds here avoid confronting the incoming breezes. Their arrival can usually be recognized from a distance by the way they come in low and swoop up to the holes.

A dozen yards farther up the mountain stands a lone copse of arbor vitae. The down-sweeping boughs float close overhead as I approach, for the climb gets suddenly steeper. Somehow these few trees have found a niche that is particularly amicable to their needs, and they have even rooted some young ones. The cleft might be a good one to dig in for ground water. In wet situations, especially those farther to the north, white cedar creates *forests* that are almost wholly of its own kind. As a result, Canadians have long since learned to turn the wood to a number of uses. Not the least of these was the forts the French put up during Captain (later Major) Rogers' time. Peter Kalm tells of the Saint Jean fortress, which

> was constructed entirely of wood. In place of masonry work they had put up heavy logs of arbor vitae of eighteen to twenty-four feet in length and height, one log being placed quite close to the other. They had chosen this tree because no other tree had been found in the whole of Canada which withstood the rot in the ground and was as durable as this one.

Kalm measured the diameters and counted the annual rings of five logs. A twelve-inch specimen was from a tree 92 years old, two fifteen-inch ones were from trees 136 and 139 years old, and two sixteen-inchers were from trees that had lived for 134 and 142 years. The 92- and 134-year-old white cedars had evidently had slightly more favored existences or else were simply better trees genetically. The trees growing along the way up Rogers' Rock are less than half the diameter of these, due perhaps to their age or to a harsher environment, especially a drier one.

Sugar maples were becoming especially prominent as I climbed higher. Botanically speaking, each vertical step compared roughly to a half-mile journey northward on level ground, and I was now well within the theoretical climate of the beech-maple forests, the Lake Forests of the Great Lakes and St. Lawrence Seaway region. Other aspects augured well for sugar maple success, such as the commonness of maple-leaved viburnum. Like sugar maples, these shrubs do best on dry, well-drained soil, which the staircase topography doubtless helped provide. Their straight stems were a favorite wood for the shafts of the Indian's arrows.

Once I reached the top I would find oaks. They had preceded the maples here, making the ground richer with their dead leaves and darker from the live ones overhead. Long ago, maple seedlings had found these conditions very much to their liking, had risen up, and were conquering the oaks, which are less tolerant of shade. Sugar maple saplings were now as thick as a crowd in a store on bargain day. And slowly, following the dictates of the wind that carried their winged seeds, the maple forest was moving upward on the remaining oaks, which had reached the upper limit to which squirrels could carry their acorns. All about the rocky summit a ring of sugar maples had closed off escape and was squeezing the earlier forest in its grip. Were the summit to be burned out and the oaks destroyed, the advance of the maples would possibly be retarded by a matter of centuries.

It was the season when the wailing of cicadas makes itself felt the most, intoning the arrival of autumn. The month was September. High on these mountains, where spring arrives later and autumn earlier, the air remained chilly until midmorning, and the cicadas came into full voice an hour or so after those down by the lake. Their songs seemed in the mood of summer's end. Some were very slow and machine-like—especially like machines that needed a good oiling. They began heavily and gradually creaked to their tired conclusions, reminding me of one species which has the memorable name "Old Scissors Grinder." You have to have heard a pair of scissors being sharpened, either at home on a rough device or in the streets as in the olden days when a grinder came by with his cart, to appreciate that name to the fullest.

I hiked a few dozen yards farther. The sugar maples opened onto a sudden plateau that, as it curves, hints of the final flatland only a hundred yards or so up. This was the sort of change in topography where Rogers would have left behind a sergeant and a half dozen or so men as a rear guard for a few minutes, to see if the Rangers were being followed. From a few species of trees the character of the forest changed to half a dozen. Sunlight spilled onto the ground cover, which changed from ferns and hepaticas and other woodland types to grasses, goldenrods, and other members of open societies. Blue jays called *oink-oink*, loudly, like many forest birds. Chickadees rushed about. And for the first time mosquitoes became a real menace. If I had been one of Rogers' men I might have taken the precaution of soaping myself or rubbing on bear grease, having observed that one of those heavily misty days was lying on the lake and mountains. But I went on, hoping the tormenting insects would drown in my gathering sweat. Dead trees lay here and there, leaving stumps with hollow boles to collect rain water, a place for these flies to pass their larval and pupal stages. Birches, signs of some past catastrophe such as burning or cutting, formed their lines of weak and fallen reminders of a past that was being devoured by maples at my back and oaks up ahead.

My favorite tree here is striped, or goosefoot, maple, unobtrusive through all seasons except fall. Then the yellow cat-faced leaves remind me of Halloween silhouettes. Their shape also suggests that of goose feet, hence the name. The tree offers little wood, and none of value to timbermen. Few people except experimenters tap its sap. Only browsing animals such as deer and moose seem to derive any economic value from it, but moose eat enough of the twigs so that it is also called moose wood. I have run several feet of color movie film just to catch this standard of autumn. The fine white slashes down the green limbs and trunk are an elegant piping that brings on the epithet "striped."

A rivulet of flattened grass led upward, becoming more or less barren during its ascent through a cleft in the bedrock. Weeds mingled with ferns and mosses of bald spots. Pipsissewa indicated that the oaks ahead were likely to be accompanied by pines. By now the old flower stalks of the pipsissewas were bearing seeds. They had lost the limber crook of youth and stood straight up, at the rigid attention of a greater age. Another crawler, wintergreen, offered more of an inducement to stop, in order to pick off the few red berries left by the regular feeders here. The stone steps were worn. How many centuries had seen travelers rest in this place where winter is not only white but green and red? The narrow path was the sort Rogers' Rangers would have created as they walked single file and spaced out so that no one bullet could kill two men.

Pipsissewa and wintergreen are both heaths, as are trailing arbutus, mountain laurel, and rhododendron. So I was not surprised when the summit began with a scarf of another heath: blueberry. Oaks rose all about, as promised earlier, but they had suffered bodily—not from the hurricane, but from the gypsy moth larvae. Pupae and cast skins swung from twigs, huddled under bark, finished off leaf stems where no blades remained. How much would the nutritional loss be reflected in a diminished crop of acorns, which might all too soon become as rare as the bullets their size that had been fired by the Rangers? The invasion was probably a massive demonstration of the long flights that can be accomplished by newborn larvae, which had reached the brow of Rogers' Rock Slide by drifting maybe seven hundred feet up from the lakeside forests. They appeared to have leapfrogged over the mixed forests in between and settled down in the dominant stand of oaks on the sunny dry pate. Here they might eventually change the character of the forest to favor trees less attractive to themselves, such as the white pines that were present now for the first time in about five hundred feet of climb. The many young pines, which have very white needles, indicated that a large part of the summit future lies with them.

Shagbark hickory and red maple had also been given safe passage to another year. In time they might compete with the pines. Possibly the worst-hit single tree was one that had evidently been struck twice. It was a small black cherry hanging in rags of green. Gypsy moth pupae swung like ornaments, while a black pouch that had been a tent caterpillar nest was stuffed into one crotch.

The summit of Rogers' Rock could actually be considered to be several hundred yards farther along the spine of the mountain, but this opening into a meadow where I stood now surmounts the cliff known as Rogers' Slide. Grasses, pincushion and other mosses, the gray lichen known as reindeer moss, wisps of goldenrod—all seemed to imply that this was the end of the road. Over mossy turf such as this, Rogers' men used to march abreast so as to make the least impressions with their feet and thus make themselves more difficult to track. I was very much sur-

prised to find a young wood frog here, far from the brook I had left four
or five hundred feet below. No body of water that I know of exists any
higher. The goldenrod had not blossomed yet, possibly delayed by the
dryness of the soil. Could the tight scalps of moss retain enough water
from rain to keep the frog eggs and larvae going?

Truly in tune with the granite crest of the slide were dusky band-
winged locusts that scaled up from bedrock just before I stepped on them
unawares. Their salt-and-pepper blackness matched the color of streaks
in the granite. When one landed it quickly aligned itself with the rock patterns. They were about the boldest set of band-winged locusts—which
take their name, incidentally, from the colorful bands on their hind wings
—I have ever run across. Usually they are easily disturbed. On dusty
roads they continually jump up before you and land ten or so yards ahead,
until they give up and swing back to drop down to the rear. At the top of
the slide I regularly walked to within a foot of them before their doubts
took over.

So precipitous is the drop of the cliff, and so shrouded at the rim
with trees, that the slide itself cannot be seen from the ledges above. The
tale of Rogers' descent is similarly hidden in a mixture of battles and
escapades, including the one that concludes the roiling winter epic known
afterward as the "Battle of Snowshoes." Possibly Rogers saved himself
by simply leaping off the cliff and tumbling safely through the drifts
to the lake below. But beyond doubt the most imaginative account is the
one stating that, in March of 1758, Major Rogers eluded punishment at
the hands of pursuing Indians by shuffling to the edge of the slide,
shoving off his back pack, which skidded down through the snow, and
then making his own way to the bottom by another route—on reversed
snowshoes! This is said to have convinced his pursuers that he had been
intercepted by an enemy, who had defeated him and hurled him off the
cliff to his death. When they saw him uninjured on the lake ice below,
though, they let him continue without chase, as possibly being favored
by the Great Spirit.

I descended the storied mountain not by a different route but by the same one I had come up by. One reason was that this was a trail that had been cut to smoothness by glaciers, spring- and rain-fed streams, and the polishing of many feet—possibly those of Rogers and certainly those of Indians during centuries of wear. But the prime reason lay in my intent to relive and see from another point of view the scenes which had given rise to so many adventures, real and imagined, in these the highest of the near woods I know best.

A Note About the Author

Millard C. Davis was born in 1930 in Utica, New York. He received an A.B. in psychology from Middlebury College, an M.S. in entomology and creative writing from Cornell University, and an M.S. in environmental communications from the University of Wisconsin. Mr. Davis has worked as an editor and a teacher, and since 1973 has been a director of the American Nature Study Society. His articles have appeared in *Nature, Nature Study, The Conservationist, The Living Wilderness,* and *The Journal of Environmental Education,* and *Ranger Rick,* among other magazines. He and his wife and five children live in New Jersey.

A Note on the Type

The text of this book was set on the Linotype in Aster, a typeface designed by Francesco Simoncini (born 1912 in Bologna, Italy) for Ludwig and Mayer, the German type foundry. Starting out with the basic old-face letterforms that can be traced back to Francesco Griffo in 1495, Simoncini emphasized the diagonal stress by the simple device of extending diagonals to the full height of the letterforms and squaring off. By modifying the weights of the individual letters to combat this stress, he has produced a type of rare balance and vigor. Introduced in 1958, Aster has steadily grown in popularity wherever type is used.

This book was composed by Kingsport Press, Inc., Kingsport, Tennessee, printed by Halliday Lithograph Corp., West Hanover, Massachusetts, and bound by The Book Press, Brattleboro, Vermont. Typography and binding design by Christine Aulicino.